Mozart
Letters and Manuscripts

Mozart

Letters and Manuscripts

Gilles Cantagrel

Harry N. Abrams, Inc., Publishers

Iconography: Roselyne de Ayala
Design: Pascale Ogée
English-language edition project managed by Cambridge Publishing Management Limited
Translated by Gray Sutherland, James Taylor, Françoise Pinteaux-Jones and Jane Carroll
Edited and adapted by Laura Davey

Published in 2005 by Harry N. Abrams, Incorporated, New York

Printed and bound in Spain
10 9 8 7 6 5 4 3 2 1

Abrams is a subsidiary of
LA MARTINIÈRE GROUPE

Preface

Once again, Gilles Cantagrel has placed his integrity and generosity of spirit at the service of a composer of genius. This time, he gives us Mozart. Using a refreshingly new approach, he introduces us in turn to the astonishingly precocious child; the adolescent avid for recognition and eager to taste life to the full; the man in his dealings with—and at the mercy of—society; his loves; his death. He brings to life the rebel nurtured by his father, driven out by his employer, forced to earn a living by giving tiresome, tiring lessons; and the composer and virtuoso who, after a moment of adulation, was cast aside.

Mozart has many faces: the man always on the move, the musician constantly working at fever pitch, but also the husband enjoying a frame of billiards with his beloved Constanze, the perpetual adolescent always ready for a joke, even if sometimes in doubtful taste, the *bon vivant* appreciative of good food and brotherhood. He lived his life carelessly, giving his heart freely to a succession of talented young women, knowing joy and sorrow and glory.

Our view of Mozart has often been idealized or distorted. Now Gilles Cantagrel returns the man and artist to us with exemplary, affectionate rigor. The illustrations are superb. This book is indispensable.

Frédéric Lodéon
Conductor and producer
(*France Inter* and *France Musiques*)

Foreword

For more than two centuries, no musician has been better known or more widely loved than Mozart. Today, he is generally regarded as one of the towering geniuses of all humankind. In the eighteenth century, the appearance of this child prodigy was seen as that of a comet in the musical firmament, and from his earliest years he was regarded throughout Europe as a miracle. Intense and tragically brief, his career was not without its painful eclipses, but admiration for him never waned, embracing kings, princes, the most illustrious of his contemporaries, including Haydn and Beethoven, and even the person in the street, fascinated by the inexpressible grace and astonishing depth of his genius.

Over the years, a Mozart legend has grown up, starting in the Romantic age, which adored him, down to the theater and cinema of today. He has been seen as a tormented hero, an angelic incarnation, a murderer's victim, and an 18th-century *galant* in his powdered wig. From the time of Goethe and Kierkegaard, philosophers and musicians, spellbound, have all sought explanations and voiced their opinions; but the popularity of the man has simply grown and grown.

Yet the mystery remains intact. Even his face, which eyewitnesses tell us was constantly in motion, is always just out of reach. We can easily picture Beethoven as he rages through life, his silhouette, his corpulence, his mannerisms. If we were to encounter Bach, Wagner, or Brahms on the street, we should recognize them instantly. Not Mozart. The lovely portrait painted of him at the end of his life by his brother-in-law Joseph Lange is probably the most moving, but—could this be a sign?—it is unfinished. And the only surviving copy of the portrait his sister Nannerl considered to be his greatest likeness is, it must be said, disappointing.

So how does one come to know Mozart? In addition to the scores and recordings of his works, which have for some time been complete, there are the Mozart family letters, translated into English by Emily Anderson in 1938, and various other kinds of documentary material, published by Otto Deutsch in 1961 and

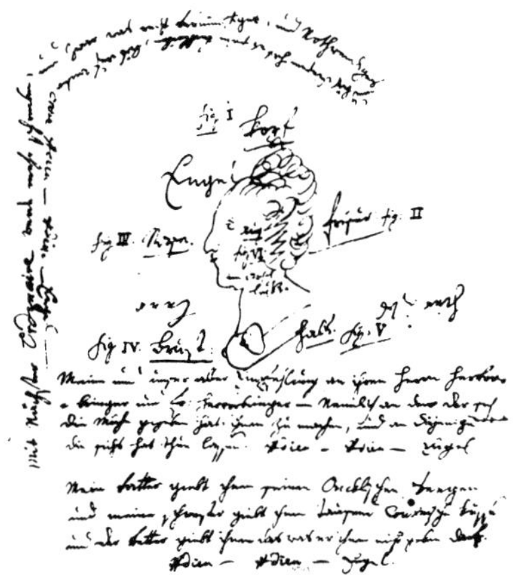

translated into English in 1965 by Eric Blom, Peter Branscombe, and Jeremy Noble as *Mozart: A Documentary Biography.*

The present volume, therefore, is not intended to be a life or yet another study of Mozart. Instead, it takes the reader on a journey, in the company of Mozart himself, among his manuscripts, his finest works. In the brief passages of commentary that seek to place his "loveliest manuscripts" in context, it seemed consistent with a pilgrimage to the sources to rely to a large extent on contemporary documents, especially his impassioned correspondence. Through letters, portraits, eyewitness accounts, and other contemporary documents, this volume tells the story of the man, his relationships, his times, and his creative life, in all their intensity. The lover and the passionate opera composer, the Christian who was the faithful companion of death, the admired genius and the generous-hearted friend. Mozart, the whole man.

Mozart's works speak for him. Whether a professional musician or simply a music lover, the reader may look upon these pages and be guided by Mozart's elegant, precise, quicksilver handwriting, which in the urgency of creation goes to the very essence, without hesitation or misgiving. See the ardor with which, as a boy, he seeks to set down on paper the memory of the music circling inside his head—and his heart, as he will later say—as ideas strike like flashes of lightning. See him take up his quill on the run. Do this knowing that no-one can ever approach, still less understand, the mystery of genius. See him write the word "requiem" or scribble down a little sketch of his cousin Maria Anna Thekla. Read one or other of his rambling, unending letters, those letters that are so spontaneous, so lively, so moving, so joyous. Stare into his face, that ever-mobile face, that dissolves before our eyes as soon as we think we have grasped it.

Mozart has no tomb that might have served as a place of veneration. Instead, his works, the works of this pure soul, are his tomb. Buried in a common grave, it was as if in some way he was offered up to all humankind.

G. C.

Attributed to Pietro Antonio Lorenzoni, this portrait of Mozart at the age of six shows the young musician dressed in the clothes that Empress Maria Theresa had presented to him, which are supposed to have belonged to her son. Salzburg, Mozarteum.

"The miraculous genius of my son"

"I could take this opportunity to amuse the reader with an account of what happens perhaps but once in a century and which has probably never occurred to such a degree before in the realm of music. I could describe the miraculous genius of my son. I could recount in detail his incredible, rapid progress in the science of music."

Leopold Mozart,
Preface to the second edition of his *Treatise on the Fundamental Principles of Violin Playing*, 1770

In Mozart's work, musical themes relating to childhood are rare. This is one: the trio of boys from *The Magic Flute* (detail of the opening). Berlin, Staatsbibliothek, Musikabteilung.

Salzburg, mid-18th century. From among the musicians in his service, Prince-Archbishop Anton Firmian singled out one Leopold Mozart to be his violin master. And rightly so, for he was not just a distinguished violinist, composer, and music theorist, but also a highly gifted teacher. A Bavarian by birth, a native of the "free city" of Augsburg, where he still had family and friends, Leopold Mozart had come to Salzburg to complete his studies, and there he soon met the gentle Maria Anna Pertl, whom he was to marry. It was to be a happy, serene marriage and a tightly knit household; Leopold never failed to show his wife signs of his affection.

The young couple—the finest in the town, it was said of them—were soon blessed with children, seven in all, but the terrible infant mortality of the time left them with only two. Of the first six children only Maria Anna was still alive when the last of the seven was born, a little boy, on January 27, 1756. He was baptized the following day and given the names Joannes Chrysostomus, Wolfgangus, and Theophilus. Of these he would retain Wolfgang, the name he was known by, and Theophilus, although he preferred the latter in its German form, Gottlieb, or the Latin Amadeus, or even the Italian Amadeo, which he often wrote in the French manner, Amadè. As a child he was often known to those close to him by his baby name Wolferl, Woferl, or Wolfgangerl, just as his sister Maria Anna would be Nannerl.

Some months later, Leopold published in his native city of Augsburg his *Treatise on the Fundamental Principles of Violin Playing*. It was an immediate success and would be regarded as a benchmark for

The Michaelsplatz (now Mozartplatz) in Salzburg, c. 1775. Unknown artist. Salzburg, Museum Carolino Augusteum.

Leopold Mozart, *Treatise on the Fundamental Principles of Violin Playing*, the original German edition of 1756. Facing the title page, a portrait of the author with his violin. Salzburg, Mozarteum.

decades to come, as can be seen in the successive reprintings of the book and its translation into other languages. Thus in 1770 a new edition appeared in Germany at the same time as a French translation in Paris, and it was in this new edition that Leopold's words expressing his teacher's astonishment at the "miraculous genius" of his son are to be found. Indeed, Leopold would never cease to be amazed by the boy, and the term "miracle" would frequently appear in his writings. He writes from Vienna in 1762, for instance, "Everyone is particularly amazed by my son, and I have heard no-one say anything but that it passes all understanding."

In 1757, shortly after the birth of his last child, Leopold's career took an important step forward when he was made court composer by the new Prince-Archbishop, Siegmund von Schrattenbach. This was a great honor for Leopold. Happy and respected outside the home, he was to know even greater joys inside it. Before his son had reached the age of three, Leopold became aware of his extraordinary gifts. Nannerl had already shown a genuine aptitude for music, and in 1759 Leopold introduced her to the harpsichord, on which she made rapid progress. But Wolfgang showed such passionate interest that his father felt compelled to sit him at the harpsichord as well, and the child learned so quickly that he soon caught up with his sister, even though she was five years his senior. Leopold would later talk of his son's "incredible, rapid progress."

Affectionate, mischievous, sociable to a fault, overflowing with love for his father, always seeking marks of affection, the boy thought of nothing but music. He was constantly at work, singing and playing, seeking to learn everything possible, and at an absurd speed, as if he were simply living faster than anyone else—a character trait that would never leave him. Music was his natural means of expression, the world in which he moved. For him, everything became music, to the point that whatever he played he learned instantly by heart. On the day before Wolfgang's fifth birthday, Leopold would record in the music notebook he had made for the children, "This minuet and this trio were learned by Wolfgang in half an hour, on January 26, 1761, one day before his fifth birthday, at half past nine in the evening."

Wolfgang understood music before he could read and write. According to many who knew him he was highly intelligent and passionately interested in everything; but he devoted himself to music alone. It was impossible to send such a child to school; his parents would see to his education themselves. His apprenticeship continued with the study of the violin. As an adult, Mozart was always happy to play the instrument, which he did brilliantly, for he was a virtuoso on the violin as he was on the viola, the harpsichord, the piano, and the organ.

Yet playing was not enough: he also had to create; he was born to compose. When at the keyboard, he would simply invent. He wanted to write music, like his father. And it surged up spontaneously within him, as if driven by some internal logic, some straightforward rhythmic essence of its own. But Wolfgang was still too young to know how to notate it, so his father wrote down his son's first fruits as soon as they blossomed forth. Today, in a display case in the Mozarteum in Salzburg, one can see the manuscript of a Minuet in F by Wolfgang notated by his father. Lost in wonder, Leopold had taken care to note the date of composition at the bottom of the page: January 1762. His son was not yet six.

Leopold wanted to share with others his wonder at this miracle of nature, this gift of God, as he liked to call it. So in the spring of 1762, he took Nannerl and Wolfgang to Munich, the capital of Bavaria, so that the Elector could hear them. While nothing else is known of this visit, the same cannot be said of the first of their many important journeys. That fall, Leopold took the family to Vienna, the capital of the Holy Roman Empire, traveling by way of Passau and Linz. At every stage of the journey he took the opportunity to appear before the local potentates, and the astonishment caused by the two prodigies spread like wildfire: in fact, the Mozart children's reputation arrived at Vienna ahead of them.

They would remain in the city for three months. Various contemporary documents have made it possible to reconstruct, almost day by day, how the family spent their time; and one is taken aback by the sheer pace of the children's lives (they were then aged eleven and six). Each and every day they played at the home of one aristocrat or another, if not indeed twice a day.

The young Mozart attends a concert, seated beside Siegmund von Schrattenbach, Prince-Archbishop of Salzburg. Martin Van Meytens, *Concert du ing the Celebration of the Marriage of Joseph II and Isabella of Parma, October 10, 1760* (detail). Vienna, Schönbrunn Palace.

On October 13, for instance, they had an audience at Schönbrunn before Empress Maria Theresa and her consort, Francis I, from three to six in the afternoon. That evening, there was an "academy" (that is, a concert) at the palace of Prince Joseph Friedrich von Saxe-Hildburghausen. This was followed the next day, October 14, by a first concert at the palace of Countess Kinsky and a second at that of Count Corfiz von Ulfeld. On the 15th, a messenger from the Empress brought gala attire for Nannerl and Wolfgang. Two concerts were held that evening. And so it went on.

The children's daily routines suffered, as Leopold himself recognized. What with the early mornings, the irregular mealtimes, the rain and the wind, Wolfgang fell ill, but before long he was back on his feet again. Sickness and exhaustion would be his constant companions on his travels across Europe.

The beginning of their visit to Vienna was a triumph, for on their way to the capital the children had already won the admiration of the local princes, and their fame had preceded them to Schönbrunn. In a letter to his friend Lorenz Hagenauer in Salzburg, Leopold could not resist recounting their triumphal entry into the city, and concluded his letter with an account of their visit to the imperial court: "Almost all I have time for is to add that we were received by Their Majesties with such extraordinary graciousness that if I were to tell it people would say I was making it all up! Suffice it to say that Wolferl leapt onto the Empress's lap, threw his arms around her neck, and kissed her unashamedly!"

But the visit dragged on and on, and Wolfgang had to recover from his sickness. The family would spend a few days not far away in Pressburg (now Bratislava, Slovakia), then capital of Hungary. And all the while Leopold was making useful contacts for the future.

On his return from Vienna, Wolfgang set himself to study the violin with redoubled ardor, for above all else this was a valuable apprenticeship for his technique as a composer. He also wanted to try his hand at chamber music, but his father judged him not yet ready. One day, when some friends of his father's were playing a new string trio, Wolfgang asked to play the second violin part. At first his father refused but in the end he relented, and soon Wolfgang had worked the part out all by himself, while his father wept with pride. "How is it that you can play the part without having taken violin lessons?" he asked. "But Papa," the boy replied, "you don't need to learn the second violin part to play it!" It was at this time, too, that he first showed evidence of his phenomenal musical memory and perfect ear.

His many gifts amazed Leopold and his entire entourage. It was time to let everyone know about this child's miraculous gifts. When peace was restored at the end of the Seven Years' War, Leopold set about putting his grand plan in motion: a European tour with his children.

Mozart among the musicians at the marriage of Joseph II. Martin Van Meytens, *Dinner in Honor of the Marriage of Joseph II and Isabella of Parma, October 10, 1760* (detail).
Vienna, Schönbrunn Palace.

Leopold, father and master

The parish register of Salzburg Cathedral, open at the page showing the entry for January 28, 1756, the day on which Mozart was baptized, which reads, "Joannes Chrysost Wolfgangus Theophilus."

Leopold Mozart, idealized portrait by an unknown artist (detail), c. 1750. Salzburg, Mozarteum.

Leopold Mozart, Wolfgang's father, has had the worst of all reputations attributed to him, that of a Dickensian villain, a domestic tyrant who exploited his children's talents. Yet such a reputation is belied by the facts. A first-rate teacher with a Europe-wide reputation, Leopold was the first to notice his son's exceptional gifts while Wolfgang was still no more than a tiny child. He then nurtured the boy's budding genius, shaped and guided him, forced him onward rather than allowing him to waste his time on easy material. It was Leopold who inculcated in his son a genuine discipline for work. Andreas Schachtner, a family friend, noted rightly that "without discipline and education he could have become a worthless fellow or a rogue." And he recalled that the boy was "ablaze with enthusiasm." Wolfgang's talent, in fact, was so great that it could easily have led him to waste his genius. Leopold understood this all too well, and at a very early stage gave his son a taste for hard work by instilling in him the mental habits without which his genius would never have blossomed fully. He was the only teacher of a child who allowed himself to be guided, and a remarkable teacher at that. As Schachtner went on to say, "What he was being made to learn hardly mattered to him at all; all he wanted was to learn, and he let his beloved papa choose which field he was to labor in. One might have said that he understood that there could be no other master in the world, even less another teacher, than his unforgettable father." And whatever the issues that later caused friction between father and son, Wolfgang remained grateful to Leopold throughout his life. As a child he would say, "Right after God comes Papa."

[...] I am pleased to inform you that on January 27, at eight o'clock in the evening, my wife was happily delivered of a boy. But, as the placenta had to be removed, she was extremely weak. Now, thank God, mother and child are both doing well. She sends her regards to you both. The child is called Joannes Chrisostomus,[1] Wolfgang, Gottlieb. I hope you will not make me await three mail coaches, for I despair to see how long it always takes. Your brother may bring the money to me. Addio.

Leopold Mozart

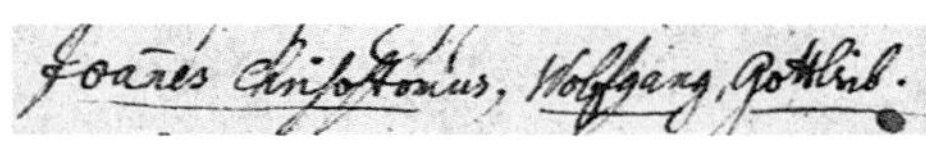

1. Mozart was named John Chrysostom because his birthday, January 27, is the feast of St. John Chrysostom. Wolfgang, the name he went by as a musician, was the name of his maternal grandfather.

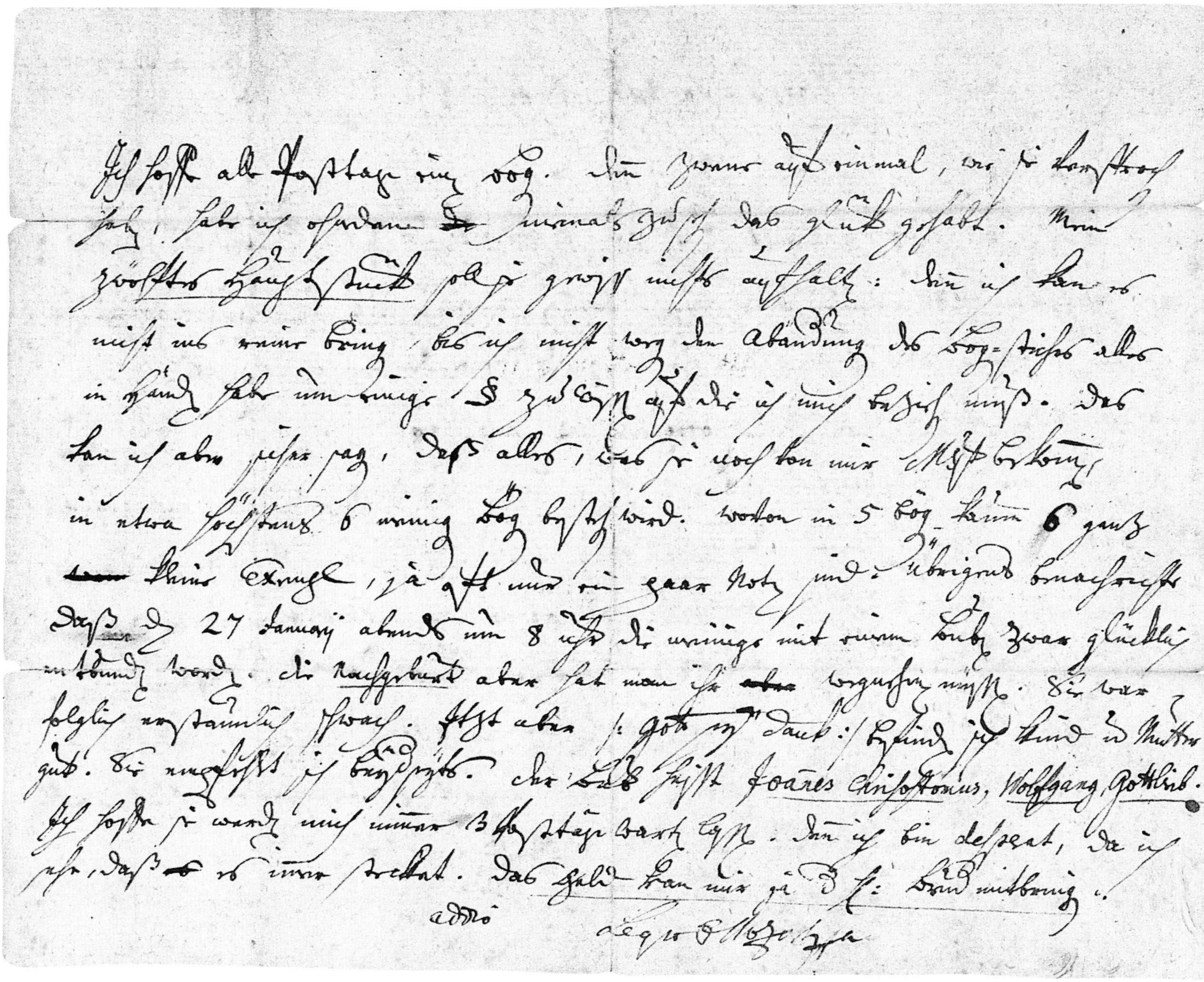

Extract from a letter from Leopold Mozart to his friend Jacob Lotter in Augsburg, announcing the birth of his son Wolfgang on January 27, Salzburg, February 9, 1756. Augsburg, Stadtarchiv.

"Ah, shall I tell you, Mama?"

Portrait of Anna Maria Pertl,
the wife of Leopold Mozart and mother of Wolfgang,
attributed to Pietro Antonio Lorenzoni, 1775 (detail).
Salzburg, Mozarteum.

Although it would seem that Mozart's mother was of no more than average intelligence, it is also clear from her letters that she lacked neither irony nor the gift of plain speech; what she says often bursts with life. Beside the celebrated trio, she led a discreet life surrounded by the affection of her husband and her children, and young Wolfgang certainly found in her the tenderness and comfort of which he more than anyone else had need. Because the piano variations on "Ah, vous dirai-je, maman" are based on a French song, it has long been supposed that they were composed while Mozart and his mother were in Paris and that he wrote the piano variations on "Je suis Lindor" and "La belle françoise" at the same time. For that was when Mozart saw his mother fall ill, and quickly went to help her in her last moments. All the more reason to sing to her, "Ah, vous dirai-je, maman, ce qui cause mon tourment?" (Ah, shall I tell you, mama, what causes my torment?). But the explanation was too good to be true. Recent studies have shown that these variations were really composed much later, during Mozart's first stay in Vienna (1781 or 1782) and were intended for a pupil; French songs were then very much in vogue. Mozart, who spoke French fluently, also composed variations for piano and violin on "La bergère Célimène" and "Hélas, j'ai perdu mon amant." None of which prevents us from hearing in the naïve freshness of these pieces, in their simplicity of tone, the childlike spirit that never left Mozart, or the memory of his mother, whom he had dearly loved.

The first page of the score of "Ah, vous dirai-je, maman" (K. 265).
Augsburg, Deutsche Mozart-Gesellschaft e. V.

Nannerl, his big sister

Portrait of Maria Anna Mozart, Wolfgang's elder sister, known as Nannerl, at the age of 12, attributed to Pietro Antonio Lorenzoni, 1763. Salzburg, Mozarteum.

Five years older than her brother, Maria Anna Walburga Ignatia Mozart, known to the family and later to the whole world as Nannerl, was Wolfgang's close companion during his learning years and the family's first journeys together. Her father gave her the best possible musical education: under his guidance she quickly showed considerable talent as a pianist. She needed no more than five years before she was good enough to accompany her brother on the great European tour of 1763–66. From London, Leopold wrote a friend, "My daughter, although she is only twelve years old, is one of the most skilful pianists in Europe." By the time she returned home, she had reached marriageable age and it was no longer seemly for her to appear in public, so she stayed in Salzburg with her mother. Although a fine example of a properly educated young lady of her times, Nannerl was nonetheless a lively soul who loved the theater and reading. She did not give up her music, and even seems to have composed, though nothing of her work survives. She remained single until she was 33, and then married a judge, Baron Johann Baptist von Berchtold zu Sonnenburg, and moved to St. Gilgen. She and her brother remained very close until their father died. Wolfgang used to compose works for her, and after his death she set down her reminiscences on several occasions. When she was widowed, in 1801, she returned with her two remaining children to Salzburg, where in 1829 she died, poor and blind, aged 78, she who had once shone as a child before the courts of Europe and who had stood beside the supernatural genius of her brother every day for a quarter of a century.

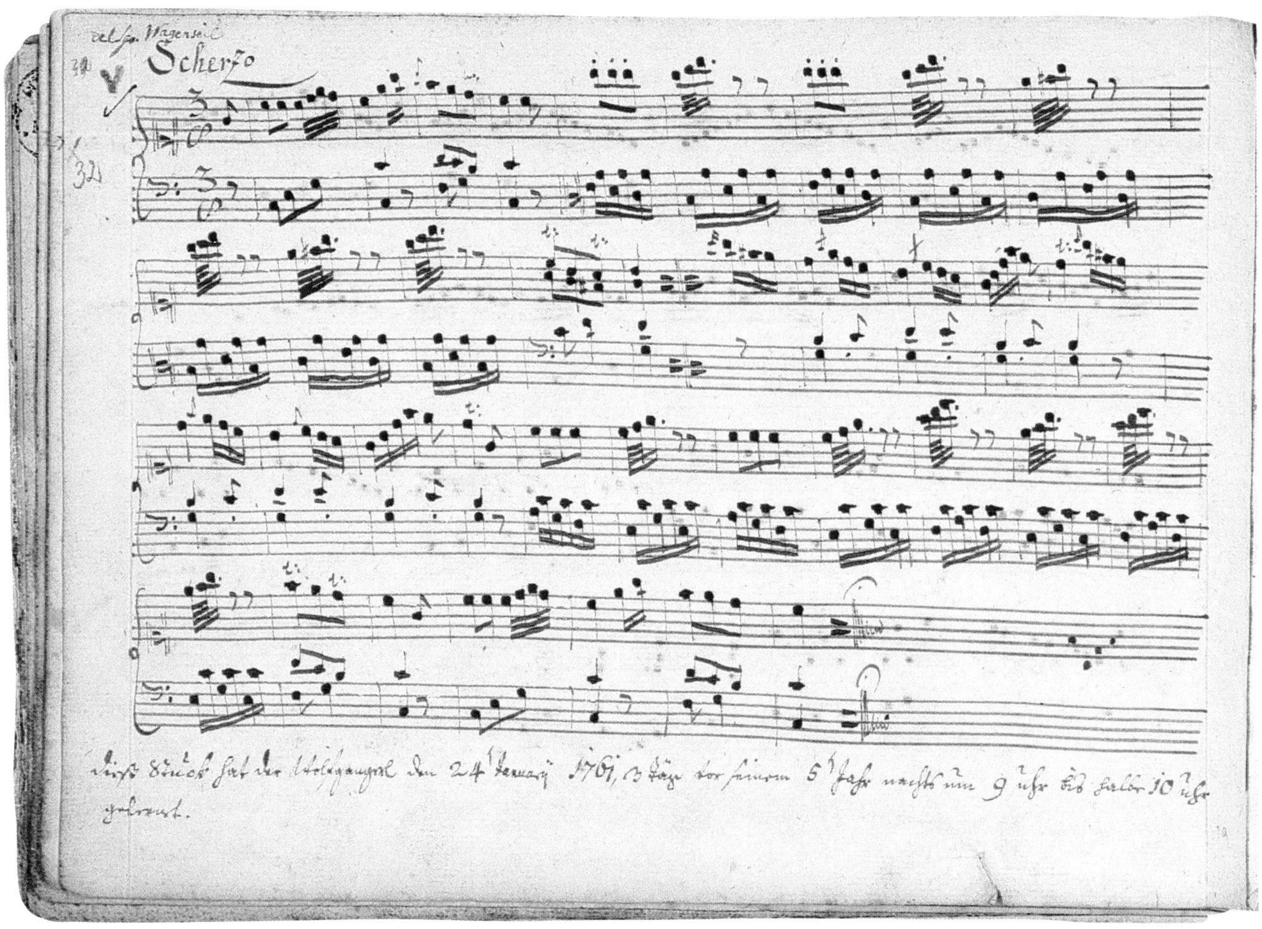

Two sheets from the music album composed by Leopold Mozart for Nannerl and Wolfgang.
Salzburg, Mozarteum.

First steps at Vienna

The Imperial Family on the Terrace of Schönbrunn Palace (detail), by Martin Van Meytens, 1750. Vienna, Kunsthistorisches Museum.

Vienna, the historic center of the Holy Roman Empire, was the seat of the palaces and mansions of countless aristocratic families from the German states and from central Europe, especially Hungary, Bohemia, Poland, and Russia. The Mozart family appeared in one palace after another, and within three months the two children and their father had become known and admired by every person of consequence in the capital. Georg Nikolaus Nissen, Constanze Mozart's second husband, tells the famous tale of how, during the Mozart family's audience at Schönbrunn, Wolfgang slipped on the polished floor and fell down, and was then picked up and comforted by Archduchess Marie Antoinette, later Queen of France, who was only a few months older than he. "You are very kind," he said to her, "and when I grow up I will marry you." The Empress Maria Theresa, who came in while this little scene was going on, asked the boy the reason for his decision, and he replied, "To reward her, for she was very kind to me." Young Wolfgang would adapt to high society's every whim, performing impromptu such tours de force as playing with one finger, or with the keyboard covered with a cloth. At the same time, although only six and a half years old, he saw fit to criticize an archduke who had made a mistake while playing, or to ask the aging composer Georg Christoph Wagenseil to turn the pages for him, all with sublime self-confidence.

[...] Almost all I have time for is to add that we were received by Their Majesties with such extraordinary graciousness that if I were to tell it people would say I was making it all up! Suffice it to say that Wolferl leapt onto the Empress's lap, threw his arms around her neck, and kissed her unashamedly! In short, we were there from three until six, and the Emperor himself took me to hear the Infanta play the violin. On the 15th, the Imperial Paymaster brought us two costumes with great pomp, one for the boy, the other for the girl. As soon as the command arrives they are to appear at court and the Paymaster will come to fetch them himself. At half past two this afternoon they are to go to the two youngest Archdukes and at four o'clock to the Hungarian Chancellor, Count Pálffy. Yesterday, we were with Count Kaunitz, the day before that with Countess Kinsky, and a little later with Count von Ulfeld. And we already have other invitations for the next two days. Please tell everybody that, thank God, we are happy and well. Sending you my warm regards, I remain your old

Mozart

Please tell Frau Niderl, the doctor's wife, that we are in good health.
N.B.: Please do not forward my letters but open them and read them. Otherwise I have to pay excessive postal fees for letters I no longer need. You can judge what needs to be sent on.

My compliments to all.

Vienna, October 16, 1762

Extract from a letter from Leopold Mozart to Lorenz Hagenauer in Salzburg, Vienna, October 16, 1762.
Salzburg, Mozarteum.

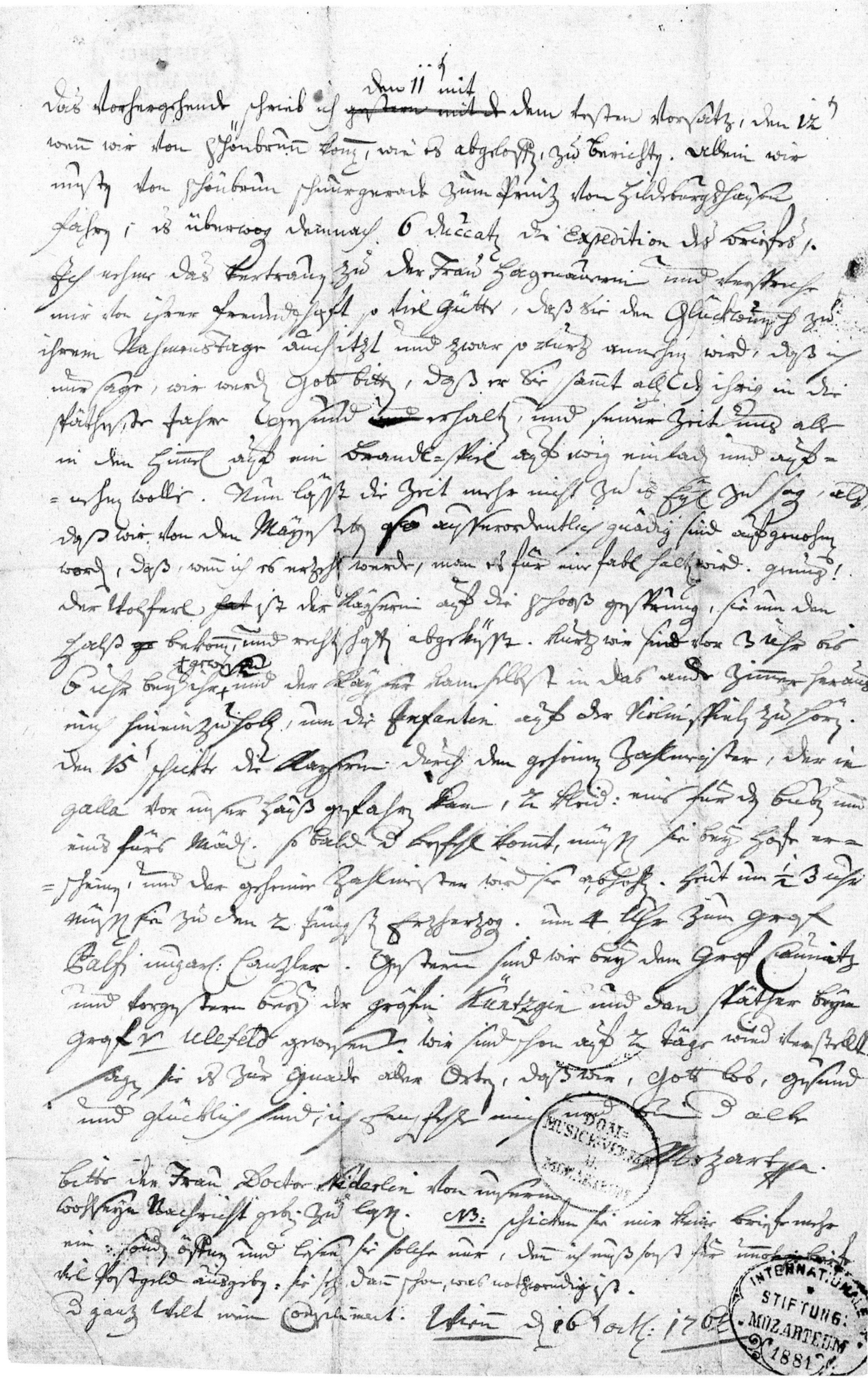

das Vorhergehende schrieb ich ~~gestern mittag~~ den 11ten mit den besten Vorsatz, den 12ten
wenn wir von Schönbrunn kommen, wie es abgeloffen, zu berichten. allein wir
musten von Schönbrunn schnurgerade zum Prinz von Hildburghausen
fahren; es überwog demnach 6 ducaten die Expedition des Briefes.
Ich nehme das Vertrauen zu der Frau Hagenauerin und ersuche
mir von ihrer Freundschaft so viel gütte, dass Sie den Glückwunsch zu
ihrem Nahmenstage aufsetze und zwar so derb annehmen wird, dass ich
mich sage, wir werden Gott bitten, dass er Sie sammt allen ihrigen in der
stärksten besten Gesundheit erhalten, und seiner Zeit uns alle
in den Himmel, auch nur ein Winkelstübl, auf ewig nimmer und auf-
=nehmen wolle. Nun lässt die Zeit mehr nicht zu, als dass ich sag, als
dass wir von den Majestäten so ausserordentlich gnädig sind aufgenohmen
worden, dass, wenn ich es erzehlen werde, man es für eine fabel halten wird. genug!
der Wolferl ist der Kayserin auf die Schoos gesprungen, sie um den
Halss bekommen, und rechtschaffen abgeküsst. Kurz wir sind von 3 uhr bis
6 uhr bey ihr gewesen, und der Kayser kam selbst in das andere Zimmer heraus
mich hinein zu hollen, um die Infantin auf der Violin spielen zu hören.
Den 15ten schickte die Kayserin durch den geheimen Zahlmeister, der in
gala vor unserm Hauss gefahren kam, 2 Kleid: eins für den Buben und
eins fürs Mädl. so bald der Befehl kommt, müssen sie bey Hofe er-
=scheinen; und der geheime Zahlmeister wird sie abhollen. heut um 1/2 3 uhr
müssen sie zu den 2 jüngsten Erzherzog. um 4 uhr zum Grafen
Palfi ungar. Canzler. Gestern sind wir bey dem Graf Caunitz
und vorgestern bey der gräfin Kinsky und dem Stadthalter Hr
graf Hr Ulefeld gewesen. Wir sind schon auf 2 täge wiederum bestellt.
sagen Sie es den guten alten Orten, dass wir, Gott lob, gesund
und glücklich sind, ich empfehle mich [illegible] alle

Mozart

bitte der Frau Doctor Niderlin von unserm
wolseyn Nachricht geben zu lassen. NB: schicken Sie mir keine briefe mehr
mit [illegible] Einschlüssen und lassen Sie solche nur, denn ich muss sonst für [illegible]
viel Postgeld ausgeben: es ist denn schon, was nothwendig ist.
das ganz Welt mein Compliment. Wien d 16 Octob: 1762

First attempts, first works

Mozart Holding a Bird's Nest (detail), by John Zoffany, 1764. Salzburg, Mozarteum.

In a memoir sent some months after her brother's death to Friedrich Schlichtegroll, who was preparing a biographical note on Mozart, Nannerl recalled how at the age of three he would "often amuse himself for hours picking out thirds at the harpsichord, and listening, with innocent pleasure, to the agreeable harmony he produced each time. [...] he made such progress that at the age of five he was already composing little pieces, which he would play on the harpsichord before his father, who would then write them down." In the wondering admiration which he felt for his son, Leopold carefully preserved all these first musical attempts, copying them down into the notebook that he had made for his daughter. Skimming through the pages, we find under the title "Compositions by Wolfgangerl during the first three months [sic] of his fifth year," in the lingua franca of the period, a cross between Latin and Italian, entries such as "Sgr. Wolfgango Mozart, December 11, 1761, followed by Minuet by Sgr. Wolfgango Mozart, December 16, 1761," and so on. He also preserved, as if they were precious relics, the first exercises in composition that he had set for his son. Wolfgang's gifts were so prodigious that he made lightning progress, and a little later Leopold would write, "My son, at the age of eight, knows everything one could expect from a man of forty."

Two of Mozart's earliest compositions. Above: Minuet in F major (K. 4), dated May 11, 1762. Below: The beginning of the Piano Sonata in B flat major, dated November 21, 1763. Salzburg, Mozarteum.

di Wolfgango Mozart d. 11 May 1762

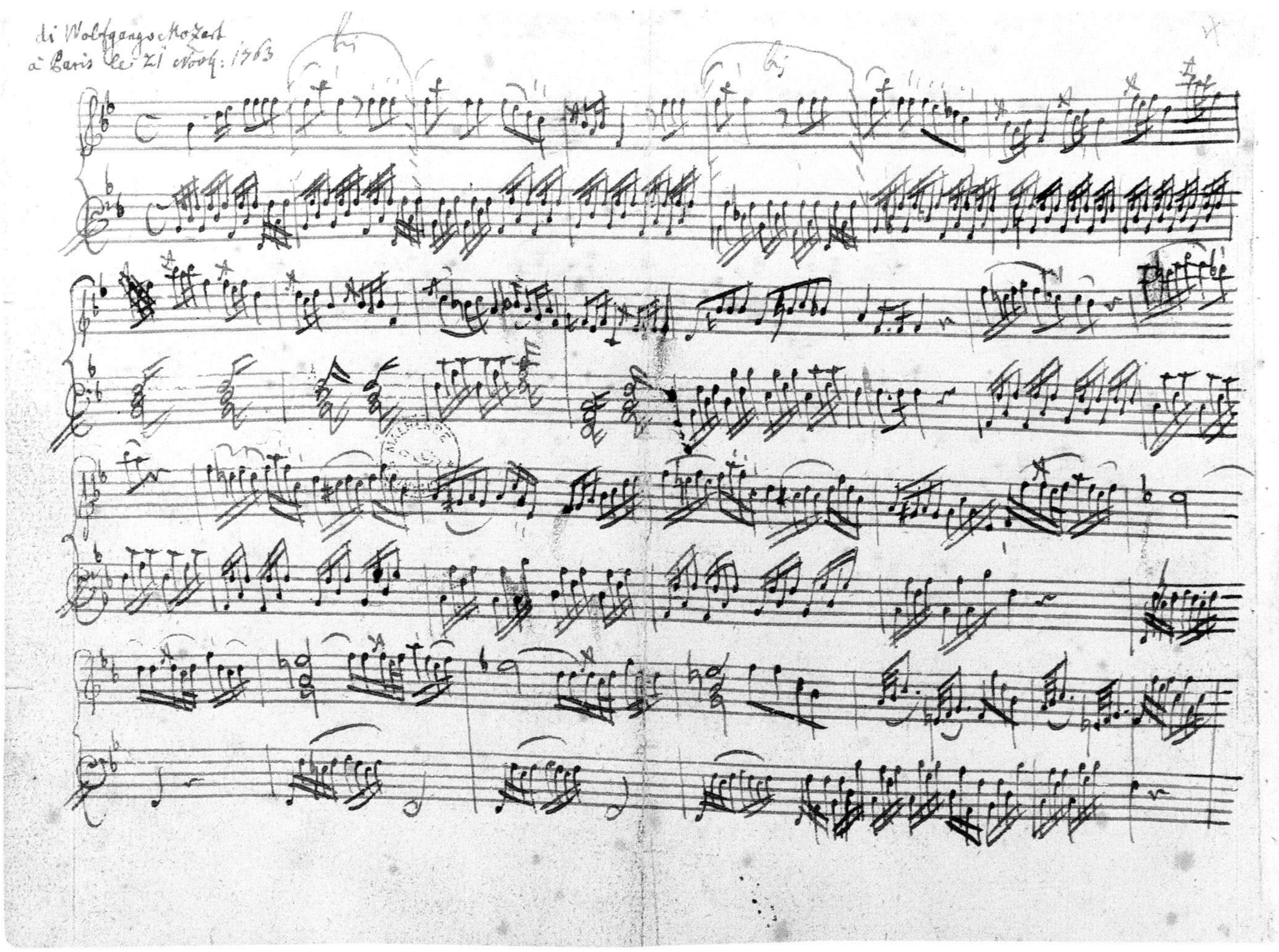
di Wolfgango Mozart
à Paris le 21 Nov: 1763

Mozart the Bavarian German

Salzburg c. 1811, view from the Mönchsberg. Color engraving by Christian Gottlieb Hammer. Salzburg, Museum Carolino Augusteum.

The house in the Getreidegasse, Salzburg, where Wolfgang was born and where the Mozart family lived from 1747 to 1773. Detail of a painting by an unknown artist, 1811. Salzburg, Museum Carolino Augusteum.

Although Austria claims Mozart as one of its sons, Salzburg became Austrian only by chance, as a result of the political and geographical upheavals accompanying the Napoleonic Wars. When Wolfgang Amadeus was born, Salzburg, the city with an archbishop for a prince, was one of 350 territorial entities that made up the Holy Roman Empire, the congeries of German states that was by then in its death throes. At that time, therefore, Salzburg was a German city, more precisely a Bavarian city. It would lose its independence in 1803 with the Final Recess of the Imperial Diet following Napoleon's defeat of Austria, when it was incorporated first into the Grand Duchy of Tuscany, then into the new Kingdom of Bavaria, and finally, in 1816, into the new Austrian Empire, which had been founded 11 years previously. Mozart, therefore, was a German from Bavaria, just as Bach was a German from Thuringia and Beethoven a German from the Rhineland. And throughout his life he would never cease to assert his Germanness. De facto, he was a European too, but that never stopped him from denouncing the fashion for things Italian that were then the rage in Vienna, or from dreaming of giving birth to a German national opera, sung in German, a dream he would realize with *The Magic Flute*.

As regards Gluck, dearest father, I have had the same idea as that of which you write. But I have something else to say besides. The Viennese (and especially the Emperor) should not imagine that I am on this earth for the benefit of Vienna alone. And while I should wish to serve no other monarch than the Emperor, I have no desire to go begging for any engagements. I think I am quite capable of doing honor to any court.

Even Gluck—has Germany made him into the great man he is? Alas, no. Countess Thun, Count Zichy, Baron van Zwieten, even Prince Kaunitz, are all thoroughly displeased with the Emperor: he no longer appreciates people of talent, and allows them to leave his lands. Just the other day, when my name came up, Prince Kaunitz told the Archduke Maximilian that such people come into the world but once every hundred years and should not be forced to leave Germany, especially when by good fortune they happen to live in the capital itself. [...]

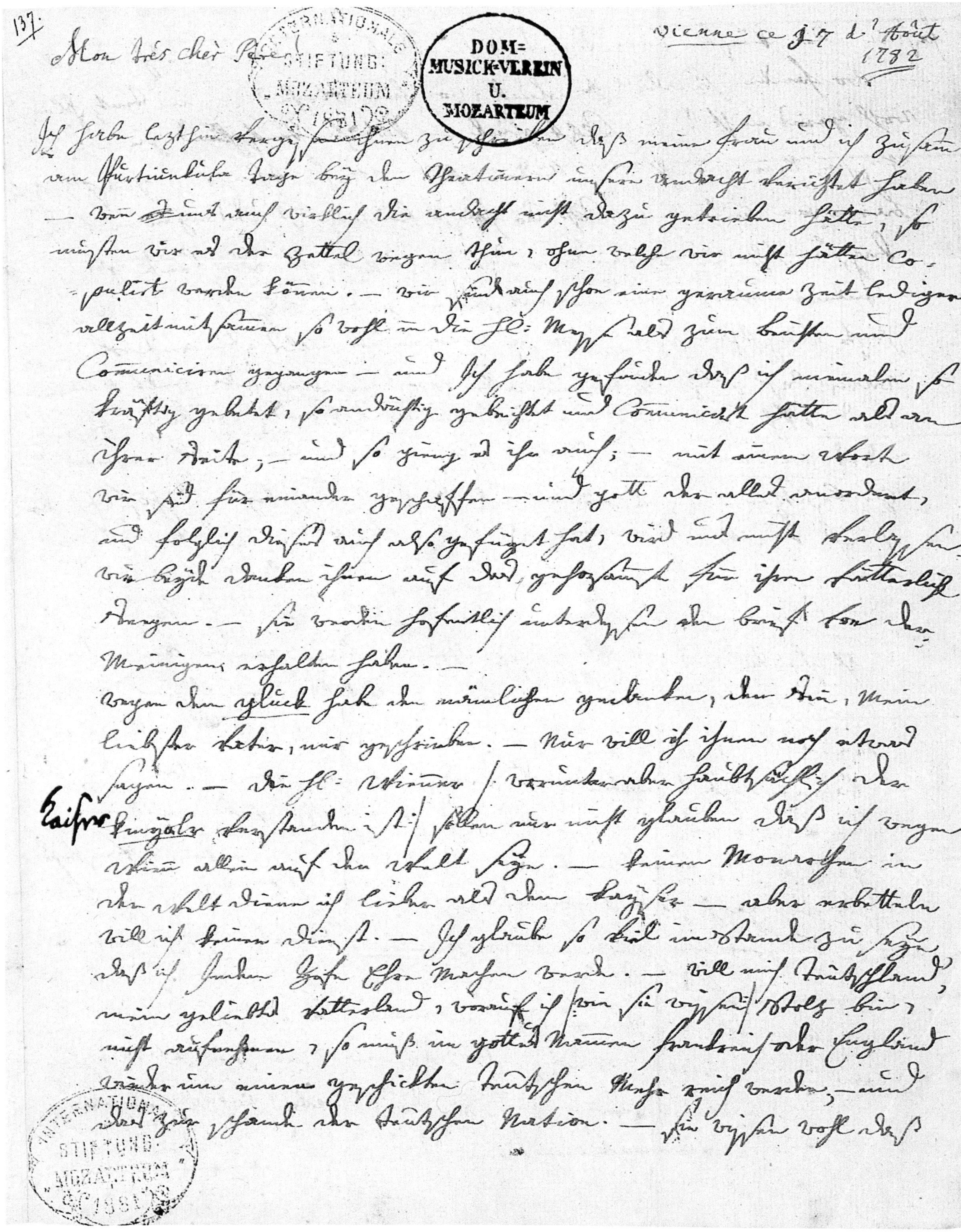

137.

Mon très cher Père! vienne ce 17 d'Août 1782

Ich habe letzthin vergessen ihnen zu schreiben daß meine frau und ich zusam-
men am Portiuncula Tage bey den Theatinern unsere andacht verrichtet haben
– wenn uns auch wirklich die andacht nicht dazu getrieben hätte, so
müßten wir es der Zettel wegen thun; ohne welche wir nicht hätten co-
=pulirt werden können. – wir sind auch schon eine geraume Zeit ledigerweise
allzeit mitsammen so wohl in die H: Meße als zum beichten und
Comuniciren gegangen – und ich habe gefunden daß ich niemalen so
kräftig gebetet, so andächtig gebeichtet und Comunicirt hätte, als an
ihrer seite; – und so gieng es ihr auch; – mit einem wort
wir sind für einander geschaffen – und gott der alles anordnet,
und folglich dieses auch also gefüget hat, wird uns nicht verlassen.
wir beyde danken ihnen auf das gehorsamste für ihren vätterlichen
Segen – sie werden hoffentlich unterdessen den brief von der
Meinigen erhalten haben. –
wegen dem glück habe ich den nämlichen gedanken, den sie, mein
liebster vatter, mir geschrieben. – Nur will ich ihnen noch etwas
sagen. – die H: Wiener /: unter welchen aber hauptsächlich der
Kaiser [illegible] verstanden ist :/ sollen nur nicht glauben daß ich wegen
Wien allein auf der Welt seye. – keinem Monarchen in
der Welt diene ich lieber als dem kayser – aber erbetteln
will ich keinen dienst. – Ich glaube so viel im Stande zu seyn
daß ich jedem Hofe Ehre machen werde. – will mich Teutschland,
mein geliebtes vatterland, worauf ich /: wie sie wissen :/ Stolz bin,
nicht aufnehmen, so muß in gottes Namen frankreich oder England
wieder um einen geschickten Teutschen mehr reich werden; – und
das zur schande der Teutschen Nation. – sie wissen wohl daß

Extract from a letter from Mozart to his father in Salzburg, Vienna, August 17, 1782. Salzburg, Mozarteum.

Mozart as a Child (detail), by Felice Cignaroli, 18th century.
Salzburg, Mozarthaus.

"I have to show the world this miracle"

"We are honest people who to the honor of their Prince and their country announce to the world a miracle that God has caused to be born in Salzburg."

Leopold Mozart, letter to Lorenz Hagenauer, Vienna, July 30, 1768

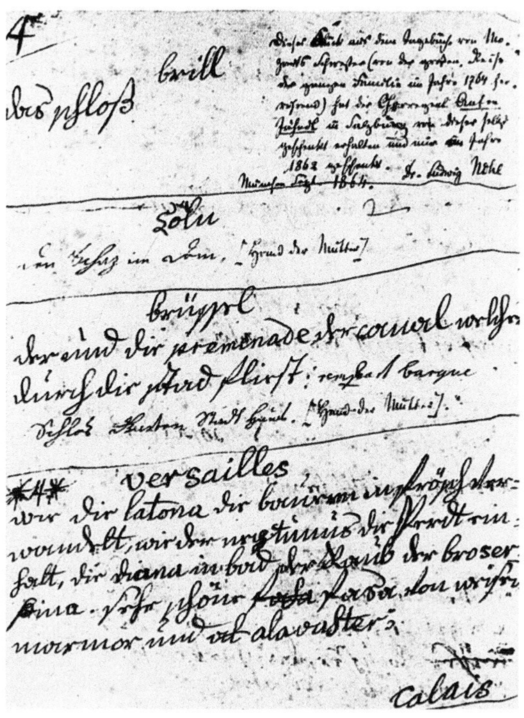

A page from the journal kept by Nannerl and Wolfgang during their tour of 1763–64. They mention Cologne, Brussels, Versailles, and Calais. Salzburg, Mozarteum.

It was indeed to the world that Wolfgang's father wanted to reveal this miracle, not for personal gain or from a perverse desire to put his children on display like some circus act, but quite simply because he had been the first to witness his son's utterly exceptional, indeed unique genius; and Leopold felt that he had to share this wonder. As he wrote in the preface to the second edition of his *Treatise on the Fundamental Principles of Violin Playing*, "The extraordinary musical gifts of my two children, this veritable gift from God, have been the reason for traveling across much of Germany and for my extended visits to France, Holland, and England."

Frontispiece from a book of 1740 by Georges Keyser, describing journeys in Germany, Bohemia, Hungary, Italy, Lorraine, and Hanover, which Leopold Mozart used when planning the tour of 1763–64.

As soon as he returned to Salzburg from Vienna, Leopold made arrangements for the great European tour that would keep the Mozart family on the road for more than three years. For young Wolfgang, this was a considerable ordeal, but also an invaluable experience, for he met the finest musicians, with whom he would talk as an equal, he frequented the noble and powerful, from whom he would later have to seek posts and commissions with which to support himself, and he formed contacts and friendships with the public. And of course Leopold, as his children's only tutor, was rigorous in maintaining their lessons, taking advantage of every encounter, of every visit. Reading his letters one can see the lively interest that this cultured man took in everything that went on around him, whatever the subject, and he doubtless shared his thoughts and his wide knowledge with the children.

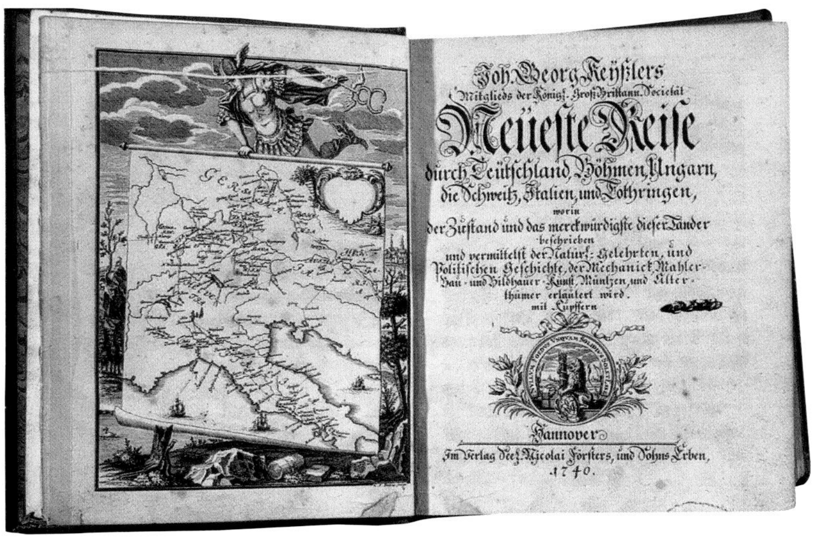

This whirlwind of activity would never cease. Even after he had settled in Vienna, Wolfgang would always be restless, changing his lodgings very frequently. All his life he would continue to travel, and it has been calculated that, on his own or with his family, he spent no fewer than 250 days in coaches of one kind or another, or on boats.

In June 1763, therefore, the Mozarts set out. They would not see Salzburg again until November 1766, nearly three and a half years later. The tour would take them through Germany to Brussels, Paris, and London, and then back to the Netherlands, Flanders, and Paris again, before returning home. The Italian pilgrimage would come later.

Their first success came on the very first leg of their journey, in Munich, which they had visited the previous year. The little prodigy had grown, to be sure, but he amazed everybody just as much as he had before. The *Europäische Zeitung* could write, "Herr Mozart afforded his fellow citizens the great pleasure of hearing for themselves the extraordinary gifts with which the Creator has endowed his two children. The Herr *Kapellmeister* is raising them with indefatigable zeal worthy of the best of fathers. The girl, who is eleven, and, almost incredibly, the boy, who is seven, are such prodigious pianists as to compel the admiration of the musical world. The experts confirm that, despite its apparent improbability, all of what one of their friends in Vienna had written is not only the truth, but often even something less than the truth."

Page 31: *Tea at the House of the Prince de Conti in the Temple* (Le Thé à l'anglaise, dans le salon des quatre glaces) (detail), by Michel-Barthélémy Ollivier, 1764. Mozart is playing the harpsichord. Versailles, Châteaux de Versailles et de Trianon.

In his native city of Augsburg, Leopold bought a small clavichord for the children, so that they could continue to work at their keyboard technique throughout their journey. At every halt, there were concerts and recitals, on harpsichord, piano, and even organ. To the wonderment of all, Wolfgang, who was too small to reach the pedals when seated, played the keys while standing. From Bavaria they traveled to the banks of the Rhine. A youth of 14 attended the concert at Frankfurt; it was the young Goethe, who would later write, "I can still quite clearly remember the little fellow, with his wig and his sword." The family then crossed from Aachen into the Austrian Netherlands, and on to Paris, which they reached on November 18. They would stay there for five months.

The stories of the concerts the Mozart family gave before the princes, and of the audiences they had at the Palace of Versailles, have been told and retold. Leopold admired the choirs in the Chapelle

Royale, but loathed the solo parts of the pieces performed there: "Everything that was supposed to resemble an aria was empty, frozen and miserable, in other words quite French." The children played for the royal family, were received by Mme de Pompadour and the Prince de Conti, were feted, and went to the aristocratic salons. They were applauded and presented with watches and snuffboxes; but the French treated them frivolously, and did nothing to help them in any way.

Only Baron Friedrich Melchior von Grimm, who had by then lived in Paris for 15 years and who quickly formed an attachment to Leopold, who was virtually his compatriot, eagerly took upon himself the charge of acting as their propagandist. He described Wolfgang as "such an extraordinary phenomenon that one is hard put to it to believe what one sees with one's eyes and hears with one's ears. For this child, to play the most difficult pieces with the greatest accuracy is but a trifle [...]. What is incredible is to see him improvise for an hour on end, giving full rein to the inspiration of his genius and to a mass of enchanting ideas, and, what is more, running them together tastefully and without confusion [...]. He writes and composes with marvelous facility, without having to approach the harpsichord to find the chords."

Yet the glory did not go to young Wolfgang's head; rather, it amused him. From his earliest youth he held his own opinions and retained his self-respect. When he once asked Mme de Pompadour for a kiss and she refused him, he cried, "Who is this that refuses to kiss me? The Empress herself has kissed me!" What was important to him, however, was meeting composers and musicians, such as Johann Schobert, the brilliant young German who had been in the service of the Prince de Conti for two years and who, tragically, was to die soon afterward. Wolfgang used Schobert's many harpsichord and violin sonatas as a model for his own first compositions. For he was now beginning to write, and from a bit jotted down here and some notes jotted down there he soon produced his two pairs of sonatas for keyboard and violin, which appeared as opp. 1 and 2, the first dedicated to Mme Victoire de France, daughter of Louis XV.

After Paris came London. Arriving in April 1764, the Mozart family stayed nearly 16 months, not leaving until the following July. By April 27, they had already been received at St. James's Palace. Leopold wrote, "The graciousness with which Their Majesties received us is beyond description; their friendly manner made us completely forget that we were in the presence of the King and Queen of England." Before King George, Mozart read at sight, improvised, and performed on the organ "so well that he is considered here a finer player of the organ than the harpsichord." Life in England was a succession of receptions, concerts, and successes.

The most important event of their stay in England, however, was young Wolfgang's encounter with Johann Christian Bach, the youngest son of Johann Sebastian. Four years earlier the "English Bach" had settled in London, where he had encountered Karl Friedrich Abel, the son of a friend and colleague of his father's, as well as a former pupil himself. The two men had formed a musical society, the Bach-Abel Concerts. Despite being 21 years Mozart's senior, Johann Christian formed a profound friendship with the boy, virtually taking charge of him during his visit and constantly giving him advice. He introduced young Mozart to Italian opera, of which he had had direct experience during his years in Italy, where he had studied with Padre Martini in Bologna (Mozart would later work with Padre Martini himself). That fall, Mozart composed six keyboard and violin sonatas, which were published with a dedication to Queen Charlotte. Shortly afterward, he completed his first symphony.

The first triumphs over, times became hard, and it was soon time to return to the road, passing through Lille, Ghent, and Rotterdam on the way to The Hague. First Nannerl fell ill, and then little Wolfgang, who had been overworked, and who lay for a while at death's door with a serious case of typhoid fever. It would be two months before he recovered. After Amsterdam, the family proceeded once more to Paris, where they stayed for two months to renewed acclaim, departing in July. Traveling via Dijon, Lyon, Geneva, Lausanne, Zürich, then Augsburg and Munich, to mention only the most important stops, they reached Salzburg in late November, having left the city three years earlier.

Young Mozart was now ten years old; the endless touring, the exhaustion, the sickness, and all the other experiences had left him considerably matured. He was a composer as well as a performer, and still astonishingly talented and highly precocious. Soon, however, he would no longer be regarded as a miracle of nature, but simply another professional musician.

After the family's return to Salzburg, new works by the young Mozart were performed in public: an oratorio, *Die Schuldigkeit des ersten Gebots* (The Obligation of the First Commandment), and a comedy in Latin, *Apollo et Hyacinthus*. Realizing that the hour of the little prodigy would soon pass and that

A Recital, by Frank Moss Bennett, 1750 (scene from an English manor house).

his son's true genius lay in composition, Leopold encouraged him to write; and Wolfgang obliged, penning work after work at an astonishing speed, his first cantatas, his first concertos, his first serenades.

That fall, the family planned to take advantage of the celebrations surrounding the forthcoming marriage in Vienna of the Archduchess Maria Josepha, daughter of Empress Maria Theresa, to Ferdinand, King of Naples, by performing in public, but smallpox was sweeping the country, and the Mozart children, who had taken refuge in Olmütz, came down with it too. When they recovered, they returned to Vienna via Brünn (Brno), arriving in January; they would remain in the city for the rest of the year. This marks the start of Mozart's professional career. He was commissioned to write an *opera buffa*, *La finta semplice* (The False Simpleton), which was not performed in Vienna, and his first *Singspiel*, *Bastien und Bastienne*, which was produced in the private theater of Dr. Anton Mesmer, the famous magnetist, who would become a close friend of the family. By the year's end, they were back in Salzburg, but not for long.

Versailles and Paris

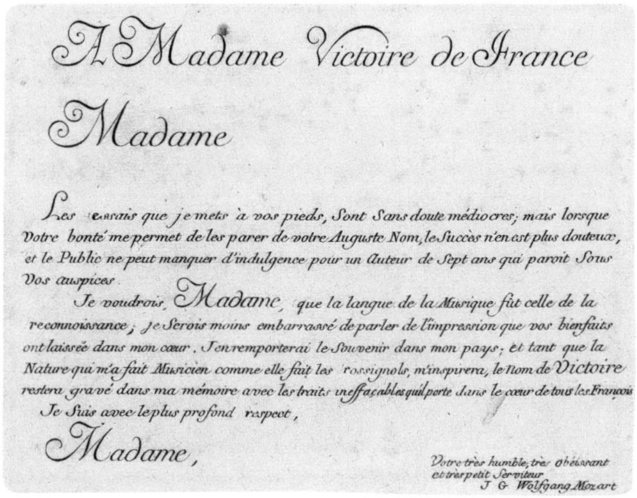

A Madame Victoire de France

Madame

Les essais que je mets à vos pieds, Sont Sans doute médiocres; mais lorsque Votre bonté me permet de les parer de votre Auguste Nom, le Succès n'en est plus douteux, et le Public ne peut manquer d'indulgence pour un Auteur de Sept ans qui paroit Sous Vos auspices.

Je voudrois, Madame, que la langue de la Musique fût celle de la reconnoissance; je Serois moins embarrassé de parler de l'impression que vos bienfaits ont laissée dans mon cœur. J'en remporterai le Souvenir dans mon pays; et tant que la Nature qui m'a fait Musicien comme elle fait les rossignols, m'inspirera, le Nom de Victoire restera gravé dans ma mémoire avec les traits ineffaçables qu'il porte dans le cœur de tous les François.

Je Suis avec le plus profond respect,

Madame,

Votre très humble, très obéissant et très petit Serviteur
J G Wolfgang Mozart

Dedication to Mme Victoire de France, written by Baron von Grimm.
Paris, Bibliothèque Nationale de France, Département de la Musique.

Leopold Mozart with Wolfgang and Nannerl (detail),
by Louis de Carmontelle, November 1763.
Chantilly, Musée Condé.

The Mozart family's first visit to France (they arrived in Paris in November 1763) is commemorated in a delightful watercolor by Louis de Carmontelle, *Leopold Mozart with Wolfgang and Nannerl*, now in the museum at Chantilly. In performing with their father, the two children gave rise to a widespread craze, and Carmontelle accordingly shows the three musicians playing together. Leopold, already a celebrated violinist, plays his instrument, while Nannerl sings, aged twelve and a half. At the harpsichord, perched atop a cushion, Wolfgang, who was soon to be eight, is playing with great concentration. Carmontelle made a number of copies of the subject, and as an engraving it was an immediate, Europe-wide success. Young Mozart, however, was not satisfied merely to appear as a keyboard prodigy; he started to compose, and not just to compose, but also to publish his work. In January 1764, his first published work, two sonatas for keyboard and violin, op. 1, was published by Mme Vendôme in Paris. It was prefaced by a dedication to Mme Victoire de France, one of Louis XV's daughters, composed in French by Baron von Grimm, which ended with the words, "I am, with the most profound respect, Madame, your very humble, very obedient, and very small servant, J. G. Wolfgang Mozart."

Sonatas for keyboard with violin accompaniment, dedicated to Mme Victoire de France by Wolfgang Mozart (his op. 1, K. 6–7). Of the copy that once belonged to Mozart, three sheets have survived, including the one reproduced here, signed by the composer.
Salzburg, Mozarteum.

London

Wolfgang Amadeus Mozart and His Sister Maria Anna, Known as Nannerl, by Eusebius Johann Alphen (1741–72). Miniature on ivory. Salzburg, Mozartmuseum.

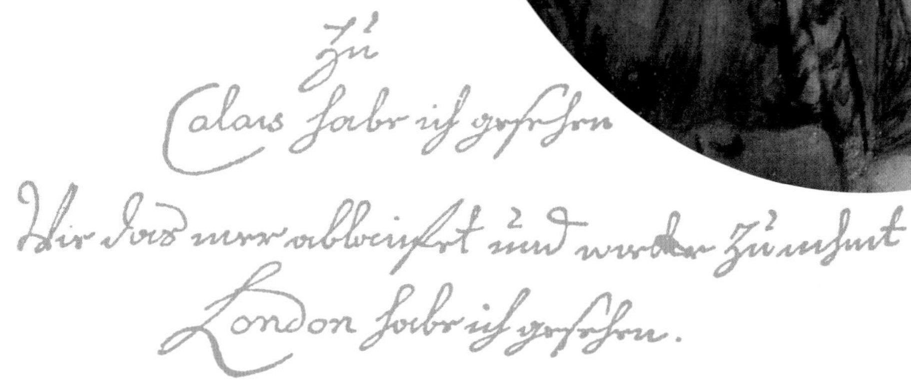

Excerpt from the journal kept by Nannerl and Wolfgang Mozart during their stay in England in 1764: "In Calais I saw …"

Mozart composed his first sacred work when he was nine years old, a motet entitled "God is our refuge" to the first verse of Psalm 46: "God is our refuge and our strength, a very present help in trouble." The seriousness of the words inspired the boy to write with equal sobriety. When the British Museum asked Mozart to leave it some tangible record of his talent, Leopold presented the museum with a copy of the Paris group-portrait engraved after Carmontelle, a copy of the sonatas published in Paris, and other items, including this motet. On July 19, 1765, a Mr. Maty, the Secretary of the British Museum, wrote Leopold Mozart, "Sir. I am ordered by the *Standing Committee* of the Trustees of the British Museum, to signify to You, that they have received the *present of the musical performances of your very ingenious Son* which You were pleased lately to make Them, and to return You their Thanks for the same." A few days later, on August 1, 1765, they left London for the Netherlands.

"God is our refuge" (K. 20), 1765.
London, British Library.

Johann Christian Bach

Johann Christian Bach, the youngest son of Johann Sebastian Bach, by Thomas Gainsborough, 1776. Bologna, Liceo Musicale.

After completing his studies in Germany, Johann Sebastian Bach's youngest son Johann Christian went to Italy, where, among other things, he worked with Padre Martini in Bologna. In 1762 he moved to England, where his compatriot Handel had recently died, and where he would very soon come to play a central role in the musical life of the country. Two years later, within a week of their arrival in England, the Mozart family was received at the Palace. The King placed before young Wolfgang "not only works of Wagenseil, but those of Bach, Abel, and Handel, and he played everything off *prima vista*." The details of the various meetings between Wolfgang and his famous elder are lost in the mists of history, although they are known to have met for the first time in March 1765. It is recorded that one day Johann Christian Bach "had begun a fugue and left off abruptly, that little Mozart hath immediately taken it up and worked after a most masterly manner." A similar report comes from the pen of Georg Nikolaus Nissen, Constanze's second husband and Mozart's first biographer: "Johann Christian, the Master of the Queen's Music, took little Mozart on his knees and played some bars, which the child continued. Taking turns in this manner, they played an entire sonata with marvelous precision." The episode must have made an impression, for we find Baron von Grimm writing in Paris, "In London, Bach took him between his knees and they played alternately on the same harpsichord for two hours together, extempore, before the King and Queen." A lively friendship developed between the two, young Mozart clearly very impressed by his illustrious colleague: his first symphonies and sonatas all show the influence of Johann Christian. Indeed, the works we know today as Mozart's first three piano concertos are in fact arrangements for harpsichord and strings of keyboard sonatas that Johann Christian had just composed and that he had doubtless shown to the boy. In the years to come, the lives and careers of Mozart and Johann Christian Bach would cross many times in their respective works and performances. In 1778, Mozart would be delighted to encounter Bach again, this time in Paris. Four years later, he would mourn his friend's death at the age of 46, writing his father, "I suppose you have heard that the English Bach is dead? What a loss to the musical world!"

The first page of the score of the three sonatas by Johann Christian Bach arranged by Mozart for piano and string orchestra.
Berlin, Staatsbibliothek, Musikabteilung.

Oratorio or opera

The Death of Hyacinth,
by Giovanni Battista Tiepolo, 1750.
Madrid, Thyssen-Bornemisza Collection.

No sooner had Mozart returned from his three-year grand tour of Europe than he was commissioned to write works for the Archbishop's court, which he began immediately. First, he had to write Act 1 of an oratorio, sacred drama, or "spiritual *Singspiel,*" *Die Schuldigkeit des ersten Gebots,* Acts 2 and 3 having been commissioned from two well-known Salzburg musicians, Anton Adlgasser and Michael Haydn. Within less than three months, the boy had finished his task, and the work was performed on March 12, 1767, in the Knights' Hall in Salzburg Castle. Immediately afterward, Mozart set about composing an intermezzo for the university's annual prize-giving ceremony. His *Apollo et Hyacinthus,* a comedy in Latin based on a scene from Ovid, was performed on May 13, 1767, in the aula of Salzburg University. Barely two months had elapsed between the completion of the first of these works and that of the second, and one can only marvel at the speed with which this 11-year-old boy worked, especially as these were no lightweight pieces: *Die Schuldigkeit* lasts about an hour and a half, and *Apollo* little less. Neither *opera seria* nor *opera buffa,* neither oratorio nor *Singspiel,* these two large scores mediate between the genres. Mozart was already tasting the lyricism that would thrill him throughout his entire life.

The first page of Mozart's opera *Apollo et Hyacinthus* (K. 38), May 1767.
Berlin, Staatsbibliothek, Musikabteilung.

A *Singspiel* in Vienna

Bastien und Bastienne was inspired by Jean-Jacques Rousseau's comic opera *Le Devin du village*, a scene from which is shown here, with Mlle Laruette and M. Suler, 1752.
Paris, Bibliothèque Nationale de France, Département des Estampes.

The little piece entitled *Bastien und Bastienne* has often passed for Mozart's first opera, although, as we have seen, this is not strictly true. Composed in Vienna during the summer of 1768, it was first performed on October 1, at the house of Dr. Anton Mesmer, who had commissioned it. In fact, Mozart had written his first *opera buffa, La finta semplice,* during his family's year-long visit to Vienna in 1768, but the world seemed to be conspiring against him, and the work was not performed as it was supposed to have been. It was at this point that a commission arrived for a *Singspiel* (the German equivalent of the Italian *opera buffa* and French *opéra comique* of the same period) from Dr. Mesmer, who wanted to stage it in the little puppet theater in his house in Vienna. With its alternation between sung arias and spoken recitative, the honest feelings of the simple villagers, and the simplicity of its plot, which was borrowed from Rousseau's *Le Devin du village* (The Village Soothsayer), this subject was much more within Mozart's reach than the fairly abstract and highly conventional sentiments of his two earlier attempts. Moreover, the wealthy Dr. Mesmer was a friend of the Mozart family. A freemason, he was given to occasional flirtation with astrology and the occult, and had made a specialty of studying magnetism, his experiments eventually leading to his being dismissed as a charlatan. The production passed off without a hitch, but so discreetly that no-one spoke of it, and so posterity has no contemporary account of the work's performance or of its reception by those present. And yet Mozart's little *Singspiel* has had its revenge: adapted for children as a puppet play, it now enjoys worldwide popularity.

Portrait of the German doctor and scholar Franz Anton Mesmer. Penciled lithograph after a contemporary portrait. The first performance of *Bastien und Bastienne* was given at Mesmer's house.
Paris, Bibliothèque Nationale de France.

Bastien und Bastienne (K. 50), overture.
Cracow, Biblioteka Jagiellonska.

Mozart at the age of 14, by Domenico Saverio dalla Rosa. This portrait was painted in Verona on January 16 and 17, 1770, during Mozart's first visit to Italy. The score on the piano is that of the Allegro for piano (K. 72a); this picture is its only source of identification.
Private collection.

"You know how I detest Salzburg"

"You, my dear friend, know how I detest Salzburg, and not only on account of all the injustices we suffered there, my dear father and I, though they were quite enough for us to wish to wipe the place from our memories forever!"

Mozart, letter to the Abbé Bullinger, Paris, August 7, 1778

Composed between May and July 1778, this "Sketch for a Ballet-Pantomime" (K. 299c) was described by Mozart to his father (in French) as follows: "The blacksmith is working ... he sees that his wife is no longer there." The sketch (of which a detail is shown here) makes use of a realistic style.
Paris, Bibliothèque Nationale de France, Département de la Musique.

During 1769, an exceptional year when the Mozart family remained in Salzburg, Wolfgang, now 13, devoted himself totally to composition, writing his first sacred works, a *Missa brevis* and a *Te Deum* for the cathedral and the Archbishop, and instrumental works, including cassations and serenades, for other Salzburg patrons. In May, the *opera buffa La finta semplice*, written the previous year in Vienna, was performed in the Archbishop's court theater, and he was appointed court *Konzertmeister* on an honorary basis.

The time had now come to complete Wolfgang's cultural and musical education, which could only be accomplished in Italy, where oratorio and opera, sonata and concerto reigned. For three years, Leopold had taken his son around Europe so that he could be heard; now they set out for Italy, where they would stay for a further three years. They made three separate journeys, which would take Wolfgang to all the great musical cities of the peninsula and bring him into contact not only with the finest composers and performers but also with ambassadors and cardinals, and with everything regarded as cultured by Italy's great families.

Bridge over the Po at Turin, by Canaletto. © Galerie Sabauda, Turin.

Breathlessly we watch father and son as they follow the roads leading south, to Verona, Mantua, Milan, Bologna, Florence (for them the greatest joy), and on to Rome and Naples, returning by the same route. They found much to admire on the way—the beauty of the countryside, the splendor of the monuments. They made a number of important stops, important because, even though the 14-year-old Mozart never failed to elicit the admiration of all who attended the many concerts he gave, the intention this time was not to win their applause but for him to complete his musical education.

In Milan, in 1770, he was commissioned to write an *opera seria, Mitridate, re di Ponto* (Mithridates, King of Pontus), for the following carnival. An opera! The sign that a composer had truly arrived! In Rome, he heard Allegri's celebrated *Miserere*, at this point still unpublished and regarded as the private property of the choir of the Sistine Chapel; on his return he transcribed it from memory. In Naples, they heard works by Nicolò Jommelli at the Teatro San Carlo. On their way back, Wolfgang was made Knight of the Order of the Golden Spur by Pope Clement XIV, the first musician so honored since Orlande de Lassus and Gluck. Yet Mozart *père* and *fils* were not overly impressed by this. Leopold wrote his wife, "You can imagine how I laugh when I hear people calling him 'signor cavaliere' all the time!"

In Bologna they stayed for more than two months with Padre Martini, the greatest musical theorist of the age. Wolfgang sailed through the difficult entrance examination of the Accademia Filarmonica. In Bologna they also met Dr. Charles Burney, who was then traveling in Europe to collect material for his *History of Music* (1776–89) and who noted in his journal, "whom should I meet but the celebrated little German, Mozart, who in 1766 astonished all hearers in London by his premature musical talent [...]. He has been at Rome and Naples, where he was much admired." Nothing, however, could distract Wolfgang from composition, above all his opera *Mitridate*, which was staged in Milan at the year's end. They then proceeded home by way of Venice and Padua, where Wolfgang received a commission for an oratorio, *La Betulia liberata* (Bethulia Liberated), on the story of Judith and Holofernes, and by Vicenza and Verona.

Returning to Salzburg in March 1771, the travelers remained barely four months before setting out for Milan for a further four months. At the end of August, Wolfgang received another commission, this time for a *festa teatrale, Ascanio in Alba*, which he composed in three weeks. It was performed for the wedding

Interior of St. Peter's, Rome, by Giovanni Pannini. Paris, Louvre.

celebrations of Archduke Ferdinand of Austria and Princess Maria Beatrice Ricciarda d'Este of Modena, held in Milan (then under Austrian rule). It was a great success, and there were five performances.

Early in 1772 an event took place in Salzburg that would be of decisive importance for the Mozarts—the election of Hieronymus, Count Colloredo, as Prince-Archbishop of Salzburg. Unlike his predecessor, Colloredo did not look kindly on them, though their period of grace continued during his early months in office, with the performance of the serenata *Il sogno di Scipione* (Scipio's Dream) at the archiepiscopal residence in early May in honor of the new Prince, who formalized Wolfgang's previously honorary position as *Konzertmeister*. This time, however, the post entailed duties.

Leopold and his son nevertheless managed to return to Milan for five months, where Wolfgang rehearsed his new opera, *Lucio Silla*. The work was first performed on December 26, with 17 further performances in three weeks. Early in March 1773, the two travelers left Italy, never to return.

Young Mozart was now tied firmly to Salzburg, leaving the city only for much shorter trips than previously, and devoting himself entirely to composition. Following the seven symphonies of the previous year, during a trip to Vienna he wrote a serenade and the six so-called Viennese string quartets, and then, back in Salzburg, his first major symphony, Symphony no. 25, in G minor. There followed more symphonies, serenades, concertos, and sonatas, and above all operatic works, such as the *opera buffa La finta giardiniera* (The False Gardener), produced in Munich in January 1775, and the *opera seria Il re pastore* (The Shepherd King), on the order of Prince-Archbishop Colloredo.

Now in his twentieth year and already master of his trade, Mozart entered a period of intense productivity during which he composed his first masterpieces, including violin concertos and incidental music

Nymphenburg Palace, near Munich, in the 18th century, by Bernardo Bellotto. Washington, National Gallery of Art.

for *Thamos, König in Ägypten* (Thamos, King of Egypt) in 1775, the "Serenata notturna" and the "Haffner" Serenade in 1776, and the Piano Concerto no. 9 in E flat major, the "Jeunehomme," early in 1777.

It was at this time that the Mozarts had their first dispute with the Prince-Archbishop. In March, Leopold requested a leave of absence, which was refused. In August, it was the turn of Wolfgang, who wanted to travel in order to earn extra income to offset his family's increased expenses. Yet despite the unimpeachable tones of humility in which he couched his petition, Colloredo remained unmoved. He intended his musicians to serve him as he saw fit. When the reply came, it was very brief, two lines in all, and very blunt: "Father and son herewith granted permission to seek their fortunes elsewhere, according to the Gospel." Colloredo's decree, however, retained Leopold in his service, while Wolfgang was summarily dismissed.

Mozart now had to find engagements to enable him to spread his wings and live his own life. And so began his odyssey. On September 23, 1777, he and his mother left Salzburg, his mother never to return. Their first stop was at Munich. After the oppressive atmosphere in Salzburg, Wolfgang could breathe again. "Ever since I managed to get away from all that endless bother I am constantly in the very best of spirits and marvelously lighthearted." There followed two weeks in Augsburg, where Leopold still had

family. But the Augsburgers took no interest in Wolfgang, and one afternoon he took them to task: "I have only come so that you, gentlemen of Augsburg, may not be laughed at in other countries, when I tell people that I spent a week in the town where my father was born without anyone taking the trouble to hear me." Wolfgang did, however, become acquainted with his younger cousin, Maria Anna Thekla Mozart, with whom he at once developed an unusually intimate relationship.

The next stop was Mannheim, where he would remain for four months. The Mannheim stay marked a turning point in the life of the young composer, first because the Elector, Karl Theodor, a friend of the poet Klopstock and a highly cultured man, kept an orchestra considered at that time to be the best in the world. Its members, virtuosi to a man, included such figures as Christian Cannabich, Ignaz Holzbauer, the Wendling family, and the unpleasant Abbé Vogler. Second, Mannheim had an opera that staged German rather than Italian works. From such conditions Mozart would distill pure nectar.

Slowly, Mozart was becoming a man as well. His heart would leap at each girl he met, and he would dedicate to them sonatas, concertos, and concert arias, while in his letters to his father, whom he would

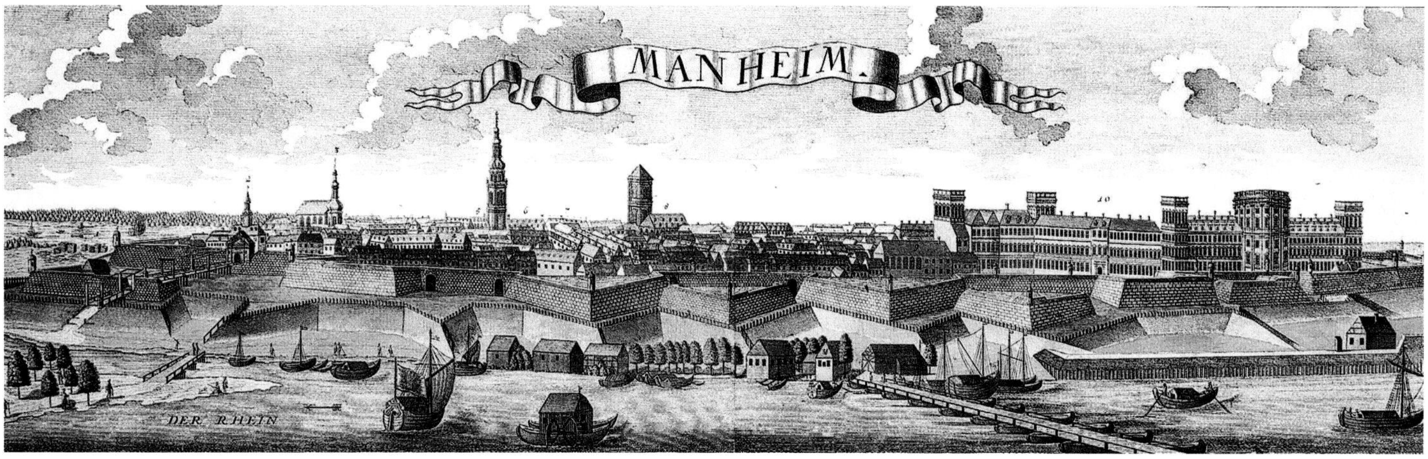

View of Mannheim (then spelt "Manheim") in 1729 (detail). Colored engraving, after Friedrich Berhardt Werner.

henceforth always address formally as "Sie," he is beginning to stand up for himself. "I imagine that all the things I have written must seem strange to you, living as you do in a town where one is used to having stupid enemies, and weak and foolish friends who, because they cannot do without Salzburg's poor fare, always have their tails between their legs and are consequently one thing one day and something else the next."

In the interminable flow of letters from Leopold, who had remained in Salzburg, one senses increasing concern. He fretted continuously about Wolfgang's daily life, admonishing him about the precariousness of his financial affairs and about his behavior, which he judged to be light-headed and thoughtless. Leopold knew his son very well, and felt that his absence deprived Wolfgang of the guidance he badly needed. His reproaches were unending: "The object of your journey was and is and must be to find an appointment or make some money!" "A journey is not a joke!" "Re-read my earlier letters often, and treat them as if they were orders!" "May I ask if Wolfgang has forgotten about confession? God must come first! From His hands we receive our temporal happiness; and at the same time we must think about our eternal salvation." And while Wolfgang never failed to show his father respect, affection, and gratitude, he now seemed to be taking a step back from his tutelage. His letters show more maturity in style, even though his facetious comments and irrepressible humor might seem to detract from it.

When Leopold discovered that his son had made the acquaintance of the young Aloysia Weber, a singer of whom he spoke enthusiastically, the ice descended. Wolfgang fell madly in love with her, to his father's chagrin and rage.

But the time came to try his luck in Paris, where he had been acclaimed 16 years earlier. He still enjoyed a certain amount of support, and received a number of commissions: the Symphony no. 31 (the

"Paris") and the *Sinfonia concertante* for wind for the Concerts Spirituels, the ballet music *Les Petits Riens* for the Paris Opera, the Concerto for flute and harp, and the Piano Sonata in A minor, with its "alla turca" finale.

Mozart himself, however, was no longer the little prodigy who had once enchanted all the grown-ups, and the nobility who had formerly feted him now inflicted affront after affront. He eked out a living, giving lessons here and there. In July, his mother fell ill and died, and was buried in the cemetery of Saint-Eustache. Echoes of this blow can be heard in the tragic Piano Sonata in A minor. One happy encounter still awaited him in Paris in the figure of Johann Christian Bach, who had gone there in August to prepare his opera *Amadis de Gaule*. "Herr Bach from London has been here for the last two weeks. He is going to write a French opera. [...] You can easily imagine his delight and mine at meeting again. Perhaps his delight was not quite as sincere as mine, but one must admit he is an honest man who does right by other people; I love him with all my heart (as you know) and respect him." Mozart received no further help from Baron von Grimm, however. Discouraged, he returned to Salzburg via Nancy and Strasbourg, where he stayed for a month with the composer Franz Xaver Richter.

The Pont Neuf and the Pompe de La Samaritaine in 1777, by Nicolas Raguenet, 1757. Paris, Musée Carnavalet.

Returning to Salzburg early in 1779, Mozart secured an appointment as court organist and in that capacity wrote a good deal of sacred music, including the "Coronation" Mass. However unwillingly, he once more resumed his place in the life of the town: "I cannot stand either the town or the people of Salzburg: I find the way they live and the way they talk utterly intolerable." Two years later, in Vienna and having to face once again the heartrending inevitability of returning to Salzburg, he would say the same thing: "It is true that I am still young, as you say, but it is nevertheless a great loss and very sad to fritter away one's youth in a dull and miserable place."

For the time being, he nonetheless continued to compose for the townspeople, for the theater, and for concerts of his own: more symphonies, the Concerto for three pianos, the *Sinfonia concertante* for violin and viola, the "Posthorn" Serenade, and the *Singspiel Zaide*.

In the late summer of 1780, Mozart was commissioned by the Elector of Bavaria to write an *opera seria* for the upcoming Munich carnival. This would be *Idomeneo, re di Creta* (Idomeneus, King of Crete), performed on January 29, 1781, in the Residenz Theater in Munich. Yet all this was most displeasing to Mozart's patron, Prince-Archbishop Colloredo, who ordered the composer to join him in Vienna. Mozart took lodgings in the city with the Weber family, who had recently moved there.

Tension grew not only between the Prince-Archbishop and Mozart, who refused to be cowed by him, but also between Wolfgang and his father, who urged him from Salzburg to be more conciliatory. On May 9, Mozart wrote, "I want to hear nothing more about Salzburg. I hate the Archbishop to the point of madness." Beside himself with rage, Colloredo berated Mozart in contemptuous terms, calling him a scoundrel, a rogue, a vagabond: "Be off with you, if you cannot serve me as you should!" Mozart resigned, and the affair came to a head on June 8 with the famous and historic kick which Count Arco, the Archbishop's Chief Steward, administered to the still unrepentant musician's backside. The break was final and Mozart decided on the spot to leave Salzburg for good and settle in Vienna.

On July 30, Mozart was given the libretto for the opera *The Abduction from the Seraglio* and set to work immediately. A new life had begun.

Michael Haydn

Portrait of Michael Haydn by an unknown artist, c. 1800. Vienna, Gesellschaft der Musikfreunde.

To Sir Wolfgang Amadé Mozart, Knight, Master of Music at *

Salzburg, November 1, 1777

Mon très cher Fils!
I have this moment returned from Mass at the Cathedral. They performed Haydn's oboe mass, with Haydn himself conducting. They also performed the Offertory and instead of the sonata the words of the Gradual spoken by the priest, which he had also set to music. There was a rehearsal yesterday after Vespers. The Prince did not say Mass himself, but Count Friedrich Lodron did instead, as the Bishops of Chiemsee, Breuner, and Dietrichstein are not here but at Augsburg for the All Saints Peremptory. I found it all extraordinarily pleasing, because there were six oboes, three double basses, two bassoons, and the castrato, who has been engaged for six months at a monthly salary of 100 gulden. Ferlendis and Sandmayr were the solo oboes. The Lodrons' oboist, a student, and then the town piper and Obkirchner were the oboes in the orchestra. Cassl and Knozenbry, the choirmaster, played the double basses, which were near the organ, beside the trombones. Estlinger was on bassoon, Hofer and Perwein were beside the oboes in the violin chorus. What I found particularly pleasing, was that since oboes and bassoons very closely approach the human voice, the *tutti* sounded like vocal pieces of great power, as the sopranos and altos, supported by the six oboes and alto trombones, balanced the many tenors and basses admirably well, and the *pieno* was so majestic that I could easily have done without the oboe solos. [...]

Letter from Leopold Mozart to his son Wolfgang in Mannheim, Salzburg, November 1, 1777 (extract).

Of all the musicians in Salzburg, one stands out for his talent, Johann Michael Haydn, Joseph Haydn's younger brother, to whom Mozart would soon form an attachment. Having settled in Salzburg in 1762, Haydn was employed first as a court musician and later as *Konzertmeister*. The two men struck up a lively friendship and Haydn's influence on the younger composer's style would be considerable.

On November 1, 1777, in one of his long letters to his son, who was then at Mannheim, Leopold Mozart wrote these words about Michael Haydn: "I have this moment returned from Mass at the cathedral. They performed Haydn's oboe mass, with Haydn himself conducting. [...] I found it all extraordinarily pleasing [...]. The whole thing lasted no less than an hour and a quarter but to me it seemed very short indeed, since it was really very well written. It all flows along quite naturally, the fugues are worked out in masterly fashion, and the themes are natural without any exaggerated modulations or abrupt transitions. If I manage to lay my hands on a copy for any length of time I shall certainly send it to you. I should add that [the soloists] kept a watchful eye on Haydn throughout the performance, who was beating time on their shoulders, otherwise it would have fallen into confusion in some places, especially in the fugues and the fast bass passages. Now most probably he will finally obtain his appointment as cathedral *Kapellmeister* or deputy *Kapellmeister*, for which he has been working for so many years."

Mon très cher Fils! 14 Salzb: d. 1 Novemb: 1777.

Diesen Augenblick komme aus dem Amt vom Dom, wo die Hauth: Mess
vom Haydn gemacht, er tactierte sie selbst. es war auch das offertorium, und an statt
der Sonaten die Worte des graduals, so der Priester bethet, ebenso daß ganz concertiert.
gestern wurde sie nach der Vesper probiert. der Fürst hielt das Amt nicht, sondern der
graf Friedrich Lodron, weil Bischof in Chiemsee, Brixen, und Dietrichstein in Aug=
=spurg auf dem Allerheiligen peremptorio, folglich nicht hier sind. Mir gefiel alles
außerordentlich wohl, weil 6 Oboist, 3 Contrabass, 2 Fagott, und der Castrat,
welcher auf 6 Monat mit monatlich 100 fl aufgenommen ist, dabey waren.
Ferlendis und Sandmayr hatten die Solo Oboen. der Oboist beym Lodron, ein gewesener
Student, dann der Verwalter und Oberjäger waren die Ripien=Oboen
Castl und der Kerschbaumer waren die Contrabässe bey der Orgel nebst dem Hofposaunist
[illegible] war mit dem Fagott, Hofer und Ferrarini [illegible] den Oboisten auf dem
Violinchor. was mir sonderheitlich gefiel war, daß, da die Oboen und Fagotte der
Menschenstimme sehr nahe kommen, die Tutti einer sehr stark besetzten Vocal=
=musik zu seyn schienen, indem die Sopran und alt stimmen, durch die 6 Oboen und
die Altposaunen verstärkt, der Menge der Tenor und Bass stimmen, das rechte gleich=
=gewicht hielten, und das piano so majestätisch war, daß die Oboe solos ganz [illegible]
[illegible] hatte. die ganze Historie dauerte 5 starke Stund, und mir war es zu kurz,
[illegible]. Es geht alles natürlich fort; die Fugen, sonderheit das
[illegible], dann das alleluja im offertorio sind meister=
Et Vitam: im Credo und das Dona nobis, [illegible] und kein übertriebener modulation oder
[illegible], die themata natürlich, und keine übertriebene modulation oder
zu gähe Ausweichung angebracht. das graduale, anstatt der Sonate, ist ein förmlicher
Contrapunct durchaus in piano. [illegible] hat hier die Stimme des Castraten gute Dienste.
Sollte ich diese Messe, über Kurz oder Lange bekommen können, so schicke ich dir solche gewiß.
[illegible] noch muß anmerken, daß der Brunetti beym Ferlendi und der [illegible]
Sadlo bey dem Fagottist, der [illegible] aber bey dem andern Oboist rückwärts stund, [illegible]
auf den Haydn sah, und ich den tact [illegible] schlug: sonst würde es manchmal
[illegible] Bass= obligation [illegible]
sonderheit in Fugen und bey laufendem [illegible]
[illegible] Kapellmeister, [illegible]
[illegible]
du musst zur Neuigkeit wissen, daß Rust in einem [illegible], so
zwar, daß ihm Dr. Barisani gesagt er solle [illegible]
diesen Winter [illegible]. Er hat demnach seine Entlassung verlangt,
die ihm der Fürst aber nicht geben will, [illegible] den Dr. Barisani [illegible]
Buchman zum Rust geschickt hat. Rust hat, da Barisani nun nicht mehr zu ihm kam,
[illegible] zum Barisani mit dem Buchman [illegible]
[illegible] Recepten hinaus gegangen, der bey Ansicht der selben [illegible]
[illegible], so werde er einige Woche [illegible]

The famous Padre Martini

Padre Giovanni Battista Martini. Unknown artist, 18th century. Bologna, Museo Bibliografico Musicale.

Giovanni Battista Martini, known as Padre Martini, was born in Bologna and lived there all his life. A Franciscan monk from the age of 15, he devoted himself to the study not only of singing, counterpoint, composition, and harpsichord but also of mathematics and the theory of music, of which he would become a master. It is now apparent that Martini was one of the very first musicologists and historians of music. At 21 he became *maestro di cappella* at the Franciscan church in Bologna, a position he would hold until his death in 1784 at the age of 78. Over the years, this highly cultured, distinguished scholar assembled a library of some 17,000 volumes, was associated with many brilliant minds as he was with countless musicians and composers, and came to be regarded as the greatest authority on music of his time. People came from far and wide to consult him and to study at his school. He made Bologna one of the most important musical centers of the century. On their way to Rome and Naples in 1770, Mozart *père* and *fils* spent six days there, as guests of the young Count Pallavicini. Leopold reported that "the famous Padre Martini was also invited, and although he never goes to concerts he came [...]. Padre Martini, the idol of all the Italians, speaks with admiration of Wolfgang and of all the proofs he has given of his skill." On their return journey, the Mozarts spent two and a half months in Bologna, where Wolfgang worked like a slave on his opera *Mitridate, re di Ponto*, which was to be staged in Milan at the end of the year. During this period he saw Padre Martini every day and also appeared as an organist and composer, astonishing all who saw him. His most signal honor, however, was to be admitted, by unanimous vote, to the prestigious Accademia Filarmonica, despite his age (candidates normally had to be at least 20 years of age, and Wolfgang was only 14). Padre Martini himself presented Wolfgang with his diploma, and on October 12, 1770, gave him a testimonial in which he stated that he had found his pupil to be "most highly versed in all the requisite musical qualities, having passed every test, above all playing on the harpsichord, with great mastery and in strict observance of all the rules, a number of themes which I had given him to develop."

Mozart's certificate of admission to the entrance examination of the Accademia Filarmonica of Bologna, October 9, 1770.

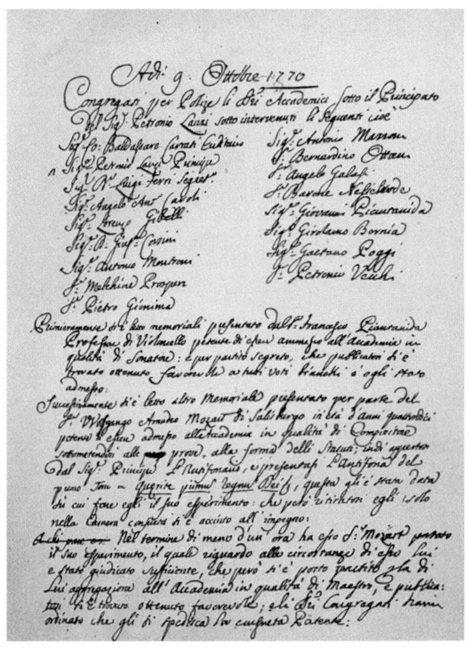

Adì 9 Ottobre 1770

Mitridate's aria from the third act of *Mitridate, re di Ponto* (K. 87), premiered in Milan in 1770, Mozart's first operatic success.
Paris, Bibliothèque Nationale de France, Département de la Musique.

Drama or rebellion?

The Court Musician (detail), by Peter Jakob Horemans, 1762.
Munich, Bayerisches Nationalmuseum.

Below:
Portrait of Tobias Philipp Freyherr von Gebler, the librettist of *Thamos,* in 1780. Copper engraving by Johann Ernst Mansfeld.

What was happening in Mozart's life in Salzburg at the end of 1773 that might explain the works he wrote during these months of intense creative activity? Not a single document exists, and almost no relevant biographical detail, that might point toward the creative source of such works as the Symphony no. 25 in G minor, with its ominous, gloomy atmosphere, predating by 15 years the other symphony he wrote in that key. (The first movement of the symphony is so powerful, so moving, that Milos Forman chose it as the theme music for his film *Amadeus.*) Mozart was not yet 18 when this tragic vehemence burst forth; a comparison with the scores of his contemporaries does nothing to dispel the mystery. Expressing himself in such personal terms was a new departure for Mozart, announcing his maturity as an artist, and one is tempted to wonder whether, deep in his soul, he perhaps had some background sense of the tragic nature of destiny? Shortly afterward, he returned to the *galant* style that Salzburg expected of him; but while writing the symphony he was also composing the incidental music for the play *Thamos, König in Ägypten.* These five interludes and two choruses are impregnated with the same ominous gravity, the same sense of the struggle between light and darkness, that one finds in *The Magic Flute,* and they absorbed all of Mozart's creative energy. Something must have happened, that much is certain, but we shall probably never discover what it was. Only the work remains.

The first sheet of the score of *Thamos, König in Ägypten* (K. 345), 1775. Berlin, Staatsbibliothek, Musikabteilung.

Siegmund Haffner

The Residentzplatz, Salzburg, c. 1776 (detail), showing St. Rupert's Cathedral, the Prince-Archbishop's Palace, and the monumental fountain. Oil on panel.
Salzburg, Museum Carolino Augusteum.

At the age of 20, Mozart might seem to have been finally settled in Salzburg. His celebrated father is cathedral *Kapellmeister* and his own position seems well established with the town bourgeoisie as well as the local nobility, whom he starts to frequent. And while, to please his clients, he willingly yields to the *galant* style then in fashion, beneath the smiling mask of charm and gaiety other more personal tones lie concealed, accents of a dreamlike melancholy and grace that are his and his alone. During this period, the mayor of Salzburg was Siegmund Haffner, a rich merchant who wished to celebrate the marriage of his daughter in a manner reflecting his wealth. Since Mozart had already written several serenades, it was to him that Haffner turned. Given that the term "serenade" means music for the evening (for the "sera"), it seems likely that this great work was written to be performed on the eve of the great affair, the young couple's last celibate evening, as an introduction to the celebrations of the following day. Mozart was in any case fully aware of what was due to the mayor's standing, so to the usual complement of strings he added pairs of flutes, oboes, bassoons, horns, and trumpets—a veritable orchestra. The work itself was on a similar scale: its eight movements took over an hour to perform, two or three times the length of a symphony. He followed this extravanganza with another serenade, the "Posthorn," also performed in Salzburg, and with that and the final serenade, commonly known as "Eine kleine Nachtmusik," this genre disappeared from Mozart's horizon. Wolfgang would, however, compose another piece in honor of Siegmund Haffner, the Symphony no. 35, which also bears his name, and which this time was composed to celebrate, in Vienna, his friend's ennoblement.

The "Haffner" Serenade (K. 250), composed July 1776.
New York, Pierpont Morgan Library, Mary Flagle Cary Music Collection.

Of the piano and pianists

Concert at the Court of the Prince-Bishop of Liège at the Château de Seraing (detail), by Paul-Joseph Delcloche, 1753.
Munich, Bayerisches Nationalmuseum.

Mozart spent the whole of 1776, the year of his twentieth birthday, in Salzburg, fully occupied with composing, performing, and teaching. He frequented high society and was much in demand. In February he wrote a new type of concerto, a Concerto for three pianos, for Countess Lodron and her two daughters. Within a few months, three further piano concertos followed, together with a multitude of other works: serenades, divertimenti, violin concertos, and a considerable quantity of sacred music, as he explained in a letter to Padre Martini of September 4, 1776: "My father is in the service of the cathedral, and this gives me the opportunity to write as much church music as I like." In January 1777, a brilliant young French virtuoso passed through Salzburg, a Mlle Jeunehomme (or Jeunomé), of whom nothing else is known. During her conversations with Mozart she must have spoken of Paris, where they would meet the following year, and of the new music then being performed in France. For this young woman he wrote a new piano concerto. Whatever the nature of their relationship—which is of little account—the tone of this concerto is quite new. The impetuous way in which the soloist takes up the material, the almost heroic brilliance of the piece, and the affirmation of the composer's own personality burst forth in defiance of the conventions of the *galant* style of the rococo era. Mozart would soon contemplate leaving the narrow world of Salzburg, with its limited opportunities, to try his luck elsewhere. He was now a professional composer and master of his trade. It only remained for him to mature into adulthood.

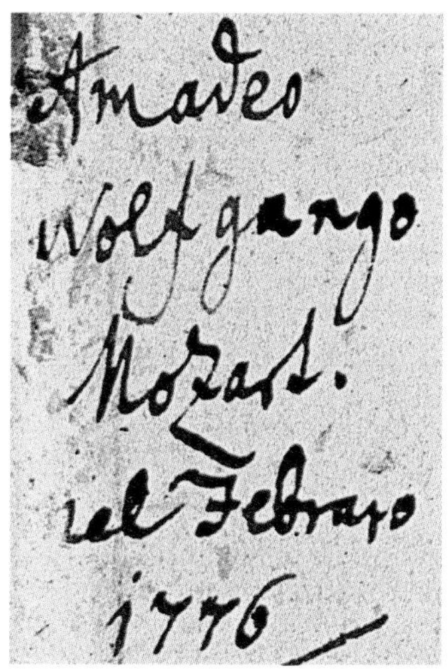

Detail of the page on the right.

Concerto for three pianos (K. 242), known as the "Lodron" Concerto. At this time, Mozart was still writing "harpsichords" (cembali) to designate the piano parts. Cracow, Biblioteka Jagiellonska.

Parisian adventure

A Concert, attributed to Jean-Honoré Fragonard. Amiens, Musée de Picardie.
Mlle Guimard is playing the harp, accompanied by three of her friends and patrons: Charles de Rohan, Prince de Soubise, playing the horn; the Abbé Louis de Rohan, the future cardinal, playing the flute (he would later be implicated in the affair of the Queen's necklace); and Jean-Benjamin de la Borde.

This time, Mozart was of no interest to anyone in Paris: the child prodigy had long been forgotten. He did find a number of old friends, however, and at first had reason to hope that things might go his way. There were plans for an opera, *Alexandre et Roxane*, lessons for the daughter of the Duc de Guisnes, who asked for a flute and harp concerto, a commission for a *Miserere*, and another for a *sinfonia concertante* for wind for the Concerts Spirituels. Then matters started to go awry. The *sinfonia concertante* was forgotten by the client who was supposed to arrange for its performance, and Mozart was asked to write a symphony for full orchestra as compensation; this was the work now known as the "Paris" Symphony, and it was a great success. Among French and Italian musicians and his German friends, Mozart was warmly welcomed, but nothing he could do would entice the aristocracy out of their shells. "I am surrounded here by brute beasts (as far as music is concerned, of course). But how could it be otherwise? For in their actions, loves, and passions they behave no differently." Then the Duc de Guisnes refused to pay for more than half the lessons Mozart had given his daughter: "They treat me here as if I were a rank beginner—all except the musicians, who know better." Yet there were happy moments, too. He visited Count von Sickingen, a German diplomat: "He is a charming man, and a passionate lover and true connoisseur of music." On one occasion, he spent eight hours with him: "Morning, afternoon, and evening, until ten o'clock, we remained at the piano, playing, praising, admiring, analyzing, discussing, and criticizing music of all kinds. He actually owns about 30 opera scores." Soon, however, Paris would no longer have a place for the young musician. Circumstances would force him away: the death of his mother, the uncertainty bedeviling his plans, some already thwarted, and then his frustrated pride, not just as a man but also as a musician and a German, his growing misunderstanding with Baron von Grimm, his separation from Aloysia, and, to cap it all, financial disaster.

Concerto for flute and harp in C major (K. 299), composed in Paris in April 1778 for the Duc de Guisnes and his daughter.
Cracow, Biblioteka Jagiellonska.

Symphony no. 31 in D major (the "Paris" Symphony, K. 297), 1778.
Berlin, Staatsbibliothek, Musikabteilung.

N. 41
Paris, Juny 1778.
di Wolfgango Amadeo Mozart
und seine Handschrift.
Sinfonia à 10 instrumenti.
All:o assai.
Violini
piano:
unisoni
Viola
Col Basso.
2 Flauti
pia:
2 oboe
2 clarinetti
Corni en Re
Trombe en Re
Tympani
Bassons.
Col Basso.
Bassi.
All:o assai.
205
121
K. 297

At the house of the Duchesse de Chabot

Musical Society (detail), by Giuseppe Zocchi, c. 1750. Pen and wash. Florence, Cabinet of Drawings and Prints.

In April 1778, Baron von Grimm gave Mozart a letter of recommendation to the Duchesse de Chabot. He presented himself but was asked to return a week later. "I kept my word and went. I had to wait for half an hour in a large, ice-cold, unheated room, without even a fireplace. Finally the Duchesse de Chabot appeared and asked me most politely to avail myself of the piano that was in the room, since none of her own was in good condition; she asked me to try it. I said, 'With all my heart I should love to play something, but that is quite impossible at the moment, as my hands are so cold I cannot feel them,' and I asked her at least to have me taken to another room where there was a fire. 'Oh oui, Monsieur, vous avez raison,' was all she said. She then sat down and proceeded to draw for a whole hour, in the company of a number of gentlemen, all sitting around a table. The doors and windows were open and I was frozen, not just my hands but my whole body, right down to my feet; and I was starting to get a headache as well. There was *altum silentium*, and for a very long time I did not know what to do, for cold, headache, and boredom. I kept thinking, 'Were it not for M. Grimm, I should leave this very instant.' Finally, to be brief, I played on that miserable, dreadful piano. But worst of all was that Madame and all the gentlemen never once stopped their drawing; on the contrary, they continued the whole time, and so I had to play for the armchairs, the tables, and the walls. In these abominable circumstances I lost patience. I started the Fischer variations, played half of them and then rose. Whereupon there was a storm of applause. But I said what had to be said, namely that I could not do myself justice on that piano and would be delighted to come back another day when there was a better instrument. But she would hear none of it, and I had to wait a further half-hour until her husband arrived. He, however, sat beside me and listened to me with rapt attention, whereupon I forgot the cold and my headache, and despite that wretched piano I started to play as I play when I am in good spirits."

The snub says much about the kind of welcome afforded to Mozart, who did not take lightly affronts to his pride as a man or as a musician. As he wrote his father, "I often see neither rhyme nor reason in anything, I am neither hot nor cold, and find pleasure in nothing; what cheers me up most of all and keeps me in good spirits is the thought that you, my dearest papa, and my dear sister, are well, that I am an honest German, and that, while I may not always have the right to speak, at least I have the freedom to think as I please."

A few weeks later Mozart's mother died. The cry of the Piano Sonata in A minor, somber and pathetic, burst forth.

Baron von Grimm in 1758 (detail), by Louis de Carmontelle. The Baron was Mozart's patron during his stay in Paris. Chantilly, Musée Condé.

Piano Sonata in A minor (K. 310), composed in 1778. New York, Pierpont Morgan Library, Robert Owen Lehman Collection.

The break with Salzburg

Count Hieronymus Colloredo, Prince-Archbishop of Salzburg, painted by Michael Greiter in 1775.
Salzburg, Museum Carolino Augusteum.

On May 9, 1781, Mozart wrote his father in Salzburg a long letter from Vienna, describing his falling out with Prince-Archbishop Colloredo. His account marks at the same time a decisive break with the world of his childhood and youth.

"Mon trés cher Pére!
I am still seething with rage!—and you, my excellent and dearest father, will certainly be as furious as I am. My patience, tried so long, has finally given out. I no longer have the misfortune to be in the service of the court of Salzburg. For me, this was a happy day. Please listen to what I have to say."
There follows the account of his row with the irascible Archbishop. The pitch of his fury increases.
"I couldn't get a word in edgeways, he was roaring away like a brush fire. I listened calmly to everything he said. He lied to my face, telling me my salary was 500 gulden. He called me a vagabond, a scoundrel, a cretin. Oh, I really don't want to write it all down. Finally, it was too much and my blood boiled, and I said, 'Your Grace is not satisfied with me, then?' 'What? Are you threatening me, you cretin? There's the door, there, I want nothing more to do with such a miserable wretch.' And at last, I replied, 'Nor I with you!' 'Then get out.' And as I was leaving, I said, 'So be it. Tomorrow you shall have it in writing.' Tell me, my beloved father, did I not say the word too late rather than too soon? Just listen for a moment: my honor is more precious to me than anything else, and I know you share the same view."
The letter ends with a brief postscript:
"Please let me know soon that you are satisfied, for that is the only thing still wanting in my present happiness. Adieu."

Letter from Mozart to his father in Salzburg, Vienna, May 9, 1781.
Salzburg, Mozarteum.

mithin schob ich meine Reise bis Samstag auf — als ich aber
heute dort schon liegst, sagten mir die Kameradinnen daß
ihr [illegible] mir ein Paquet mitgeben will — ich frag
ob es pressirt; so sagten sie bey, es wäre ihr [illegible]
— so ist es mir leid daß ich nicht die Ehre haben kann [illegible]
[illegible] zu bedienen, [illegible]
[illegible] vor Samstag nicht [illegible] — ich bin [illegible]
[illegible] meinen eignen [illegible]
[illegible] ist es nun ganz Natürlich daß ich nicht [illegible]
kann, [illegible]
und meine [illegible] — [illegible]
[illegible] Moll,
— als ich zu ihr [illegible] — [illegible]
[illegible]
[illegible] Alkohol [illegible]
[illegible] — [illegible]
als ich [illegible] zu ihr [illegible], so war [illegible] —
Nun! wann geht er zu [illegible]? — [illegible] Ich habe wollen
heute [illegible] allein der Platz war schon bestellt.
[illegible]
[illegible]
[illegible] — er [illegible]
[illegible] zu gehen, sonst schreibt er [illegible] daß
die [illegible] Besoldung [illegible] — [illegible]
[illegible] — ich hätt
alles [illegible] — er [illegible]
500 fl. Besoldung — [illegible]
[illegible] — O [illegible] nicht [illegible]
[illegible]

Portrait of Mozart at the age of 14, by Louis-Gabriel Blanchet, c. 1770. Private collection.

"Adieu, my angel, my sweetheart"

"Adieu, my angel, my sweetheart. I am aching to see you."

Mozart,
letter to his cousin Maria Anna Thekla Mozart,
Kaisersheim, December 23, 1778

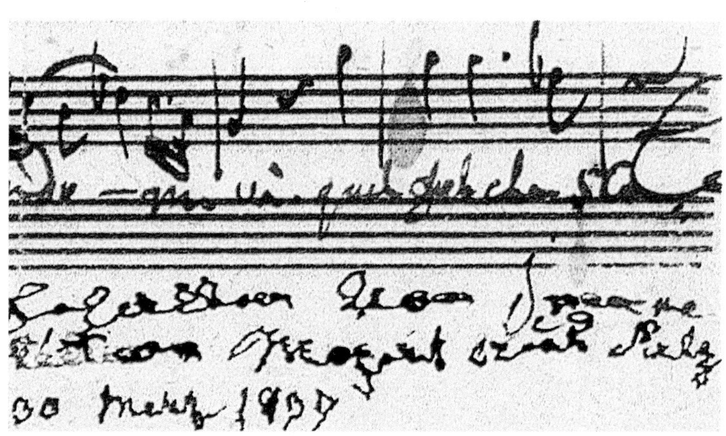

Detail of the aria "Alcandro, lo confesso ... Non sò d'onde viene" (K. 294).

These loving words come at the end of a letter from Wolfgang to his first cousin, a letter full of scatological humor. That was how Mozart was, constantly overflowing with love and tenderness, as ready to give as to receive. The phrase "make happy" recurs again and again in his letters. For him writing and playing music were an act of love.

At first such emotional outpourings were reserved for Wolfgang's immediate family, primarily his father, whom he would always address in correspondence as 'Mon trés cher Pére' (in French, with the accents usually pointing the wrong way), but also his mother and sister. As his father's friend Johann Baptist Becke wrote Leopold, "I have never seen a child so filled with love and respect for his father as your son."

Portrait of Aloysia Weber, of whom Anna Maria Mozart wrote to her husband Leopold, "When Wolfgang makes new acquaintances he would immediately give his heart and soul for them. It is true she sings marvelously" (letter from Mannheim, February 4, 1778).
Unknown artist, 18th-century German school.

Even when Wolfgang was in Vienna and relations between father and son became strained, the respect, affection, and gratitude he felt for Leopold never left him. And the tender relationship he had with his sister Nannerl would also continue, at least until their father died, and even then they would play together works for two pianos or for four hands, works that Wolfgang had written for the two of them.

When Wolfgang was 22, his mother, Anna Maria Mozart, died in his presence in a wretched room in Paris. In the letter in which he conveys the sad news to his father, he cries out like a child, "My dearest father! Take care of yourself! My dear sister! Take care of yourself! You have not yet seen what a kind heart your brother has, for he has not yet had an opportunity to show you. My dears! Look after your health, remember you have a son, a brother, who will use all his strength to make you both happy."

Once Mozart reached adulthood, he naturally turned toward other women, and first, remaining within the family, toward his little first cousin Maria Anna Thekla Mozart, who lived in Augsburg and whom he called "Bäsle" ("cousin" in Swabian dialect). Mozart met her in Augsburg in October 1777. Four days later, on October 17, he wrote his father, "Our little cousin is beautiful, intelligent, charming, talented and gay; and that is because she has been out in the world and has even spent some time in Munich. To tell the truth, we get along well together, because she's a bit of a scamp too. We both like making fun of people, it's most amusing."

Very soon, the letters exchanged by the two cousins—their correspondence would last for four years—became very free in tone, as was characteristic of the Mozart family's letters. Unlike the pompous style that had been *de rigueur* in Germany since the beginning of the century, according to

Autograph of the aria "Alcandro, lo confesso ... Non sò d'onde viene" (K. 294), which Mozart wrote for Aloysia Weber in 1777. Subsequently, in her memory, he would ask that no-one else should sing the aria.
Paris, Bibliothèque Nationale de France, Département de la Musique.

which the correct way to address even intimate friends was "Well-born honored Sir" and the polite "Sie" form had to be used, the Mozarts' letters were never less than extremely frank. Some people have gone so far as to describe them as pornographic, though nothing in the seven volumes of the family's letters even remotely approaches pornography. Indeed, one may well wonder whether they were perhaps somewhat reticent about discussing sex, whereas they were joyfully scatological in their language, as was very common at that time. Even Anna Maria, Mozart's worthy mother, talked about asses and farts in her letters, without mincing her words, as if it were the most natural thing in the world.

None of which detracts from the fact that Mozart's relationship with his *Bäsle* seems to have been one of affectionate, intimate complicity, and was certainly very free, as sometimes happens between young cousins. Was his *Bäsle* licentious? Surely not, but equally surely, a "bit of a rogue" and "nothing less than bawdy," in Wolfgang's own words. And she may well have initiated him into various love games. How else to explain certain allusions? Wolfgang does not speak, like Proust, of "doing catleya," but of "doing *spuni-cuni*." Would there have been much difference?

As Mozart's confidante and consoler, his *Bäsle* probably also helped him to get over his first heartbreak, which he experienced soon after he first met her. On January 17, 1778, Mozart wrote his father from Mannheim about "a certain Herr Weber. I don't know whether I've written you about his daughter. She sings most admirably and has a lovely, pure voice. The only thing she lacks is acting experience; with that she would be able to take the stage as *prima donna* in any theater. She is only 16 and her father is a thoroughly honest German who is raising his children properly; that is why his daughter is so sought after here. He has six children in all, five girls and a boy [...]. She sings the aria I wrote for De Amicis remarkably well, with all its horribly difficult passages [...]. She is quite able to teach herself and accompanies herself well. She also plays *galanterie* quite passably." Mozart would give her music lessons himself ... and fall hopelessly in love with her.

Some days after their first meeting, he writes, "I shall not say much about her singing: in a word, it's wonderful! [...] What astonishes me most of all is how well she reads music. Just imagine: she sight-read my difficult sonatas—slowly, I grant you, but without missing a single note [...]. I have become so fond of this unfortunate family that I want nothing so much as to make them happy. [...] My sister will find in Mlle Weber a friend and companion, for she has here, just as my sister has in Salzburg, a reputation for behaving properly." Mozart is already hatching plans for traveling with the Webers. And in a postscript to the letter his mother adds, for her husband to read, "You will see from reading this letter that when Wolfgang makes new acquaintances he would immediately give his heart and soul for them."

Then, on his return from his mid-year visit to Paris, Mozart stops off in Munich, wanting to see the girl he calls "my dear Weber," only to find that she is indifferent to him. Concerned about her career, which was just beginning, and still very young—she was only 18—Aloysia was not contemplating marriage. Wolfgang tells his father nothing, revealing only that he is unhappy. On December 29, 1778, he writes, "Today I can only weep [...]. In all my life I have never written as badly as this; I cannot—my heart is too ready to weep! I hope you will write me soon and comfort me."

And he would soon need comforting, for two years later Aloysia married Joseph Lange, an actor with the Burgtheater and a painter who afterward made a fine portrait of Mozart. But the embers never really ceased to glow. "It's true, I was a fool over the Lange woman," Mozart would write, "but what will a man not do when he's in love? I truly loved her, and I still care for her even now, I can feel it. How lucky I am that her husband is madly jealous of her and won't let her go anywhere; that way, I see her only rarely."

The careers of Wolfgang and Aloysia sometimes ran side by side, especially in Vienna, and once they were brother- and sister-in-law they became friends, as well as being fellow professionals. On March 12, 1783, he would write, " My sister-in-law, Frau Lange, gave her concert today in the theater and I played a concerto." It was Aloysia who created the role of Madame Herz (Mrs. Heart) in Mozart's *Der Schauspieldirektor* (The Impresario), beside her husband as Herz, and more importantly that of Donna Anna for the Vienna premiere of *Don Giovanni* in 1788. Some years earlier, Leopold had come to Vienna to hear Aloysia sing and play the piano, and had written, "There is nothing one can object to. She sings with the greatest expression [...]. Her portamento and all of her expressive notes are astonishingly strong, and the tender parts, the passagework and ornaments, and the high notes are all extremely fine." The arias Mozart wrote for Aloysia provide a detailed picture of her talent and confirm the judgment of his father.

With Aloysia spoken for, Mozart took pity on her younger sister Constanze, whom he would eventually marry, following what has justly been seen as the machinations of Frau Weber. Constanze would later claim to have fallen in love with Mozart the moment he set foot in the Weber household, and it would appear that relations between the two sisters, Constanze and Aloysia, were tempestuous in the extreme. It is by no means easy to tease out the truth from the welter of contradictory stories. Mozart nevertheless now turned to Constanze. She was 20, he 26. In the letter in which he introduces his "beloved Constanze" to his father, and as if to reassure him, he paints a picture of her that is horrifying for a young man claiming to be in love, the picture of a modest, thrifty soul—something in which he was in fact much mistaken, for Constanze's desire to dress "prettily and cleanly" would lead her to great extravagances.

Clearly, Mozart wanted to be seen as an adult by his father and by society. At the same time, it is highly likely that Frau Weber wanted to see her daughters settled, and had set her heart on a talented young composer with a promising future. It is even possible that, unable to marry Aloysia, Mozart turned to Constanze, who was also a singer, out of lover's spite, and assumed the role of savior of the unloved member of a family he had taken pity on—he himself even spoke of "saving the poor girl." What is certain, however, is that he can be seen here trying to rationalize a situation that had gotten slightly out of hand, trying to convince himself that he was happy and in love.

And in this, he succeeded. Whatever clouds may sometimes have darkened their marriage—the slightly chaotic style of their household and their carelessness with money—Mozart formed a close attachment to Constanze and never ceased to show her the greatest affection. With her by his side, a couple came into being. All the letters he sent her during his last years, when she was taking cures in Baden, are the letters of a gentle, attentive husband. They all begin, "Dearest, most beloved little wife of my heart," or "Dearest little wife." On September 30, 1790, he writes her from Frankfurt, "Dearest little wife of my heart," and ends, "I am as excited as a child at the thought of seeing you again. If people could look into my heart, I would almost feel ashamed. Everything seems cold to me, as cold as ice. Ah, if only you were near me, then I might be able to feel greater pleasure in people's attentions to me. But as things are, everything is so empty. Adieu, my love. I am ever your Mozart, who loves you with all his soul."

There can be no doubt about the deep affection that Mozart felt to the end of his life for his little wife—who bore him six children—even if she often showed herself to be frivolous, and even if her brilliant husband's behavior could sometimes be childish and, if not exactly dissolute, certainly a little fickle.

"Madamina ...," "Fair lady, here's a list I'd show you of the beauties my master has loved. A list, yes, but 'twas I who made it. Look now, read it with me!" Mozart was not Don Giovanni, but neither was he the angelic character some have made him out to be. One has only to listen to his operas to realize that love lies at the very heart of them. From the one extreme, ideal love, with its apotheosis in *The Magic Flute*, to the other, perverse love, culminating in *Così fan tutte* (All Women Behave Thus).

Constanze Weber, Mozart's wife, in 1782, attributed to Joseph Lange, Mozart's brother-in-law. Glasgow, Hunterian Art Gallery.

During Mozart's ten or so years of married life, his encounters with talented female singers, the intense, intimate collaboration between the composer and his singers that was needed to bring this sublime music to a point of exaltation, all this would have led to much temptation, or in any case to relationships as close as they were fleeting, as Tolstoy so admirably described in *The Kreutzer Sonata*. The voluptuous, even erotic aura of a very beautiful voice, its texture and its body, and the fact that it seems to reflect a personality quite out of the ordinary, is a potent stimulus for a musician's creative sensitivity. He will then write an aria for her, or more than one, for her voice alone, for its technical abilities, for the subtlest, most intimate colors and nuances of its timbre, for her particular talent as a singer. Composing for an exceptional diva is like embarking on a sort of love affair with her. Whether Mozart yielded to this, and whatever happened with Nancy Storace or Josefa Duschek, is immaterial. What matters is the fierce emotional charge that his scores still impart to us.

Looking beyond all the possible love affairs or sudden infatuations, we find only Mozart's extraordinary ability to love and be loved, and his constant, all-consuming urge to communicate with all beings, which found its highest expression in his music and which enabled him to see so clearly into the deepest recesses of the human soul. Late on the evening of April 11, 1787, at a time when Mozart had just learned that his father was very seriously ill and was turning his thoughts to *Don Giovanni*, and doubtless after an evening spent discussing matters aesthetic, his friend Gottfried von Jacquin wrote in his album, "True genius without heart is an absurdity, for genius is not made by lofty understanding alone, nor imagination alone, nor both together. Love! Love! Love! is the soul of genius." He could not have described Mozart's personality more accurately.

Das Bäsle, Maria Anna Thekla

Mozart's cousin Maria Anna Thekla Mozart (the *Bäsle*) in 1777. Drawing.
Salzburg, Mozarteum.

On October 13, 1777, in Augsburg, Mozart first met his cousin, the daughter of Leopold's brother. He would shortly be 22 and she was still 19. When the two cousins were apart, they corresponded, until October 23, 1781, at which point she disappeared from Mozart's life. The *Bäsle* would later have an illegitimate son by a canon in Augsburg, would marry at 35, and would end her days in Bayreuth in 1841, at the age of 83. One of the most famous letters Mozart wrote her is that of May 10, 1779:

"Dearest, best, most beautiful, most lovable, most charming little bass or little violoncello infuriated by her unworthy cousin!

Salzburg, May 10, 1779

Blow into my behind.
It's good, cheers!

Whether I, Joannes Chrisostomus Sigismundus Amadeus Wolfgangus Mozartus, will be able to calm, assuage or soften the rage that enhances your charming beauty (*visibilia et invisibilia*) certainly by the height of a good slipper heel is a question I am quite happy to answer. To soften means as much as carrying someone softly in a soft chair. By nature I am soft and mild and like to eat my mustard, especially with beef. So it is fine with Leipzig, even though Herr Feigelrapée insists on maintaining or rather beheading that nothing good will come of the pie—but I can't really believe that—it wouldn't be worth bending down for it. Now were it a purse full of convention kreutzer—then for something like that one might be able to claw up or lift up or stretch out. So, as I've said, I couldn't let it go for less, that's my last price—no haggling, I'm no woman; and there's an end to it. Yes, my dear little violoncello, that's the way the world doth go: one has the purse and another the silver, and he who has neither has naught, and naught as is much as very little, and little is not much; thus naught is still less than little, and little still more than not much, and much still more than little, and—thus it was, and is, and ever shall be. Put an end to your letter, seal it up and send it off to its destination. Coward!
Your most obedient servant on his knees
My ass it is not Viennese."

After several more jokes and a "Tender Ode," Mozart fills the third page of the letter with a little drawing of his cousin's face, and ends with these words:

"My own and all our greetings to the lady and gentleman who brought you forth, namely those who took the trouble to make you, and to the one who let herself be made. Adieu—Adieu, Angel. My father sends his avuncular blessing and my sister sends you a thousand cousinly kisses. And your cousin gives you what he ought not to give you.

Adieu—Adieu—Angel.

I shall write more when the mail next goes, something very sensible and necessary, but until then, and until further notice, that's it. Adieu—Adieu—Angel."

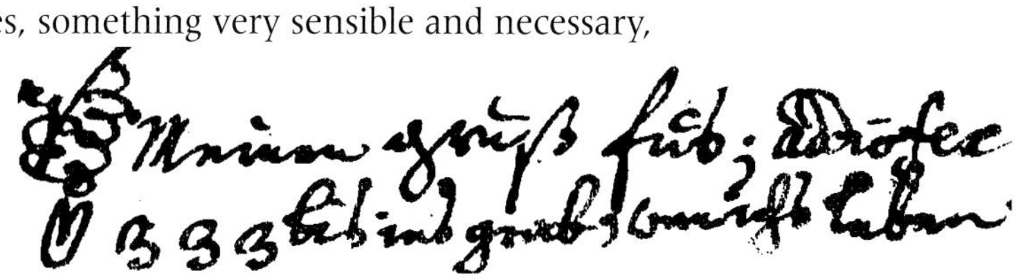

Best beloved cuzzy bunny:
I have received your so precious letter and see therein it makes my head spin that my uncle dunkle my auntie taunty and your elf self are all well smell, as are we safe and sound hound, thank the Lord. I have also received conceived the letter better from my papa haha in my claws hee-haws. I hope you too will have received believed the letter wetter I sent you from Mannheim. So much the better, better the much so. And now for something rather clever.
[*There follows a four-page letter, an amazing combination of jokes, mostly scatological, puns, rhymes, and sometimes indecipherable nonsense, only a little of which seems to contain a real message.*]
Ecce provatum est, Mama was right. Keep well, I kiss you 10,000 times and am as always the old young sow's tail
Wolfgang Amadé Rosenkranz
From us two travelers a thousand greetings to uncle and auntie.
To all my good friends amends
Greetings bleatings; adieu fex hex
[a drawing of a heart] 333 to the grave, while I still have life
Miehnnam eht ht5 rebotco 7771.
[*Mozart uses the name of Rosenkranz to rhyme with "Sauschwanz" (sow's tail, a vulgar Bavarian epithet). The number 333 (in German, "drei drei drei") rhymes with "treu treu treu" (true true true). The date has been written backwards, as has "Mannheim."*]

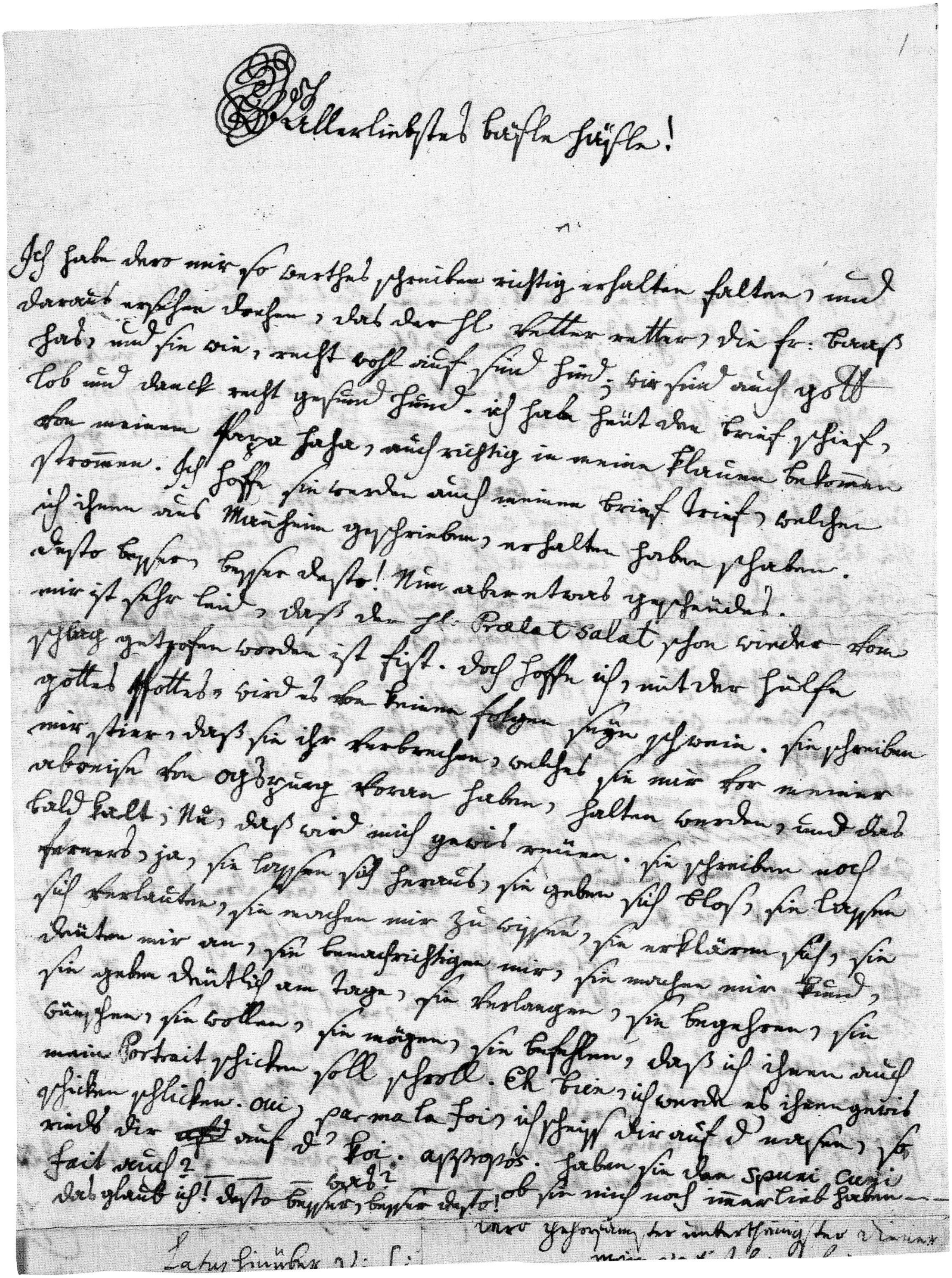
Allerliebstes bäsle häsle!

Ich habe dero mir so werthes schreiben richtig erhalten falten, und
daraus ersehen drehen, daß der H: vetter retter, die fr: baaß
has, und sie wie, recht wohl auf sind hund; wir sind auch gott
lob und danck recht gesund hund. ich habe heüt den brief schief
von meinem papa haha, auch richtig in meine klauen bekommen
strommen. Ich hoffe sie werden auch meinen brief trief, welchen
ich ihnen aus Mannheim geschrieben, erhalten haben schaben.
desto besser, besser desto! Nun aber etwas gescheüdes.
mir ist sehr leid, daß der H: Prälat Salat schon wieder vom
schlag getroffen worden ist fist. doch hoffe ich, mit der hülfe
gottes spottes wird es von keinen folgen seyn schweyn. sie schreiben
mir stier, daß sie ihr versprechen, welches sie mir vor meiner
abreise von augsburg gethan haben, halten werden, und das
bald bald; Nu, das wird mich gewis reuen. sie schreiben noch
ferner, ja, sie lassen sich heraus, sie geben sich bloß, sie lassen
sich verlauten, sie machen mir zu wissen, sie erklären sich, sie
deüten mir an, sie benachrichtigen mir, sie melden mir kund,
sie geben deütlich am tage, sie verlangen, sie begehren, sie
wünschen, sie wollen, sie mögen, sie befehlen, daß ich ihnen auch
mein Portrait schicken soll schooll. Eh bien, ich werde es ihnen gewis
schicken schlicken. Oui, par ma la foi, ich schiß dir auf d' nasen, so
rinds dir auf d' koi. apropos. haben sie den spuni cuni
fait auch? — was? —
das glaub ich! desto besser, besser desto! ob sie mich noch immer lieb haben —

Letter from Mozart to his *Bäsle*, Maria Anna Thekla Mozart, in Augsburg, Salzburg, November 5, 1777.
London, British Library.

"It is true she sings marvelously"

Aloysia Lange, née Weber, in the title role of Grétry's opera *Zémire et Azor*, by Johann Baptist Lampi. Private collection.

With these words Anna Maria Mozart confirms her son's impassioned description of Aloysia Weber. Mozart's youthful ardor would lead him to write arias for his beloved Aloysia, first "Alcandro, lo confesso ... Non sò d'onde viene," and shortly afterward "Popoli di Tessaglia ... Io non chiedo," a great dramatic *scena* designed to make her shine. This bravura piece was still unfinished when the girl rejected him, but Mozart completed it, dedicating it to the end of a love never consummated. Five other arias followed, among which "Vorrei spiegarvi, oh Dio" occupies a special place. Aloysia was singing Clorinda in *Il curioso indiscreto*, an opera by Pasquale Anfossi to a libretto probably by Lorenzo Da Ponte. Mozart wrote two arias for her, intended to substitute those by Anfossi but setting the same words, a common practice at the time. Aloysia's reputation was based on the extraordinary suppleness of her voice, which somewhat compensated for her lack of stage presence. Mozart, however, chose to highlight not her amazing if somewhat cold virtuosity but rather her extended tessitura. A hesitant creature who has already suffered, with a nobility of spirit that sublimates all pain, Clorinda sings, "I would tell you, O God, wherein my torment lies. But fate condemns me to silence and to weep. For him who would love me, my heart cannot burn, and cruel duty makes me appear inhuman!" In a plot worthy of *Così fan tutte*, Clorinda thus addresses her seducer; she is at the point of yielding when she pulls herself together and sends him back to his betrothed with this violent imprecation, "Ah, Count, leave me, run, fly far from me!"

The aria "Vorrei spiegarvi, oh Dio" (K. 418), 1783. Cracow, Biblioteka Jagiellonska.

N.12. Il curioso indiscreto. Atto Primo.
per la Sig:ra Lange
di Amadeo Wolfgango Mozart
Adagio
Con sordini
Violini
Pizzicati
Viole
2 Oboe
2 fagotti
Clorinda
Bassi
Adagio
185.
418

vorrei spiegarvi oh Dio! qual è l'affanno mio; qual

"Two little black eyes"

Constanze Weber and Mozart at the time of their wedding, 1782. Copies of miniatures on ivory.

[...] In my eyes a bachelor is only half alive. That is how I see things, and there is nothing I can do about it. I have thought the matter over, weighed everything up, and my mind is set.
So now, who is the object of my love? Do not be alarmed again, I beg of you. Not one of the Webers? Yes, one of the Webers—not Josefa, not Sophie, but Constanze, the middle one. I have never come across such differences of temperament in a single family. The eldest is a lazy, gross, perfidious woman, more cunning than a fox. The Lange woman is false, malicious, and a coquette. The youngest—she is still too young to be anything. She is just a kind-hearted person but much too light-headed. God keep her from being seduced. But the middle one—that is, my good, my dear Constanze—she is the martyr of them all, and perhaps for that very reason is the kindest-hearted and the cleverest—in short, the best of them all. She is the one who looks after the whole household but can never satisfy them. Ah, wonderful father! If I wanted to describe all the scenes that have taken place in that house on our account I could fill pages. If you wish, I shall do so in my next letter. But before delivering you from my chatter, I must make you a little better acquainted with the character of my beloved Constanze. [...]

Toward the end of 1781, Mozart wrote a number of letters to his father announcing his intention, against Leopold's wishes and despite his many cautionary admonitions, to marry Constanze Weber, having been unable to capture her elder sister's heart. On December 15, he paints the following portrait of his fiancée:
"I must make you a little better acquainted with the character of my beloved Constanze. She is not ugly, though she is anything but beautiful. Her whole beauty lies in two little black eyes and a pretty figure. She is no great wit, but has enough sound common sense to be able to do her duty as a wife and mother. She is not inclined to extravagance—that is completely false; on the contrary, she is accustomed to dressing badly. For what little her mother has managed to do for her children, she has done for the other two but not for her. It is true that she would like to dress prettily and cleanly, but without going overboard. And she is capable of making most of the things a woman needs herself. She also dresses her own hair every day. She knows all about housekeeping, and has the kindest heart in the world. I love her and she loves me with all her heart! Tell me: could I wish for a better wife?"

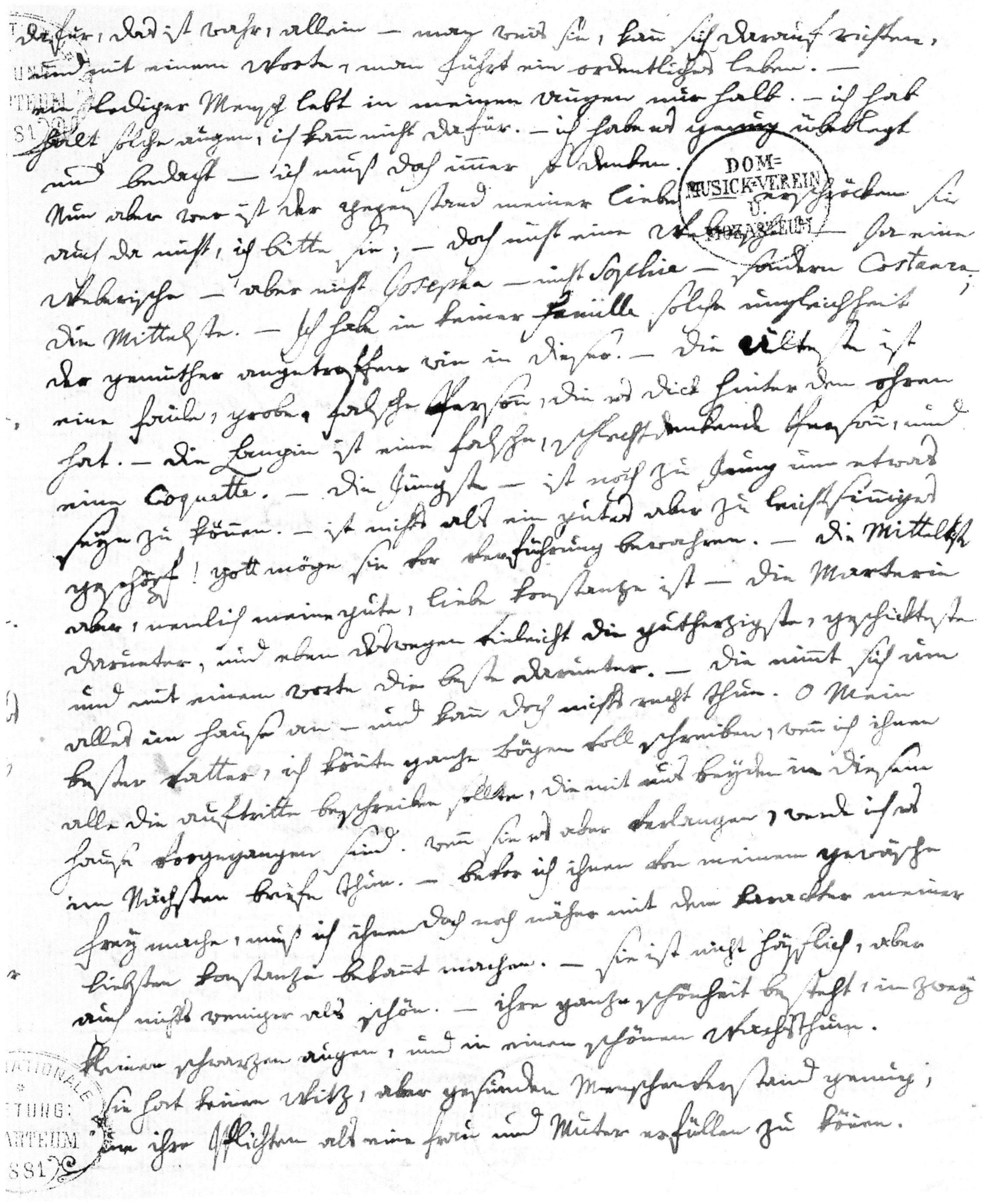

Letter from Mozart to his father about Constanze Weber, Vienna, December 15, 1781 (extract). Salzburg, Mozarteum.

Games of love and chance

Count Almaviva asking his wife's pardon in Act 4 of *The Marriage of Figaro*. Watercolor, 18th-century Austrian school. Private collection.

Mozart's opera arias, concert arias, and lieder talk constantly of love, of hearts being overwhelmed and on the point of succumbing. One has only to listen to the first of Cherubino's arias in that showcase of the games of love and chance, *The Marriage of Figaro*:

> "I no longer know who I am or what I do,
> One moment I am made of fire and another of ice,
> Every woman makes me change color,
> Every woman makes me tremble.
> [...]
> I speak of love when I am awake,
> I speak of love when sleeping,
> To the waters, to the shadows, to the mountains,
> To the flowers, to the grass, to the fountains,
> To the echoes, to the air, to the winds
> That bear away with them
> The sound of my helpless cries.
> And if there is no one to hear me,
> I speak of love to myself."

Later, in Act 4 of the same opera, Susanna sings the so-called chestnut-tree aria, which Mozart wrote for Nancy Storace:

> "Ah, come, tarry not, divine joy!
> Come where love calls you to savor its delights,
> Before the nocturnal star lights up the skies,
> While the night is still dark and the world silent.
> Here murmurs the brook, here plays the breeze
> That with gentle sighing restores the heart;
> Here the flowers laugh, here the grass is cool.
> Here everything invites us to love's pleasures.
> Come, my love, within these hidden trees!
> Come, with roses I would crown your brow!"

Mlle Contat in the role of Susanna in Beaumarchais's play *Le Mariage de Figaro* (detail). Watercolor, 18th-century French school.

Susanna's aria "Deh vieni" from Act 4, Scene 9, of *The Marriage of Figaro* (K. 492), 1786.
Cracow, Biblioteka Jagiellonska.

"For Mlle Storace and me"

In 1783, on their way home from Italy, the Storaces, an Anglo-Italian family of musicians, stopped in Vienna. Mozart struck up a great friendship with the young Stephen Storace, a composer, and his sister Anna, known to her friends as Nancy. Nancy, then 18, had a marvelous voice, and had made her debut in London before she was eight. After a brilliant career in various cities in Italy, she was engaged by the Vienna Opera, where she gave full rein to her great dramatic powers. Shortly thereafter she married the composer John Abraham Fisher, who treated her very badly. In 1786 she sang the part of Susanna in the first performance of *The Marriage of Figaro*. In February 1787 she left Vienna with her brother and mother for London, never to return. It was the last Wolfgang saw of her, but they continued to correspond, and when she died she left instructions that Mozart's letters to her were to be placed in her coffin. What transpired between them? Was Nancy one of Mozart's great loves? The facts are unknown, but that matters little. For the answer lies in the music, which bares its soul in the eloquent dramatic aria "Ch'io mi scordi di te ... Non temer, amato bene," for soprano and piano obbligato with orchestra, which Mozart wrote for her shortly before her departure, inscribing the work *"Für Mselle Storace und mich."* There can be no doubt about it: the music is an avowal writ large, an idealization of love, a declaration in which the two protagonists confess to each other their mutual passion, Mozart at the keyboard addressing Nancy who is quick to respond, the amorous dialogue forming the weft and warp of the aria. Beneath the apparent serenity, their hearts are sinking: "My soul grows faint," confesses the singer, to a piano accompaniment that seems almost panic-stricken. Later, the lightning flashes of the piano answer the soprano's complaints of her lover's cruelty. The lovers' dialogue penetrates to the deepest core of their love. Rarely has a melodic line seemed so sensually vocal, while the piano part, so purely, so essentially instrumental, matches the most beautiful passages in Mozart's concertos. "That I should forget you? [...]Ah no, my life would be worse than death. [...] Do not fear, beloved, My heart will always be yours. I cannot bear such pain, My soul grows faint. You sigh? O woeful grief! Think at least what a moment this is! [...] Gentle souls, you who see My pain in this moment, Tell me if a faithful heart Can bear such torment!"

Musical scene by Gasparo Vizzini, 18th century. Naples, Museo San Martino.

Above left:
Nancy Storace in the role of Euphrosyne in Milton's *Comus*, c. 1790. Etching.

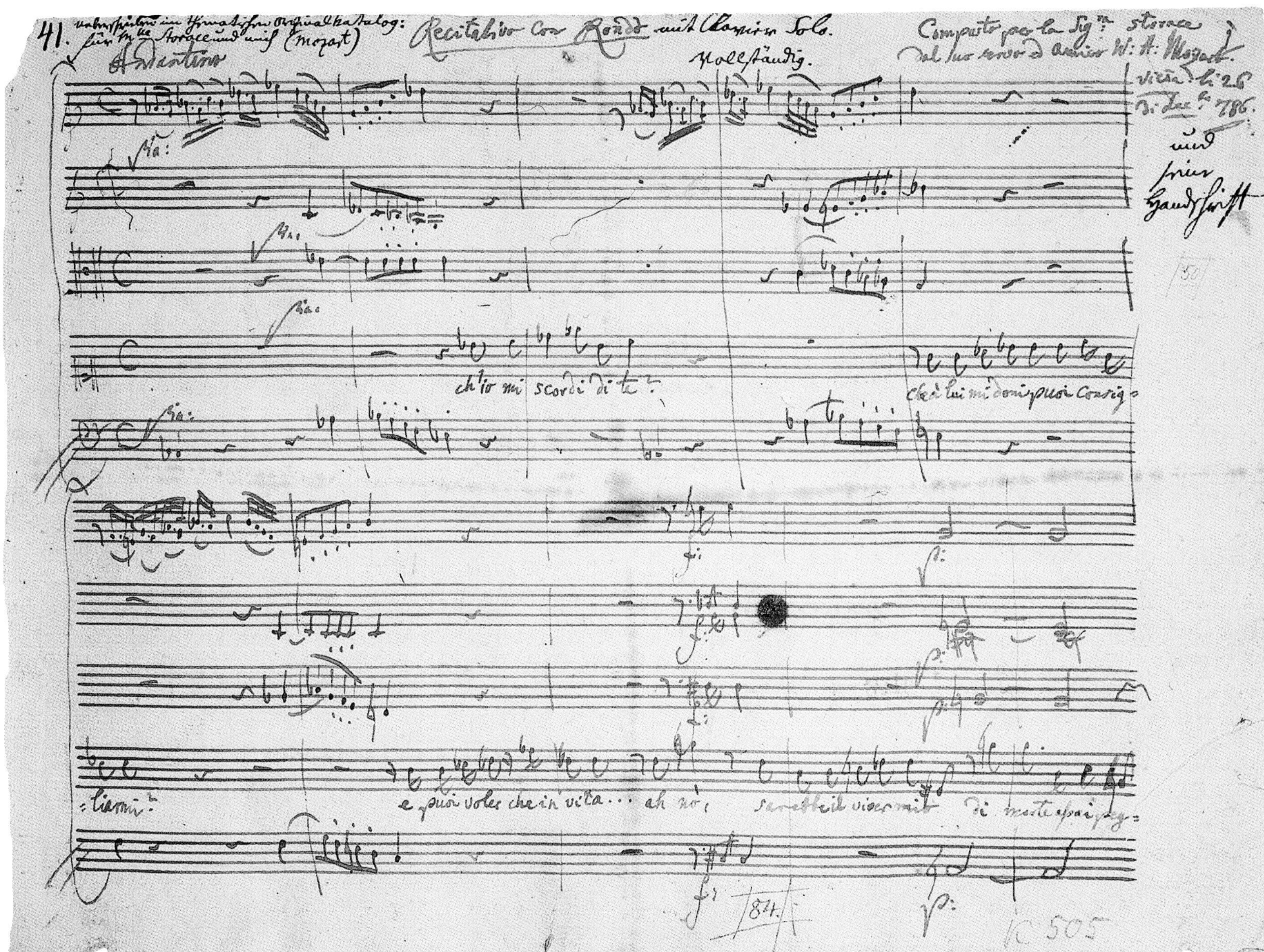

The aria "Ch'io mi scordi di te … Non temer, amato bene" (K. 505), 1786.
Cracow, Biblioteka Jagiellonska

"Adieu, beautiful flame!"

Mozart in the Duschek's house in 1787 (detail). Painting on glass. Prague, villa Bertramka.

Another concert aria, another masterpiece, "Bella mia fiamma, addio! ... Resta, o cara" is also connected with an opera, and with a friend who was also a singer. Prague, November 3, 1787: Mozart was staying at Bertramka, the Duscheks' villa outside the city, where he had completed his opera *Don Giovanni*. Five days after it was performed, Wolfgang and Josefa Duschek found themselves in conversation. They had known each other for ten years and Mozart had already dedicated a concert aria to her. But this time Josefa demanded a new composition; it is even said that she locked him up until the aria was written; but in return he demanded that she sight-read the piece, which would explain its tricky intonation, which Josefa would make light of. Mozart took his text from the aria in Jommelli's *Cerere placata* in which the condemned hero, Titan, bids farewell to those he loves. An aria for a man, which Mozart writes for a woman: is this another piece of vocal cross-dressing, so useful for making confessions? Or a bit of role-switching, with Mozart singing through Josefa's voice? At first, the farewells are restrained, lacking the vocal effects characteristic of the genre: sad resignation in the face of the soul's dreadful loneliness. But then the shell breaks under the pressure of the intense pain that has so far been repressed. Freed from all conventional restraint, the aria seems to follow the logic of rising emotion, until the pain bursts forth in animal violence: furious cries, breathless vocalizations, and obsessive repetitions. Donna Anna may perhaps never have shown such madness as in this aria of farewell.

> "Beautiful flame, adieu!
> Heaven chose not to make us happy.
> Here, sundered before it was even tied,
> This purest knot
> That bound our souls
> With a single will! [...]
> Stay, my love; cruel death
> Takes me from you, oh God! [...]
> I go ... Alas! Farewell forever!
> This pain, this grief,
> Are terrible to me!"

The concert aria "Bella mia fiamma, addio! ... Resta, o cara" (K. 528), 1787.
Berlin, Staatsbibliothek, Musikabteilung.

Mozart in 1773. Miniature on ivory, attributed to Martin Knoller. Salzburg, Mozartmuseum.

"God is ever before my eyes"

"God is ever before my eyes. I realize His omnipotence and fear His wrath. But I also know His love, His compassion and mercy to His creatures. He will never abandon those who serve Him."

Mozart, letter to his father, Augsburg, October 24, 1777

Excerpt from the "Dies irae" from the Requiem. Vienna, Österreichische Nationalbibliothek.

These words, which might almost come from one of the Psalms, in fact flowed from the pen of the 21-year-old Mozart. Having spent two weeks in Augsburg, he sent his father a lengthy account of the events of the previous days, and ended by thanking him for his congratulations on his name day. On this sort of occasion, it was perfectly natural to invoke divine Providence: "If His will is done, all is well—according to mine. Thus I can lack nothing—I cannot but be happy and satisfied. I shall surely strive to follow the instructions and advice that you have been good enough to proffer and to live strictly by them."

As a child, Mozart received a complete religious education of the highest quality. There was nothing unusual about this at the time, especially in southern Germany, which was fervently Catholic. But in Mozart this religious upbringing awakened and nourished a deep, burning faith, such that there can be no doubt as to the sincerity of the religious convictions underlying what appear to be expressions of a purely formal kind in his correspondence. Indeed, according to some biographers, he may even have undergone crises that, if not actually mystical, at least strengthened his religious faith and practice.

For instance, when explaining to his patron Prince-Archbishop Colloredo his reasons for requesting a leave of absence—his principal argument being that he wanted to help his father financially—he does so in pious terms, as was fitting when addressing a prelate. But then he goes much farther than talking about circumstances, and his language takes on a most ardent quality: "The greater the talents children receive from God, the more they ought to use them to improve their lot and that of their parents, to help them and to see to their own advancement and their future. The Gospel teaches us that we must make our talents fruitful. In conscience, then, I am accountable to God for all the pains my father has taken tirelessly and incessantly in providing for my education. I am therefore bound to use my strengths to lighten his burden and provide for my needs as well as those of my sister, for I should be sorry if she were to have spent so many hours at the piano without being able to put this training to some use."

The religious education that Leopold gave his son was no cursory affair but rather an ongoing process; for the Mozarts were devout, practicing Catholics. Before Wolfgang left Mannheim for Paris, Leopold, no doubt fearing that his son would be exposed to all sort of temptations in France, wrote him, "Live as a good Catholic Christian, love and fear God, pray with fervor and confidence with all your soul, and lead the life of a Christian, so that if I were never to see you again I should have nothing to fear at the hour of my death."

Shortly afterward, on the day his mother died, Mozart sent his father a preliminary letter to prepare him for the news that he would only convey some days later: "I have completely surrendered to the will of God—and trust that you and my dear sister will both do likewise. Is there any other way to remain calm? [...] I know that God orders all things for our good (even though we may believe that everything is going awry) and wills it thus; for I believe (and no-one will convince me otherwise) that no doctor, no man, no misfortune or chance can give or take away the life of a man, this only God can do. [...] Come now, God will see to all things! I have an idea in mind, for which I pray to God daily: if it is His divine will, it will be done, and if not, then I shall be equally satisfied—at the very least I shall have done what it fell to me to do [...]. Place your trust in God, for it is there that you will find solace."

The terrible news followed on July 9. And once again Wolfgang invokes the will of God and divine Providence: "Monsieur, mon trés cher Pére! I hope that you will now be strong enough for me to tell you the saddest, most painful news—my letter of July 3 will have prepared you for the worst. On the same day, the 3rd, my mother fell blessedly asleep in the Lord, at twenty-one minutes after ten in the evening. When I wrote you, she was already tasting the joys of Heaven—everything was already over. I wrote you the same night. I hope you and my sister will forgive me this slight piece of deception, but I thought it most necessary: understanding from my own pain and sadness what yours would be, I could not find it within me to announce such dreadful news brutally. I hope you are now prepared to hear the worst and, after you have allowed your pain and tears to take their natural, understandable course freely, to surrender yourselves finally to the will of God and worship His ineffable, unfathomable, and all-wise Providence."

For Mozart, religion was also a question of practice. Shortly after his marriage, he wrote to reassure his father on this account: "For some time already, my wife and I had always gone to

The Mozart myth in the 19th century: young Mozart playing the organ in a Franciscan church in Vienna in 1762, by Heinrich Lossow, c. 1864.

Mozart as a Knight of the Golden Spur, painted in 1777 for the Bologna Academy. Bologna, Museo Bibliografico Musicale.

Mass and confession and had taken Communion together, and I discovered that I had never prayed so fervently or confessed or taken Communion in such a spirit of devotion as I did with her by my side; and she found the same. In a word, we were made for each other, and God who arranges all things and who therefore has also willed this will not forsake us."

At the same time, his faith was a moral code. Fundamentally, Mozart was an ethical being. As he wrote from Mannheim on February 4, 1778, "I know myself, and I know I have enough religious sense never to do anything that I could not admit to the whole world [...]. Friends who have no religion are not friends for long."

The music Mozart wrote for the Catholic liturgy is ample proof of his religious convictions. In the whole of his professional career he never held a post that obliged him contractually to write music for the church. His sacred works were occasional pieces, works that had been specially commissioned or written as circumstances dictated. And while he was, inevitably, placed under certain constraints in each case, he found himself all the freer to express himself as he wished. On September 4, 1776, he wrote (in Italian) to Padre Martini from Salzburg, in terms both respectful and affectionate: "Most Reverend Padre Maestro, Most esteemed Master, the veneration, esteem, and respect in which I hold your most worthy self lead to me trouble you with this letter and to send you a feeble specimen of my music, which I submit to your masterly judgment." He goes on, "Our church music is very different from that of Italy, especially in that a Mass with the whole Kyrie, Gloria, Credo, Epistle sonata, Offertory or motet, Sanctus, and Agnus Dei, even if it is the most Solemn Mass and celebrated by the Prince himself, may not last more than three-quarters of an hour. Special study is needed for this sort of composition; and yet the Mass must have all the instruments—trumpets, drums, and so on."

The score that Mozart sent to Padre Martini was a motet that he had written shortly before, "Misericordias Domini," for the Elector of Bavaria. Martini took the time to read it and in his reply wrote, "I have studied it, with pleasure, from beginning to end, and I tell you in all sincerity that I like it remarkably well, finding in it everything required in modern music: good harmony, sound modulations, moderate movement for the violins, and vocal lines that flow naturally and are agreeably handled." It is interesting to note that these comments could equally apply to a chorus from an opera in the "modern" style. There was no substantial difference, therefore, between music for the church and music for the stage; indeed, this had been true since the Baroque period. Only later, in the 19th century, did many musicians turn to an archaicizing style for the church, a "sacred" style, with strict counterpoint, one that was quite different from the music of their times. This change started toward the end of the 18th century. On April 12, 1783, acknowledging that church music had become unfashionable, Wolfgang wrote his father, "Baron van Swieten and Starzer both know as well as you and I that taste changes, but also that this change in taste has unfortunately extended to church music, which ought not to be so. As a result, true church music is to be found under the roof, all but eaten by the worms."

Most of Mozart's creative life was played out to the accompaniment of sacred music, from the brief motet "God is our refuge," his first known sacred work, which he wrote in London in August 1765, when he was nine, to the Requiem, which he left uncompleted at his death. Unsurprisingly, the bulk of his church music dates from his Italian journeys and his Salzburg years—Masses, Offertories, litanies, motets for Vespers, all under the frowning, authoritarian eye of the Prince-Archbishop. In Vienna, however, aside from the brief, sublime motet "Ave verum," he wrote only the Mass in C minor and the Requiem, both unfinished. Without requests for works and released from his obligation to write for the Prince-Archbishop, Mozart seems no longer to have felt the need to compose for the church. Might this perhaps be a sign of disaffection, of a cooling of his faith? Certainly not. He was occupied with other genres, opera in particular, and was having to face the difficulties of a risky professional life, with neither a formal position nor a regular salary, one in which there were no commissions for Masses. And then there was his freemasonry, to which he would soon turn, without there being any contradiction between his faith and his philosophical commitment: indeed, it is quite likely that his religious feelings were able to flourish more freely in that context than within Catholic liturgical practice.

The Vienna Pfarrkirche. Engraving by Ziegler. Vienna, Historisches Museum der Stadt.

Music for the Passion

The Crucifixion, by Franz Joachim Beich, 1720. Vaduz, Princely Collection.

Written in Salzburg in 1767, when he was just 11, the *Grabmusik* (Passion), is one of Mozart's earliest sacred works. The youthful prodigy had then just returned from the three-year tour that had taken him around much of western Europe, and it was now at Salzburg that he astonished his audience, and where he would have to prove his budding genius as a composer. This cantata for soprano (the Angel of the Resurrection) and bass (the soul of the Christian), choir, orchestra, and organ may have been written for an Office during Holy Week, probably Vespers on Good Friday. It is a little like a fragment of a Passion, but for the Catholic rather than the Lutheran liturgy. The accents that Mozart finds to express the anguished spiritual meditation following the death of Christ are already highly personal, as can be seen here, in the text of the second aria:

"Rocks, break open your abyss,
And grieve with piteous sound!
Stars, moon, and sun, flee!
Nature, grieve, and I with you.
Roar thunder! Lightning and flames,
Strike down with fire
Him who has committed the crime of wounding this heart!"

Mozart is supposed to have written the final chorus some years later, when the work was performed again in Salzburg.

Introduction to the *Grabmusik* (K. 42), 1767.
Berlin, Staatsbibliothek, Musikabteilung.

"Exsultate, jubilate"

VUE DE LA PLACE DU DÔME DE MILAN.

Milan, Piazza del Duomo (detail).
Optical view, late 18th century.
Paris, Bibliothèque des Arts Décoratifs.

Nowadays, Mozart's motet "Exsultate, jubilate," for soprano solo, two violins, viola, two oboes, two horns, bass, and organ, is, with his Requiem, his most famous piece of sacred music, especially its extraordinary final "Alleluia." This bravura aria demands breathtaking virtuosity and a great vocal range; yet beside serving as a showcase for any soprano, its sunny lyricism and melodic generosity are guaranteed to uplift an audience. Curiously, the aria was not originally written for a woman. In December 1772, Mozart's opera *Lucio Silla* was performed to great acclaim, the role of Cecilio being sung by the celebrated soprano castrato Venanzio Rauzzini, and it was for him that Mozart composed the motet, which in reality is a grand three-part concert aria. In a letter full of his beloved word-games, Mozart wrote his sister on January 16, "I have for the *primo* a *uomo* motet to write had, which tomorrow at Theatine Church the performed be will." The following day, January 17, 1773, Rauzzini sang the aria at Sant'Antonio Abate, the Theatine Church in Milan. That is all that is known. Then 27, Rauzzini was born in Venice and had trained at Rome and probably at Naples. He then entered the service of the Elector of Bavaria, but had to leave the court on account of certain amorous indiscretions with society ladies. That he was an honorable musician and exceptional singer is beyond doubt; he also composed and played the harpsichord. For much of his subsequent career he worked in England, where among other things he was Nancy Storace's voice teacher.

Excerpt from the opera *Lucio Silla* (K. 135), composed in 1772, which inspired the motet "Exsultate, jubilate." Cracow, Biblioteka Jagiellonska.

The "Alleluia" from the motet "Exsultate, jubilate" (K. 165), 1773.
Cracow, Biblioteka Jagiellonska.

The "Coronation" Mass

St. Rupert's Cathedral, Salzburg, at the end of the 18th century (detail), by Karl Schneeweiss, 1790. Salzburg, Museum Carolino Augusteum.

How this Mass acquired the nickname "Coronation" remains a mystery, but it was certainly not of Mozart's doing. It was long supposed that the piece had been composed for the annual crowning of the shrine of the Virgin in the Maria Plain Basilica overlooking Salzburg, but in actual fact it was completed in March 1779 and was most probably performed shortly thereafter in Salzburg Cathedral. It is also possible that it was performed once more in 1791, this time under the direction of Antonio Salieri (who was not, as has long and too often been asserted, Mozart's sworn enemy), for the coronation of Emperor Leopold II as King of Bohemia in Prague. Whatever the truth of the matter, the "Coronation" Mass follows the pattern set by its 13 predecessors, the first of which saw the light of day in 1768. In principle, it was a *Missa brevis* (short Mass), as was required at Salzburg; but Mozart expanded the musical content and the instrumentation, adding two oboes, two horns, two trumpets, three trombones, and timpani to the usual soloists, chorus, strings, and organ. In its structure and its diversity of musical techniques, the Mass also marks a sort of culmination of everything Mozart had hitherto composed in this genre. Most striking of all is the scrupulous care with which the composer, a firm believer, treats the liturgical text, to great musical effect: the adoring quality of the "Qui tollis," the terror in the face of sacrifice and suffering in the "Crucifixus," the acclamation on the word "pax," referring no doubt to the restoration of peace following the Austro-Prussian War. And what can one say about the compassion of the "Agnus Dei," for which the composer borrowed the sublime melody of the Countess's aria "Dove sono" in *The Marriage of Figaro*—an expression of pain, sacrifice, and love.

The "Agnus Dei" from the "Coronation" Mass (K. 317).
Cracow, Biblioteka Jagiellonska.

The last Mass

Constanze Weber, Mozart's wife, in 1790. Pastel by an unknown artist. Vienna, Mozarthaus.

As his time in Salzburg drew to an end, it was in his sacred music that Mozart came to express himself most personally. Once he moved to Vienna, the struggle to make a fresh start, the attraction of opera, and soon his involvement with freemasonry all distracted him from the Catholic liturgy, and his religious vein seems to abate. If he is to be believed, Mozart composed the Mass in C minor, which would be his last, to fulfill a vow he had made for Constanze's recovery from illness before marrying her. "As proof of the sincerity of my vow, I have here the score of a half-written Mass, which is awaiting completion." The composition of the Mass seems to have taken much longer than usual. Mozart started it in August 1782 and it was finally performed 14 months later, on October 26, 1783, in St. Peter's Abbey Church, Salzburg. Constanze sang one of the soprano parts, as Nannerl records in her diary: "23rd. Mass at eight. Rehearsal for my brother's Mass in the Kapellhaus, where my sister-in-law is singing the solo [...]. 26th. Mass at St. Peter's, where they performed my brother's Mass. All the court musicians were playing." But exactly which score did they play? What remains of the Mass is incomplete. Did it remain unfinished, as is generally believed? Could the missing parts have been lost, which seems most unlikely? Or did they use parts of earlier works to fill in the gaps? This is possible. Yet the mystery remains: with the exception of the Requiem and the "Ave verum," Mozart never wrote for the church again during the eight, crucial, years he had left to live.

The "Kyrie" from the Mass in C minor (K. 427).
Berlin, Staatsbibliothek, Musikabteilung.

"Ave verum"

St. Stephen's Cathedral, Vienna, in 1792.
Etching by Carl Schuetz.

The tiny piece of music presented here is a short, simple motet for four voices with strings and organ, which in all lasts no more than four minutes. And yet it is one of the most moving, most intense moments in all of Mozart's sacred music. Composed for the Corpus Christi procession in June 1791, it was dedicated to Anton Stoll, a friend of Mozart's who was choirmaster at Baden. That is all that is known about this insubstantial sheet. Yet it expresses Mozart's spirituality probably with greater intensity than any other piece. Here the believer addresses his prayer to Christ, to the true body of Christ, His side pierced by the spear, dying on the Cross, in a meditation on the mystery of the Incarnation and Redemption, in a truly mystical experience, in a climate of silent worship, without effects, but in which the slightest musical inflection is an act of belief in the Christian mysteries. That this fragment recalls the no less sublime trio from *Così fan tutte* of the previous year and its song of disembodied love should come as no surprise: whether it seeks to express mystic or human love, the music remains the same.

The first and second sheets of the "Ave verum" (K. 618), 1791.
Vienna, Österreichische Nationalbibliothek.

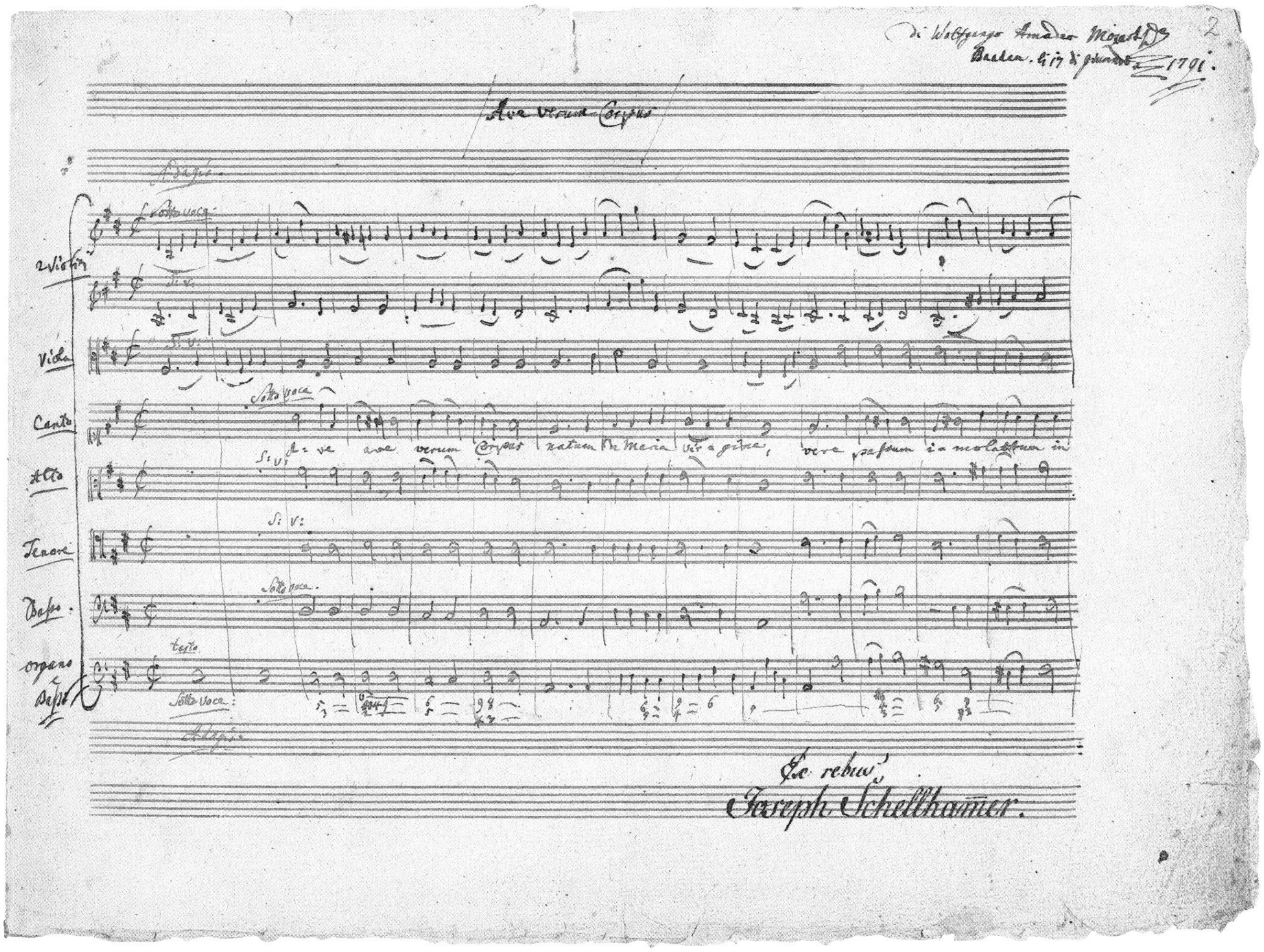
di Wolfgango Amadeo Mozart
Baden li 17 di giugno 1791
Ave verum Corpus
Adagio
sotto voce
2 Violini
Viola
Canto
Alto
Tenore
Basso
organo e Basso
tasto
A- ve ave verum Corpus natum de Maria virgine, vere passum immolatum in
Ex rebus
Joseph Schellhamer.

Cru- ce pro ho- mine.
Cujus latus per- fo- ratum unda fluxit et
in Cruce pro homi- ne.
Cujus latus perforatum unda fluxit et

Portrait of Mozart by an unknown 18th-century artist. Vienna, Gesellschaft der Musikfreunde.

"Not for the Viennese, but for the people of Prague"

"This opera [*Don Giovanni*] is not for the Viennese, but for the people of Prague."

Mozart, quoted by Friedrich Rochlitz, Vienna, 1788

Fugue in C major for pianoforte (K. 394). .
Paris, Bibliothèque Nationale de France, Département de la Musique.

Mozart followed the Prince-Archbishop to Vienna, where relations with Colloredo were to deteriorate beyond repair. He was all too aware of the contrast between the capital of the Empire and the little town of Salzburg to which he would soon have to return, a contrast that only exacerbated his discontent. As it transpired, he did not go: he simply stayed in Vienna. For Mozart, the move to Vienna and his new life there represented the triumph of his freedom and his dignity as a man. When the row with Colloredo first broke out, he wrote his father, "I had no idea that I was a valet, and that was my downfall."

But from the moment Mozart began to enjoy greater independence, his relationship with his father changed. Leopold continued to bombard him with very long letters, but his son responded to them less and less frequently, and with increasing formality. As he grew older, Leopold became if anything more determined to guide his son, in both his career and his personal life, and even in his composition: it was as though his son were still 15 years old. But now that he had grown up, Mozart lived his life as he saw fit. Yet they would always feel profound affection for each other. For even though Mozart behaved very stubbornly toward his father, he never ceased to show him great respect and appreciation.

Indeed, rather than putting Leopold in the dock, we would perhaps do better to remember how he admired his son's talent, which, as an outstanding musician himself, he had been able to recognize. His son had a rare gift which, in Leopold's view, should have brought him enormous success as a professional musician. Yet, as far as he could tell, his prodigious son simply did not achieve this. He was too independent, quite incapable of compromising or adapting to a more conventional mould, and so he was only modestly successful as a court musician, especially in Vienna. After his early triumphs, he became neither the most famous nor the best paid musician of his time, honors which, his father believed, his abilities should have earned him. Hence, Leopold was very resentful of what he perceived as his son's failure.

What Leopold did not realize was that his son's genius as a composer was on an altogether higher plane, and could not be constrained by any professional norms. Had Mozart been nominated as a court musician, had he even become the supreme master of music in Vienna, London, or Paris, in receipt of a substantial salary and living a glamorous life, there would still have been no room for his genius. It would still have transcended everything, and everyone, around him.

Leopold was, nevertheless, a good father: he urged his son to be prudent with his money, did his best to keep in touch with him, and showered him with advice. From the moment Wolfgang moved away from him, he could tell that he had changed. In February 1778, after almost five months of separation, Leopold wrote his 22-year-old son, "You have not put enough trust in me, even though I am very concerned about you, and you have not written me to ask for my advice [...]. My son, you are too excitable, too impetuous! You have totally changed since you were a child. When you were a child, and even a teenager, you were very serious, and when you were at the piano, or otherwise occupied with music, nobody dared distract you in the slightest. So grave was your expression, that many feared you would die young, since your talent had blossomed too quickly." This was all true, and Leopold could not understand why his son was slipping away from him. Mozart's genius was flourishing freely, but his father could make no sense of him. Eventually, their correspondence almost dried up altogether.

In Vienna, for the first time in his career, Mozart had no official post or function: he was not employed by a prince, a church, a town, or a theater. He had no employer at all. Up to that time, only a few princes and Italian dilettantes had been in the position of being able to compose what they wanted, rather than having to earn a living by it. Even Handel, who organized concerts of his own works, was subsidized by the British Crown.

For his own part, Mozart depended upon commissions—especially for operas—concerts, and lessons. But in spite of his father's best efforts, his money management was hopeless, and Constanze was, if anything, even worse. Even in favorable circumstances, when he made significant sums of money, Mozart could not help spending more than he earned: money would just slip through his fingers. Yet he was good at making it, not because he was avaricious, but because he was acutely aware of his own worth. In June

1781, he wrote his father that he had only one pupil. "Of course, I could have more if I agreed to lower my price. But this would lose me credit: I charge six ducats for 12 lessons, and I make it quite clear that I am being generous."

At first, things went extremely well in Vienna, and Mozart enjoyed both freedom and success. In response to his father's (perfectly justified) homilies about the importance of financial security, Mozart replied, "I can assure you that this is a marvelous place, and the best in the world for one in my profession—everyone says so. I am in very good health and thus am thoroughly enjoying life here. You may rest assured that there is only one thing on my mind: making as much money as possible." Two days later, he wrote, "Being in Vienna is a pleasure in itself," then, the following month, "Here I have made the most wonderful and useful acquaintances in the world. I am loved and appreciated in the best houses. I am honored in every way imaginable, and—what is more—I am paid."

He was a success, both in society and in concert. Even when he was still in Colloredo's service, he performed as a pianist. He described his performance at the Kärtnertortheater on April 3, 1781, in glowing terms: "I am very happy with the Viennese public. [...] I had to restart twice, because they kept on applauding." He later returned to his success in the capital of the Empire: "What really delighted and surprised me were their extraordinary silence and their cries of 'Bravo!' while I was playing. In Vienna, where there are so many good pianists, this is a great honor indeed." He also had one of his symphonies, probably the "Paris" Symphony, performed at the same concert. He wrote his father, "Last time, I forgot to mention that the symphony went magnificently: it could not have been more successful. They had doubled the number of wind instruments, so there were 40 violins, 10 violas, 10 double basses, 8 cellos, and 6 bassoons."

Portrait of Leopold Mozart (detail), attributed to Pietro Antonio Lorenzoni, 1765. Salzburg, Mozarteum.

In 1782, Mozart made the acquaintance of the famous Baron Gottfried van Swieten, the Dutch ambassador in Vienna, a composer in his own right but primarily a patron. Every Sunday, from noon to two in the afternoon, his drawing rooms and his library filled with an exclusive audience, and the finest musicians in the city, even Haydn himself, played Handel and Bach. But this was by no means the only major musical gathering in Vienna. Councillor von Kees, the Storaces, and the Mozarts themselves—Wolfgang and Constanze, who were married on August 4—all hosted their own events.

Mozart was very proud, both as a man and as a musician, of all this success. Though a native of Salzburg, he was a European as far as his music was concerned. "The Viennese (and especially the Emperor) should not imagine that I am on this earth for the benefit of Vienna alone," he wrote his father.

Of his concert on March 12, 1783, he wrote, "I am overjoyed that the public gave me such a warm reception. Even after I had left, they carried on applauding, and I had to repeat my rondo. Their applause was like a tidal wave. It all augurs well for my academy on March 23." This "academy," a concert

Morning concert in the Augarten, Vienna (detail). Etching, 1783. Vienna, Wienmuseum.

which Mozart organized at his own expense, was also a success. As the Vienna correspondent for the Hamburg music journal *Magazin der Musik* wrote, "Today, at the Nationaltheater, Mozart gave an *accademia,* in which several of his well-known and well-loved compositions were performed. It drew a considerable audience, and he also played two new concertos and some new fantasias, all of which were rapturously received. Even our monarch, far from leaving early (as is his wont), stayed right to the end. Of all our composers, none has earned such unanimous approval from his public."

Mozart was a star. In March 1784 he organized a cycle of three academies on successive Wednesdays in the Trattner Palace—at his own expense, as usual. They were "subscription only" events, aimed at an aristocratic audience, and after only one concert he had an impressive 174 subscriptions. Everyone who was anyone in Vienna was on the list, which he sent to his father. "I have 30 more subscribers than Richter and Fischer combined," he wrote. "The first academy, on the 17th, went well: the hall was packed. And the new concerto I played was remarkably well received. Wherever you go, people have only good things to say about the academy." This is a reference to his Piano Concerto no. 14 in E flat major. He was similarly successful some days later, at the first performance of his Quintet for piano and wind, "which got a remarkable reception [...]. To tell you the truth, I had played so hard that I was tired at the end. I was quite honored that my audience did not at any point share my fatigue."

His life in Vienna reached its zenith in 1785. Leopold came to visit him on February 11, and on that same evening attended one of his son's academies. It was the first of a cycle of five, and Wolfgang played his Piano Concerto in D minor for the first time. Leopold was overwhelmed. He wrote his daughter, "The concert was beyond compare, the orchestra remarkable [...]. They performed Wolfgang's excellent new keyboard concerto." His son's superb apartment behind the cathedral, with its rococo room and "delights of all sorts," profoundly impressed him. (The apartment is now a Mozart museum, called the Figaro Haus, as it was here that Mozart worked on *The Marriage of Figaro*.) The next day, the Mozarts hosted a chamber music event attended by Haydn. Leopold was dazzled, and left Vienna on April 25. His son would never see him again.

On May 1, 1786, at the Burgtheater, *The Marriage of Figaro* was a triumph.

Soon, Mozart felt the desire to travel again, especially to England. The success of *Figaro* in Vienna inspired a production in Prague, to which Mozart was invited by the Italian director Pasquale Bondini. On January 12, 1787, Leopold wrote Nannerl: "Your brother will be in Prague with his wife by now: he wrote me last Monday that he was on his way there. His opera *The Marriage of Figaro* has been so popular that the orchestra and a society of great connoisseurs and amateurs have sent him letters of invitation and a poem which has been written about him."

It was to his young pupil and friend in Vienna, Gottfried von Jacquin, that Mozart described his success in Prague, not to his father, to whom he would write only one more letter. At a ball he had attended, "I noted with great pleasure that everyone was dancing to music taken from *Figaro*: it had been adapted for contredanses and allemandes. Here, no-one talks about anything except *Figaro*; no-one plays, rings, sings, or whistles anything except *Figaro*; no-one goes to see any operas other than *Figaro*—which is certainly a great honor for me."

Franz Xaver Niemetschek, the author of the first biography of Mozart of 1798, comments, "In Bohemia, all of Mozart's works received due recognition and appreciation." As a citizen of Prague who

Mozarthaus in Vienna, Domgasse 5, where Mozart composed *The Marriage of Figaro*. Watercolor by Huser, 18th century.

witnessed the triumph of *The Marriage of Figaro* at first hand, he could reaffirm the composer's own observations: "It was made into suites for wind instruments, into quintets, into allemandes: in short, arias from *Figaro* filled the streets and gardens, and even cabaret harpists had to play 'Non più andrai' if they wanted anyone's attention. [...] Only a public with such a fine sense of musical beauty, and comprising so many learned connoisseurs, could immediately recognize the value of such art."

Soon after the production of *The Marriage of Figaro* in Prague, Mozart gave a concert at the Opera House, in which he appeared at the piano and conducted the symphony known today as the "Prague" Symphony. As Niemetschek recounts, "Never had the theater been as full as on that occasion, nor had anything ever enchanted an audience like his divine playing. We did not know what to admire more, his compositions or his playing: they were equally extraordinary, and the combined effect of the two seemed to cast a delicious spell upon our very souls. But when Mozart finished a half-hour improvisation at the end of the concert, having brought our rapture to its zenith, we emerged from this state of enchantment, and gave him endless applause and acclaim."

It was here, in Prague, that he was commissioned to write what would become *Don Giovanni*; but he was beginning to miss Vienna. "Although I have received every grace and honor imaginable, and although Prague is a very beautiful and pleasant place, still I long to return to Vienna," he wrote.

After his father died on May 28, Mozart returned once more to Prague. It was there that he finished *Don Giovanni*, which was first performed under his own direction on October 29 at the Nostitz Theater (now the Stavovské Divadlo, or Theater of the States). The German-language music journal *Prager Oberpostamtszeitung* reported, "Nothing of this kind had ever been staged in Prague before. Herr Mozart conducted the orchestra himself, and as soon as he took up his position, he was greeted by three cheers, which were repeated at the end, when he left the orchestra. After all, this is a very demanding opera, and everyone expressed rightful admiration for the performance, which was very good, despite the difficulties and after so few rehearsals. All the singers and musicians performed to the very best of their ability, honoring Mozart with their outstanding endeavors. [...] There were many in the audience, and all of them were delighted with this opera."

In Vienna, however, the tide was turning. At the Burgtheater, *Don Giovanni* was poorly received. His love affair with Vienna, already on the wane, was over. The following summer, he wrote three more symphonies—his last—but it seemed that they would never be performed: the Viennese no longer wanted to hear music of that sort.

Before relations between them had deteriorated, Mozart had been warned by Count Arco, one of Archbishop Colloredo's principal officers, "Believe me, you are too easily impressed: no-one is famous here for very long. At first, one is heaped with praise and makes a lot of money, it's true; but for how long? After a few months, the Viennese will want something new."

On December 7, 1787, Mozart was made Musician of the Royal Imperial Chamber by the Emperor, and was finally in receipt of a regular salary. But it was not enough to pay off his debts, nor even to cover household expenses: Constanze was in poor health, and he had to pay for her spa treatment in Baden.

So he decided to look for work elsewhere. In 1789, he traveled to Saxony and Prussia, returning via Leipzig and playing the organ at St. Thomas's Church. After two months' absence, he returned to Vienna, where his financial problems were getting worse: he had to take out numerous loans just to make ends meet. In 1790, he traveled to Frankfurt to perform at the coronation of the new Emperor, Leopold II. A great honor, but not at all profitable. In 1791 he gave only one concert in Vienna—his last.

By this point, in spite of generous support from his freemason friends, he was in dire financial straits. He could no longer live off his commissions, lessons, and increasingly rare concerts. No sooner had he realized his dream of artistic freedom than it was exposed as an illusion.

Prague. The Nostitz Theater, inaugurated in 1783, where *Don Giovanni* was first performed on the night of October 29, 1787, and Charles University, Prague.

"My greatest work"

The concert hall in the Nationaltheater, Mannheim, in 1793, by Franz Anton Mal. Mannheim, Städtisches Reiss-Museum.

At the Burgtheater in Vienna on April 1, 1784, Mozart staged another successful academy, performing a number of new compositions: two new symphonies, no. 35 (the "Haffner") and no. 36 (the "Linz"); two new piano concertos, no. 15 in B flat major and no. 16 in D minor; two arias; and a Quintet for piano and wind which he had finished only two days previously. He was particularly happy with this last: "As far I am concerned, it is the greatest work I have ever composed. I wrote it for oboe, clarinet, horn, bassoon, and piano. I wish you could have heard it! They played it so well!" This radiant work succeeded in giving the Viennese public all they had come to expect from their favorite musician in the way of elegance and charm, while representing for its composer the profound expression of a talent at the very peak of its powers. And indeed balance is the key to this score, which has elements of both chamber music and concerto—a sort of "chamber concerto"—and which combines woodwind and piano by means of either dialogue or contrast. Thirteen years later, the young Beethoven would use it as a model for his own quintet.

Quintet for piano and wind (K. 452).
Paris, Bibliothèque Nationale de France, Département de la Musique.

"A remarkable concerto"

Maria Anna Mozart, known as Nannerl, in 1792 (detail). Salzburg, Mozarteum.

During Lent 1785, Mozart staged no fewer than five "subscription only" concerts, which he gave at the Zur Mehlgrube inn, located near the Neumarkt in Vienna. He had to prepare new compositions for all of these: his public expected nothing less. On the very day of his first concert, his father arrived in Vienna with a friend, and they attended the concert. Leopold wrote his daughter, "They performed Wolfgang's remarkable new concerto, which was still being copied out when we arrived: there was no time for your brother to rehearse the rondo even once, because he was supervising the copiers!" He was referring to his son's Piano Concerto in D minor, no. 20, renowned and revered by pianists for more than two centuries. As usual, Mozart conducted from the piano and improvised his own cadenzas. It was his first concerto in a minor key, and one that prefigures the tragic accents of *Don Giovanni,* written two years later—a bold move on his part, and the first sign that he and his somewhat frivolous Viennese public would not be on good terms forever.

Piano Concerto in D minor (K. 466), composed in 1785.
Vienna, Gesellschaft der Musikfreunde.

A symphony for Prague

View of Prague at the beginning of the 19th century. Paris, Bibliothèque Nationale de France.

Prague, January 19, 1787. Two days after the first performance of *The Marriage of Figaro*, Mozart gave a concert at the Nostitz Theater. He played a number of fantasias and variations on the piano, and conducted a new symphony, written especially for the occasion. Completed a month and a half earlier, it was composed at the same time as the Piano Concerto no. 25 in C major, and, as so often with Mozart, the two works seem to complement and echo each other. At the end of the concert, the audience was ecstatic. Mozart improvised for a full half-hour to rapturous applause, and had to return to the piano more than once, until at the cry of "*Figaro*!" he was obliged to improvise on his famous aria "Non più andrai." The accounts of the performance paint a very touching picture of Mozart in action, radiant with delight. The symphony had three movements, and three sharps in the key signature, which clearly had some masonic significance (Mozart had been invited to Prague by members of the lodge). Still only 32 years of age, the composer of this work comes across as having all the exuberant confidence of youth, as well as profound warmth, humanity, and sympathy for those in distress. Based on a motif from *The Marriage of Figaro*, which had been so successful in Vienna, the finale of the symphony had everything that was needed to delight the citizens of Prague.

The "Prague" Symphony (K. 504), composed in 1786.
Cracow, Biblioteka Jagiellonska.

An opera for Prague

Poster for the first Viennese performance of *Don Giovanni* at the Vienna Burgtheater, May 7, 1788.

The success of *The Marriage of Figaro* in Prague came just in time to rescue Bondini, the director of the Nostitz Theater, from bankruptcy. But he not only avoided catastrophe: he actually made money, for Mozart as well as himself. He therefore wasted no time in commissioning another opera from Mozart, to be performed before the end of the year. This was to be *Don Giovanni*. Its composition did not come easily, and, for a number of reasons, the theater kept having to postpone. Mozart himself fell behind schedule, finally completing the work in Prague. According to Niemetschek, he confided in a *Kapellmeister* by the name of Kucharz, "It does not matter to me how much work I must do, nor how much pain I must endure, to give the people of Prague something excellent. And it would be quite wrong to imagine that my art comes easily to me. I can assure you, dear friend, that no-one has studied composition as assiduously as I have." Two days before the first performance, the overture was still unwritten, so Mozart sat down at his table to compose throughout the night. Constanze told him stories to make him laugh, and prepared punch for him to drink. It is said that when his work ground to a halt, she told him to lie down and rest for a while. He dozed off at three in the morning, and she woke him at five. The copiers turned up at seven, by which time, without a single crossing out, the overture was complete.

Case made to hold the autograph score of *Don Giovanni*, bought by the great singer Pauline Viardot in 1885. Viardot donated it to the library of the Paris Conservatoire in 1892. It is now held by the Bibliothèque Nationale, Paris.

Overture to *Don Giovanni* (K. 527).
Paris, Bibliothèque Nationale de France, Département de la Musique.

The last concert

In Mozart's time, concerts were held in private houses, as here, at the Ismaning court in 1773. Detail of a painting by Peter Jacob Horemans. Munich, Bayerisches Nationalmuseum.

At the end of the 18th century, there were still very few concert halls—barely more than there were permanent orchestras. Musicians played wherever they could—in the homes of aristocrats, on theater stages, or in public places such as inns and cafés, even outdoors. On March 4, 1791, no longer having the funds to organize his own concerts, Mozart performed in a concert organized by the clarinetist Joseph Bähr, which also featured the singer Aloysia Lange, in a hall belonging to the court caterer Ignaz Jahn in the Himmelspfortgasse. Mozart had not written a piano concerto for two years, even though it was in performing these works that he had formerly made such an impression in Vienna. On January 5 of this year, however, he had completed a new concerto, in B flat major, hoping to be able to perform it one day, perhaps on tour ... It would be his last piano concerto—indeed, his last public appearance. There is no record of how it was received. The work shows no sign of what he was going through at this time, and we will never know whether he was hiding his emotions, restraining himself, or simply resigned to his fate. In its sobriety, its total lack of empty virtuosity, the concerto is a masterpiece.

The opening of the Piano Concerto no. 27 in B flat major (K. 595).
Cracow, Biblioteka Jagiellonska.

Farewell to Prague

View of Prague in the 18th century. Colored engraving, Austrian school. Prague, Mozartmuseum.

Mozart left Prague after the first performance of *La clemenza di Tito* (The Clemency of Titus) on September 6, 1791, returning to Vienna with a view to staging *The Magic Flute* at the end of the month. As a farewell to his friends, he left them with an aria for bass and string quartet, "Io ti lascio, o cara, addio" (Farewell, my love, I am leaving you). (Constanze later denied its authenticity, but it is now generally attributed to Mozart.) It is not known to which "love" it is addressed: possibly Josefa Duschek, who provided accommodation for the Mozarts at the villa Bertramka. But it was also a more general farewell to his friends and to his beloved Prague, and one can certainly hear the composer himself speaking in the words, "I am leaving you ... be happy and forget me!" This short, intimate piece has nothing in common with his concert arias, the use of Italian seeming no more than a nod to convention. Above the low throbbing of the strings, the vocal line expresses an inner fervor, restrained at first but intensifying in the course of the three stanzas. Mozart's last concert aria is in fact nothing of the kind: it is rather a lied, and was very soon transcribed and published as such for soprano and piano, with German words ("Lassen muss ich"). Niemetschek records that, at the moment of his departure from Prague, Mozart was overwhelmed by such sadness at leaving his friends that he burst into tears.

The aria "Io ti lascio, o cara, addio" (K. 621a), composed in 1791.
Salzburg, Mozarteum.

Mozart Composing. Colored etching by Giovanni Antonio Sasso, c. 1815, after G. B. Bosio.

"I must say, I am very happy with this opera"

"We are having the first rehearsal [of *The Abduction from the Seraglio*] on Monday. I must say, I am very happy with this opera."

Mozart, letter to his father, Vienna, May 29, 1782

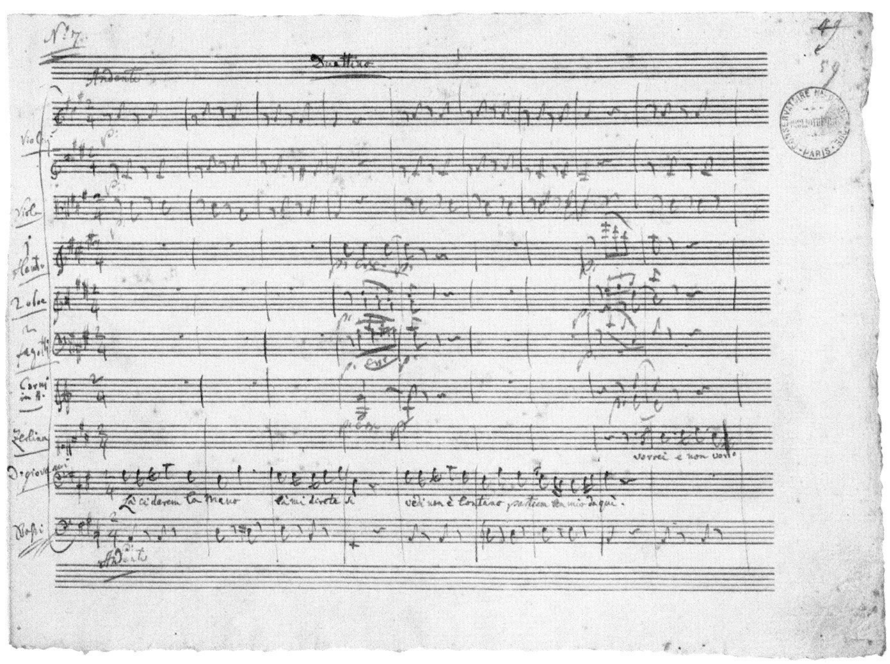

The aria "La ci darem la mano" from *Don Giovanni*.
Paris, Bibliothèque Nationale de France, Département de la Musique.

By the end of the 18th century, opera was more fashionable than ever. In Vienna, Prague, Munich, Milan, Venice, Naples, Paris, and London (to name only those places to which Mozart himself traveled), many new works were being performed, some of them written in a matter of weeks. Old favorites in the repertory were not enough: the audience wanted new material. Far from bucking this trend, Mozart embraced it wholeheartedly. Here was a new composer to reckon with, and in no time at all, all his commissions were for operatic works.

Opera, or rather the expression of human emotion in song, was a real passion for Mozart, one that he evinced from an unusually early age. He was just eight years old when his father wrote, "He is contemplating an opera, which he would like to stage in Salzburg with child performers." One wonders why he was so enthusiastic about the genre. Perhaps it was the love he felt so passionately for others, the empathy so often noted by commentators, that made him want to know and understand them, and to share in both their suffering and their joy. Few artists have explored the secrets of the human soul so thoroughly: even his concertos and sonatas reverberate with human drama, like scenes from an opera.

He was no more than 11 when he wrote his first lyric works, *Die Schuldigkeit des ersten Gebots* and *Apollo et Hyacinthus*, to be performed in Salzburg. Arriving in Vienna in early 1768, Mozart and his father immediately came into contact with the world of opera, but were very disappointed. Leopold wrote his friend in Salzburg, Lorenz Hagenauer, "It is well known that the Viennese are not generally interested in any serious or intelligent spectacle, that they are empty-headed, and that, hence, they are interested only in undemanding entertainment: dances, demons, phantoms, sorcery, Hanswurst, Lipperl, Bernadon, magicians and ghosts. Every day, it is the same: you just have to go to a Viennese theater! Even decorated noblemen will applaud cheap innuendos and lame jokes, and will be helpless with laughter, yet during any remotely serious scene, when the action is most touching and beautiful, and the dialogue quite spiritual, they will chat with their ladies so loudly that no-one else can hear anything."

Mozart nevertheless accepted commissions for *La finta semplice* and *Bastien und Bastienne*—at the age of 12, surely the most precocious opera composer of all time. Later, aged 14, he wrote a conventional *opera seria, Mitridate, re di Ponto*, to be performed in Milan. This required a lot of hard work, which stretched the young composer to his limits. Two months before the first performance at the Regio Ducal Teatro, he wrote his mother, "I cannot write very much, as I have written so much recitative that my fingers hurt." He added, "I ask Mama to pray for me, so that the opera goes well and we can be together again."

He switched between the various established genres, and explored different theatrical formats, composing the serenata *Il sogno di Scipione*, the *dramma per musica Lucio Silla*, the *opera buffa La finta giardiniera*, another serenata, *Il re pastore*, music for Baron von Gebler's drama *Thamos, König in Ägypten*, and the *Singspiel Zaide*. This long early period, dominated by genres borrowed from Italy, concludes with a masterpiece, the *dramma per musica Idomeneo*, the music of which far transcends the rather conventional libretto by the Abbé Varesco: "In my opera, there is music for everyone—except the cloth-eared."

But alongside his conventional material, Mozart was gradually refining his dramaturgical skills and his use of music to represent situations and characters, always acutely aware that he needed a good libretto to work with. He judged a number of librettists and librettos very harshly, and became more and more selective. In the famous letter he sent his father on October 13, 1781, from Vienna, where he developed his ideas about the relationship between words and music, and where he was working on *The Abduction from the Seraglio*, he made his views very clear: "for the best thing is when a good composer, who knows the theater and is himself in a position to make suggestions, finds himself an intelligent poet." This is exactly what happened: it was no accident that he made friends with Gluck, the operatic reformer, by whom he was much admired. After a performance of *The Seraglio* in August 1782, Mozart wrote, "My opera was staged again yesterday—as requested by Gluck! Gluck paid me a number of compliments. I am dining with him tomorrow."

The Teatro Regio in Turin, by Pietro Domenico Olivero, c. 1741. Turin, Museo Civico.

After *Idomeneo,* Mozart breathed new life into the genre with *The Seraglio,* a work that was very dear to his heart. For this time, the libretto, over which Mozart maintained tight control, went right to the heart of the human condition, transcending all convention. Moreover, the work combined speech and song, elements of both popular and high culture, the comic and the tragic. Mozart wrote, "Would you believe that I am writing a comic opera as if it were an *opera seria*? In an *opera seria,* there should be little jesting and much more that is wise and sensible, while in an *opera buffa* there should be few serious things and many more playful and amusing things. Now, if you want as much humorous as serious music in an *opera seria,* then I cannot help you; but doing the opposite is not a problem." Crucially, his new work, a *Singspiel,* was sung in German.

For Mozart, to compose an opera in his mother tongue, rather than in Italian, was a dream come true. When in Mannheim toward the end of 1777 and the beginning of 1778 he had seen operas performed in German, he had written his father, "I know for certain that the Emperor intends to establish a German opera company in Vienna, and that he is trying to find a young *Kapellmeister* who understands German, is talented, and could try something new: Benda and de Gotha are going to try their luck, and Schweitzer is determined to make the job his. I reckon that it would suit me very well—if it is well paid, of course. If the Emperor gives me a thousand florins, I'll write him a German opera, and if he does not want to employ me, then that makes no difference to me. Please ask as many of our Viennese friends as possible to spread the word that I am in a position to honor the Emperor. If this does not sway him, then I will prove my worth to him by writing an opera. What he does after that is neither here nor there." In fact, Joseph II did establish a German national opera, which he set up in the Burgtheater. Inaugurated in 1778, it closed only five years later, in 1783.

This desire for a national opera that rejected the fashion for things Italian—the Italian language, Italian singers and genres—had been gaining in strength for several decades, and now had all the fervor of a nationalistic conflict. Mozart wrote Councillor Anton Klein in Mannheim on March 21, 1785, "I have no news to give you about the proposed German opera because (apart from the fact that it will be established in the Kärtnertortheater) everything is cloaked in the greatest secrecy. The grand opening is in October. If you ask me, it is unlikely to be very successful. As far as I can tell from the way people are already behaving, they are not really trying to bring German opera back to life and to help it survive (for its demise may only have been temporary), but to destroy it completely. Only my sister-in-law Lange has been allowed to join the German opera. Cavalieri, Adamberger, and Teyber, all Germans in whom we can take pride, have to remain at the Italian theater and do battle with their own compatriots! There are too few German singers! And if there are any as good as the ones I have mentioned, let alone better, which I very much doubt, the theater directors seem to be thinking too much about saving money and too

The great hall of the Old Burgtheater, Vienna, c. 1800 (detail). Copper engraving.

little about patriotism, and would rather pay a lot of money to bring foreign singers here than employ German ones, who are just good, if not better, for nothing! [...] Unfortunately, there are too many theater directors and conductors who have—as much through ignorance as incompetence—ruined their own work. If there were even one patriot supporting this project, then everything would change for the better! But then perhaps the National Theater, which has started very promisingly, would flourish too, and what a terrible shame it would be for Germany if we Germans started thinking in German, acting in German, speaking in German, and even—singing in German!!!" Clearly, debates about the management of opera are as old as opera itself, as are those about singers and, nowadays, directors. If we were to replace a few of the names in Mozart's letter, it would read like a contemporary critique of the profession.

After the success of *The Seraglio,* Mozart began to look for another excellent libretto—which, he insisted, had to be in German. "Every nation has its own opera—why should we Germans not have ours too? Is the German language any less suited to song than French or English? Is it not in fact more singable than Russian?" Resigned to having to translate an Italian libretto into German, he decided to adapt Goldoni's comedy *Il servitore di due padroni* (The Servant with Two Masters), which was to become *Diener zweier Herren.* At the same time, he accepted a commission from the director of Viennese theaters for *L'oca del Cairo* (The Goose of Cairo), which he eventually abandoned. In any event, the German opera closed in March 1783, and he had to go back to writing in Italian. But he still needed a good libretto: "I have cast my eye over a hundred librettos, maybe even more, but I have found almost none to be satisfactory—not, at least, without a lot of modifications. And even if a poet agreed to make such changes, it would be easier for him to start afresh. It is always best to write something new. There is a fine poet, by the name of Da Ponte, but he is snowed under at the moment, with all the corrections he has to make for the theater. He is also contracted to write a brand new libretto for Salieri, which will take him at least two months. He has promised to write me one, but who knows if he will be able—or willing—to keep his word?"

While he was still looking for the right libretto, and because comic opera was popular in Vienna, Mozart composed *Lo sposo deluso* (The Disappointed Husband), possibly to a libretto by Da Ponte, and began work on *Il regno degli Amazoni* (The Kingdom of the Amazons), of which only a single aria has survived. In these works he returns to the familiar themes: true love, fidelity and fickleness, ill fortune and changes of heart.

But the decisive encounter came when, at the behest of the Emperor himself, Da Ponte made a free adaptation of Beaumarchais's *La Folle Journée, ou Le Mariage de Figaro* (The Mad Day, or The Marriage of Figaro), duly editing out its more vitriolic attacks on the established order. In *The Marriage of Figaro, Don Giovanni,* and *Così fan tutte,* Mozart and Da Ponte explored the games of love and chance to the point of tragedy, in a sort of descent into hell. Then, finally, came *The Magic Flute,* a work of light and transcendence.

While Mozart was working on *The Marriage of Figaro,* he also composed *Der Schauspieldirektor,* a "comedy with music," or *Singspiel,* based on a libretto by Johann Gottlieb Stephanie, the author of *The Seraglio.* At once a caricature of lyric theater and its mores and a reflection upon the genre itself, this short one-act work, intended for a private performance in the Orangery at Schönbrunn, was written in German, as requested by the Emperor. Performed in the first part of the program, Mozart's *Singspiel* was interestingly followed by *Prima la musica e poi le parole,* by Salieri.

Finally, written at the same time as *The Magic Flute,* came *La clemenza di Tito,* to be performed at the coronation of Leopold II as King of Bohemia in Prague. Mozart accepted this commission at a time of severe financial hardship, and finished it in under three weeks. But while the work marks a return to *opera seria,* and is extremely weak dramatically, it must have been of at least some interest to Mozart. The king's clemency is, after all, similar to that shown by the Pasha Selim in *The Seraglio,* and in his generosity of spirit he is not unlike Sarastro in *The Magic Flute.* In any event, Mozart produced a score of great beauty that deserves rather more attention than it has generally received.

Scene from Mozart's Opera "Don Giovanni", by Alexandre-Evariste Fragonard, 19th century. Clermont-Ferrand, Musée Bargoin.

Idomeneo

Set design by Lorenzo Quaglio for the first performance of *Idomeneo*, 1781.
Private collection.

When Mozart received a commission for a new opera in Munich in 1780, it seemed as though his chance to write a German opera had finally come. But the libretto he was offered by the Abbé Varesco was once again in Italian. Moreover, he was far from satisfied with it, and obliged the Abbé to make a great many substantial changes. For the first time in his career, Mozart had imposed his will on a librettist, with highly significant results. Little by little, he had the whole text rewritten. In structural terms, he moved as far away as possible from the conventions of Italian *opera seria*, with its succession of arias and recitatives, to embrace the model favored by Gluck and French tragedy, in which acts and dramatic situations were linked by choruses and ensembles. His lively recitative, subtle musical language, and nuanced instrumentation breathe life into the figures on stage, who are no longer stereotypes, but creatures of flesh and blood, who experience their passions with great intensity, and who develop throughout the course of the drama, inspiring fear or arousing pity. With the demise of the older form of *opera seria*, modern psychological drama was born.

Elektra's recitative preceding the aria "Idol mio" in the second act of *Idomeneo* (K. 366), composed in 1781.
Cracow, Biblioteka Jagiellonska.

"Prima la musica"

Orientalism was all the rage in the 18th century: *Harem Scene* by Giovanni or Francesco Guardi, c. 1743. Düsseldorf, Museum Kunst Palast.

In a letter to his father from Vienna, dated October 13, 1781, Mozart wrote mostly about Stephanie's libretto for *The Abduction from the Seraglio*. He realized that, while "the poetry is not of the highest quality," the words at least had the merit of being psychologically credible and dramatically effective, and would lend themselves very readily to a musical setting. He developed his thoughts along the more general lines of the relationship between words and music, a preoccupation for all musicians. Five years later, Salieri would announce, "Prima la musica e poi le parole" (Music first, then words), an idea Richard Strauss would later make the subject of his opera *Capriccio*. On this point, Mozart had no doubt whatsoever; there could be no debate on the matter: "In an opera the poetry must be the obedient daughter of the music. Why, after all, are Italian comic operas so popular, in spite of their dreadful librettos? Even in Paris—I saw it with my own eyes! It is because the music dominates, and all else is forgotten. An opera will be all the more successful, the better it is worked out, with the words written for the music, and not for the sake of some wretched rhyme (by God, rhymes do nothing for any kind of theatrical performance—if anything, they are harmful to them), where complete stanzas spoil a composer's every idea. Verse is absolutely essential for music; but rhymes for the pleasure of rhyming are downright pernicious. Those gentlemen who approach their work with such pedantry will only bring ruin to themselves and to their music. The best thing is when a good composer, who knows the theater and is himself in a position to make suggestions, finds himself an intelligent poet, a real phoenix. In such cases, you have nothing to fear from an ignorant audience."

Vienna, October 13, 1781

Mon trés cher Pére!

I thank you along with Fräulein von Auernhammer for the concertos. Yesterday morning, M. Marchal brought young Herr von Mayern to my room and in the afternoon I drove out to fetch my things. Herr von Mayern hopes to be taken on at Count Jean Esterhazy's as a private tutor—and Count Cobenzel has given him a letter of recommendation for the Count. He said to me, "J'ai donné une lettre à Monsieur votre protégé," and later, speaking to Marchal, said, "D'abord que j'aurai de reponse, je le dirai à M. Mozart votre protecteur."
Now to the libretto of the opera. As far as Stephanie's work is concerned, you are quite right—yet the poetry is perfectly in keeping with Osmin's stupid, coarse, wicked character. I know the poetry is not of the highest quality—yet it is so close to my musical ideas, which were already buzzing around inside my head, so in agreement, that it could not fail to please me; and I would wager that it will lack nothing in performance. As far as the poetry in the piece itself is concerned, I really could not bring myself to despise it. Belmonte's aria "O wie ängstlich" could hardly be better written for music. Except for the "hui" and "kummer ruht in meinem schoos," the aria is not bad either, especially the first part. I don't know—in an opera the poetry must be the obedient daughter of the music. [...]

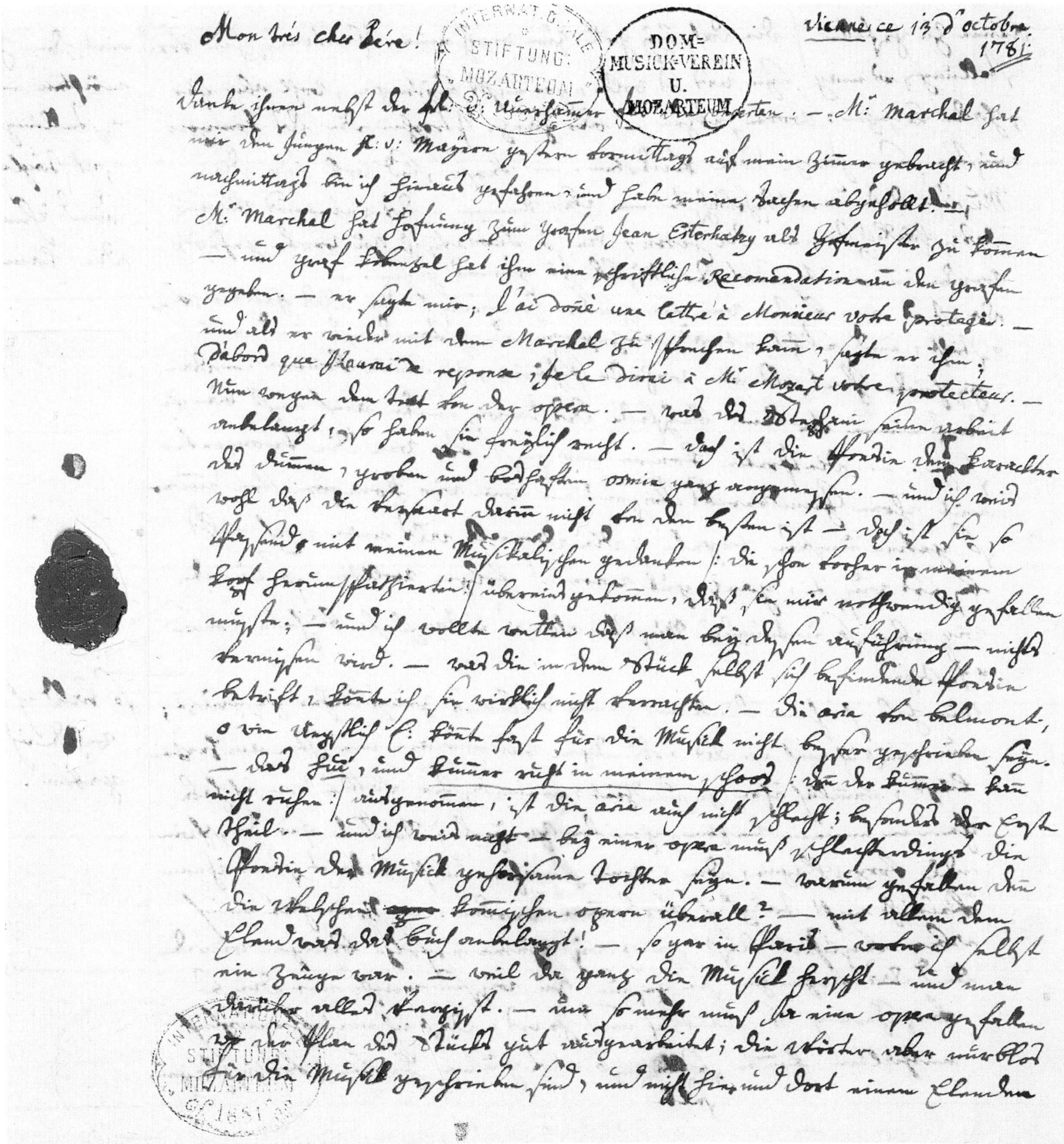

Mon très cher Père! Vienne ce 13 d'octobre 1781

Danke ihnen nebst der Schw: für übersandten … – Mr: Marchal hat mir den jungen H: v: Mayern gestern vormittags auf mein Zimmer gebracht, und nachmittags bin ich hinaus gefahren und habe meine Sachen abgeholt. – Mr: Marchal hat Hofnung zum grafen Jean Esterhazy als hofmeister zu kommen – und graf Cobenzl hat ihm eine schriftliche Recomendation an den grafen gegeben. – er sagte mir; J'ai doné une lettre à Monsieur votre protegé. – und als er wieder mit dem Marchal zu sprechen kam, sagte er ihm; D'abord que j'aurai de reponse, je le dirai à Mr: Mozart votre protecteur. – Nun wegen dem text von der opera. – was die arbeit des Stephani anbelangt, so haben sie freylich recht. – doch ist die Poesie dem karackter des dummen, groben und boshaften osmin ganz angemessen. – und ich weis wohl daß die versart darinn nicht von den besten ist – doch ist sie so passend mit meinen Musikalischen gedanken (die schon vorher in meinem kopf herumspatzierten) übereinsgekommen, daß sie mir nothwendig gefallen muste; – und ich wollte wetten daß man bey dessen aufführung – nichts vermissen wird. – was die in dem stück selbst sich befindende Poesie betrifft, könnte ich sie wirklich nicht verachten. – die aria von belmont, O wie ängstlich etc: könnte fast für die Musick nicht besser geschrieben seyn. – das hui, und kummer ruht in meinem schoos (denn der kummer – kann nicht ruhen) ausgenommen, ist die aria auch nicht schlecht; besonders der erste theil – und ich weis nicht – bey einer opera muss schlechterdings die Poesie der Musick gehorsame tochter seyn. – warum gefallen denn die welschen komischen opern überall? – mit allem dem Elend was das buch anbelangt! – so gar in Paris – wovon ich selbst ein Zeuge war. – weil da ganz die Musick herrscht – und man darüber alles vergisst. – um so mehr muß ja eine opera gefallen wo der Plan des Stücks gut ausgearbeitet; die Wörter aber nur blos für die Musick geschrieben sind, und nicht hier und dort einem elenden

Letter from Mozart to his father, Vienna, October 13, 1781 (folio 3).
Salzburg, Mozarteum.

The Abduction from the Seraglio

"Too many notes, my dear Mozart!" the Emperor is said to have cried after the first performance of this work, in July 1782. To which Mozart is said to have responded, "No, sir, not one too many!" The richness, splendor, and originality of this work must certainly have seemed astonishing. In spite of its fashionable Turkish setting and the banality of its plot, this was Mozart's opportunity to write, in German, an opera that went right to the heart of his human and philosophical preoccupations. Happiness and love have to be earned and the challenges of life overcome, and in this way we grow up. This is also the philosophy underlying *The Magic Flute*. Prefiguring Sarastro, the "evil" pasha finally reveals his magnanimity and gives us a lesson in compassion, renouncing vengeance and the favors of his captive in order to bring happiness to the two young people he has put to the test. In spite of a cabal, the opera was a triumph. Staged wherever German was spoken, it was an unprecedented success, unique for its genre. Shortly afterward, Goethe wrote, "All our efforts to express the very essence of things were rendered futile by the appearance of Mozart. *The Abduction from the Seraglio* has defeated us all."

A scene from Act 2 of *The Abduction from the Seraglio*: Pedrillo persuades Osmin to drink while Blonde looks on. Watercolor, 18th century. Private collection.

Osmin's aria "Ha! wie will ich triumphieren" in the third act of *The Abduction from the Seraglio* (K. 384). Cracow, Biblioteka Jagiellonska.

19
Allo vivace
Violini
Viole
Flauto Piccolo
2 Oboe
2 Corni
2 Fagotti
2 Clarinetti
Osmin:
Bassi
Allo: vivace
33

O, wie will ich triumphiren

The Marriage of Figaro

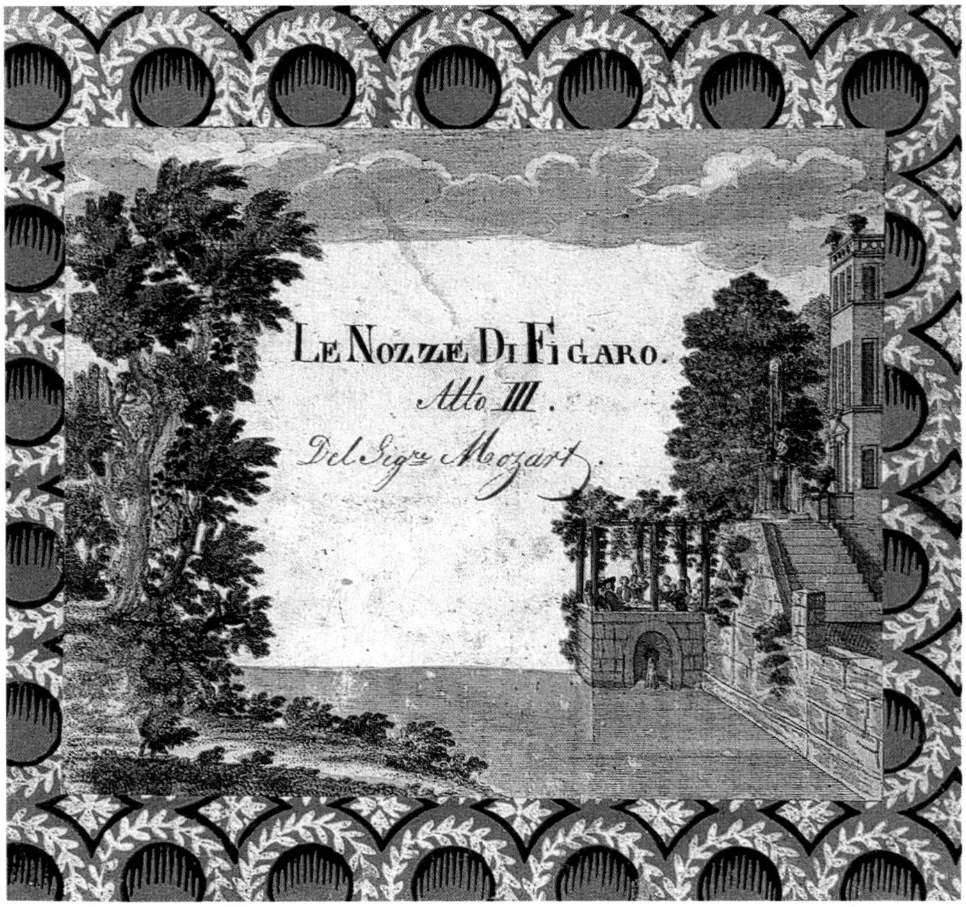

Title page (detail) of Act 3 of Lorenzo Da Ponte's libretto for *The Marriage of Figaro*, after the play by Beaumarchais. Colored copper engraving, 1788.

Portrait of Lorenzo Da Ponte, the librettist for three of Mozart's operas, including *The Marriage of Figaro*. Colored copper engraving by Michele Pekenio, c. 1820, after a miniature by Nathaniel Rogers.

In November 1785, Leopold Mozart sent his daughter news of Wolfgang: "He must hurry to finish the opera *The Marriage of Figaro*. [...] I know this piece: it involves a great deal of work, and the translation from the French must surely have been very free for it to work as a libretto. Pray God that the drama is well received. I have no fears for the music. There will have to be a great deal of toing and froing and plenty of discussions before the libretto is as he wants it." Da Ponte certainly removed all the more subversive elements from Beaumarchais's original: one simply did not make fun of the establishment, and censorship reigned supreme. If *The Seraglio* is a hymn to liberty, then *Figaro* is a hymn to equality, while *The Magic Flute* is a hymn to fraternity. Mozart was certainly a man of the Enlightenment. But as he himself wished, *Figaro* is more psychologically than socially orientated. He himself called it an *opera buffa*, but while its situations and comic misunderstandings are highly entertaining, its passions and jealousies, its rage and eroticism, and the energy that drives its characters belong to the world of serious drama. But it is all farcical enough to drive one mad, and from the very overture the audience is thrown headlong into the turbulent world of *La Folle Journée*.

Overture to *The Marriage of Figaro* (K. 492), composed in 1786.
Berlin, Staatsbibliothek, Musikabteilung.

Draft of the recitative and Susanna's aria no. 27 from *The Marriage of Figaro*.
Paris, Musée des Autographes et Manuscrits.

The Marriage of Figaro

De Begnis in the role of Figaro at the King's Theatre, London, in 1823. Pen and watercolor by M. Gauci. London, City of Westminster Archive Centre.

Cherubino in Act 2 of *The Marriage of Figaro*. Copper engraving by Johann Heinrich Ramberg, 1815.

It is not so much Figaro as the Countess, Rosina, who is the focal point of the work: the rest of the action goes on around her. She is a pure and idealized figure, portrayed in two wonderful arias expressing her isolation. Passive and innocent at first, she increasingly seizes the initiative, in a vast ballet that is driven relentlessly by a complex of different passions—love of money for Marcellina and Bartolo, morality for Antonio the gardener, jealousy for Figaro and the Count. And of course, they also fall prey to their sensuality: the Count feels a burning desire for Susanna, who is in turn pursued by Cherubino, a young man who is discovering love for the first time, and who both seeks and receives plenty of female attention, including that of the Countess herself, who is unable to remain indifferent to him. Even the music of the young Barbarina trembles with inexpressible desire. From the gardener to the Count, from the Countess to the soubrette, Mozart is fascinated by all of their lives, no one of which he regarded as having greater value than any other. And in all these schemes and stratagems, Mozart paints a prodigious tableau of the human psyche through the powerful magic of his music. Amidst the languid games of a summer night, this "mad day" comes to a happy end ... but for how long? *Don Giovanni* would soon follow.

Cherubino's aria no. 6, "Non so più cosa son," from Act 1 of *The Marriage of Figaro*.
New York, Pierpont Morgan Library.

Don Giovanni

Manuel García, the brother of Pauline Viardot, in the role of Don Giovanni. Lithograph, 1824.

Leporello serenading Donna Elvira in place of Don Giovanni, who is standing behind him (Act 2, Scene 1). Austrian school, 18th century. Private collection.

With the character of Don Juan, Mozart takes on what is one of the great themes of Western culture, together with those of Faust and Tristan. And while the story may have its roots in the *commedia dell'arte*, he raises it to the level of a myth. *Dramma giocoso*? *Opera buffa*? Maybe so. But Mozart breaks all the rules. The very first scene, for example, far from being the traditional exposition of characters and plot, shows us destiny sealed in an instant, in a few moments of astonishing violence, under the twin signs of sex and death, *eros* and *thanatos*, in the rape of Donna Anna and the murder of her father. The whole drama leads inexorably to the resolution of the conflict, through a variety of seduction rituals. Don Giovanni is a glutton at the table and a monster toward women, but, though he gives full rein to his terrifying lusts, he is merely trying desperately to overcome his existential angst. His lack of moderation is that of a hero of Greek drama, as is his absolute authenticity. Even behind his mask, Don Giovanni never flinches and never lies.

The first two pages of the canzonetta no. 17 from Act 2 of *Don Giovanni* (K. 527), composed in 1787. Paris, Bibliothèque Nationale de France, Département de la Musique.

Allegretto
Viola
Mandolino
Allegro

ch'hai la bocca dolce più del mele
tu che il zucchero porti in mezzo il core

Don Giovanni

Don Juan and the Statue of the Commander (detail), by Alexandre-Evariste Fragonard, 1830. Strasbourg, Musée des Beaux-Arts.

No-one knew better than Mozart how to convey the ambiguity of the characters that surround Don Juan. Is Donna Elvira his wife or not? Is what she feels for him love or hatred, repulsion or compassion? All at once, to be sure. Was Donna Anna seduced or not? Is it her father's murderer she is pursuing, or the man to whom her body will belong forever more? And whom does Zerlina prefer, her peasant fiancé or the lord? Is not Leporello the wicked, devious, shameful face of his master, to the point where he actually exchanges with him his cloak, his hat, his identity, and his conquests? Certainly, the music suggests as much, revealing each character's profoundly troubled soul. Don Giovanni himself is unfettered by convention or morality. As the art of time, music presents this irrepressible lothario as someone who lives in the present, and always at the fastest possible tempo: and this is why only death, which stands outside time, can get the better of him. The stone guest will reestablish the moral order and punish the criminal. Yet this is not the central point of the opera. Don Giovanni's meteoric impact upon the other characters' lives exposes their own weaknesses, and reveals the secrets of their souls. Nothing will ever be the same again for them, and they have to make the best of it.

In the cemetery, Leporello, threatened by Don Giovanni, invites the statue of the Commander to dinner.
Paris, Bibliothèque Nationale de France, Département de la Musique.

Violini
Viole
Leporello:
Bassi
Allo
O statua gentilissima del gran Commendatore … padron … mi trema il core non

poso non poso terminar
ti metto questo acciar. ti metto questo acciar.

Così fan tutte

Set designed by Anton Brioschi for *Così fan tutte*, 19th century.
Salzburg, Mozarteum Archives.

The third work in the famous "Da Ponte trilogy" pushes psychological analysis further than either of the two previous operas. It is said that the Emperor himself told Mozart and Da Ponte to use a story which had supposedly taken place recently in Trieste, and which everyone in Vienna was talking about. Two young men agree to test the fidelity of their fiancées by disguising themselves, and sure enough, within a single day this stratagem lands each girl in the wrong man's arms. There is no classical intrigue, leading to a hero's death: here, the tragedy lies rather in the dreadful emotional solitude which all six characters must endure in the pursuit of love. The misunderstanding that forms the basis of the plot reveals an unbearable truth: that each of the two sisters is really attracted, both personally and physically, to the other's fiancé. When the men unmask, they have to return to the old "reality," even though they are fully aware that it is a based on illusions and lies. The men are no better off than the women, and the general outlook is very bleak. Yet the music is as sublime as the characters are ignoble, even while exposing their most intimate feelings. The descent into hell within the most secret depths of the human soul takes place to the accompaniment of an ideal sonic beauty. The work was for a long time misunderstood, being regarded as nothing more than an indecent sexual farce. Only with the rise of psychoanalysis was it recognized as a terrifyingly perceptive insight into human psychology.

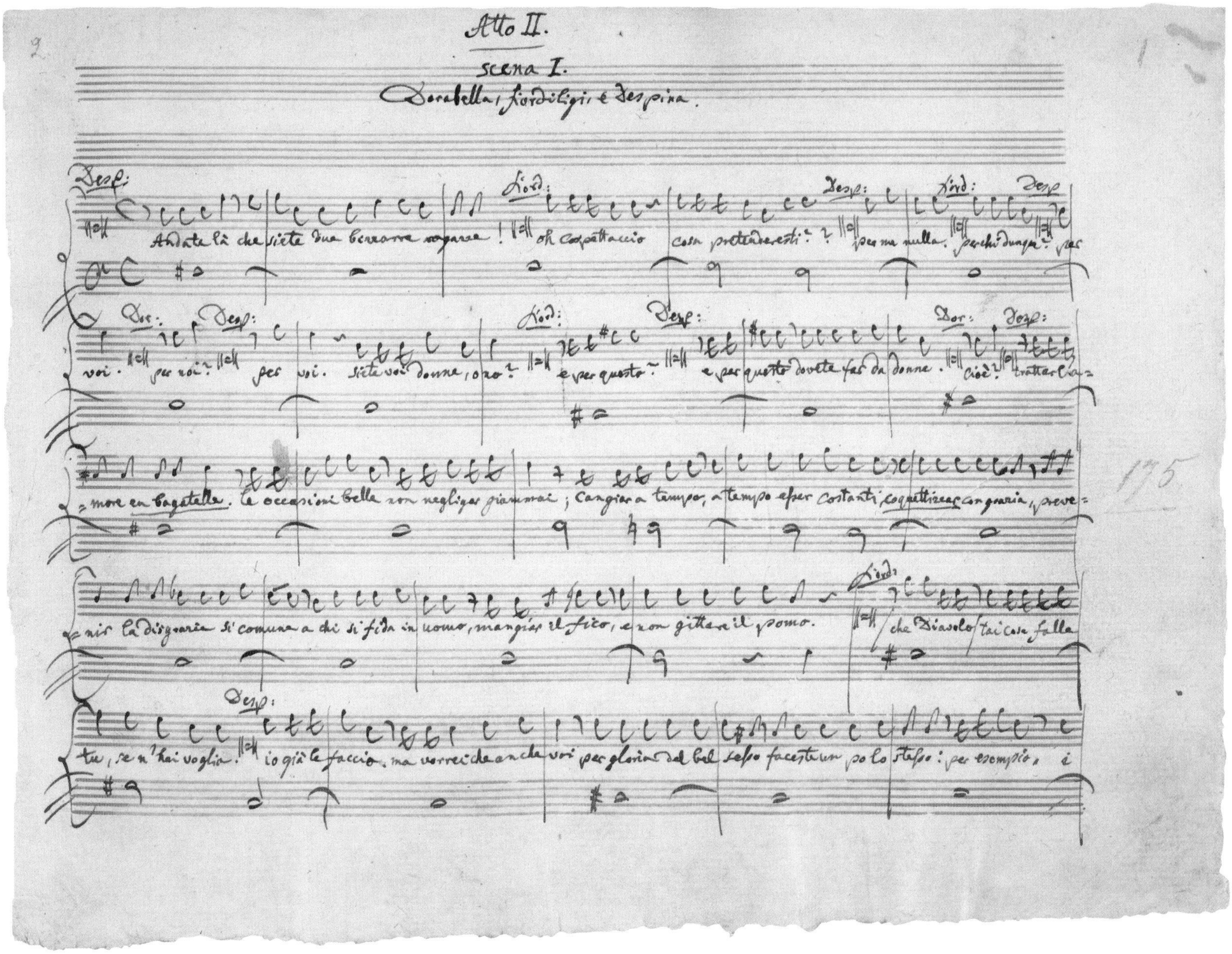

Act 2, Scene 1, of *Così fan tutte* (K. 588), composed in 1790.
Berlin, Staatsbibliothek, Musikabteilung.

La clemenza di Tito

The ceremonies held in Prague in 1791 for the coronation of Leopold II (Holy Roman Emperor since 1790) and Empress Marie Louise as King and Queen of Bohemia. Colored etching by Johann Balzer.

This *opera seria,* which Mozart agreed to write for purely financial reasons, was at first treated with scorn and then praised to the skies. In fact, it deserves "neither such excessive honor nor such indignity." The libretto, which is adapted from Metastasio, who had himself drawn heavily on Corneille's *Cinna,* is certainly not free of the standard clichés of the genre, and with its conventional situations and inconsistent characters is vastly inferior to the three great operatic masterpieces that preceded it. Mozart himself was well aware of its shortcomings, and set it to music as quickly as he could at the same time as writing *The Magic Flute,* which was much dearer to his heart, even entrusting its interminable recitatives to his pupil Franz Xaver Süssmayr. Yet, while the drama has little to commend it, the same cannot be said of the music. Though somewhat uneven by Mozart's standards, it has some wonderful highlights, such as the arias of Sextus and Vitellia (whose orchestral accompaniments include, respectively, clarinet and basset-horn), the finale of Act 1, and the two trios and finale of Act 2.

Overture to *La clemenza di Tito* (K. 621).
Berlin, Staatsbibliothek, Musikabteilung.

Mozart Composing, by Ernest Meissonier. Paris, private collection. 19th century.

"The greatest composer …"

"Before God, and as an honorable man, I tell you that your son is the greatest composer known to me either in person or by name: he has taste and, what is more, the most profound knowledge of composition."

Haydn to Leopold Mozart, quoted in a letter from Leopold Mozart to his daughter, Vienna, February 16, 1785

Opening of the Piano Concerto no. 21 in C major (K. 467), composed in 1785. New York, Pierpont Morgan Library, Dannie and Hettie Heineman Collection.

With these words, Joseph Haydn, who was then regarded in Vienna and throughout the world as the greatest living composer, publicly acknowledged Mozart's genius. The endorsement would certainly have been seen as the most authoritative possible, and would prove to be an invaluable asset in Viennese artistic circles.

The imperial city's artistic life stimulated a fundamental development in Mozart's musical thinking, first as he witnessed his own success, but also through the concerts he attended, the operas he saw, the scores and librettos he studied, and of course his regular contacts with men of letters and composers—Gluck, in particular, Dittersdorf, and Vanhal, as well as Paisiello, Martin y Soler, and many others.

The Italian musician Antonio Salieri (1750–1825), by an unknown artist, c. 1800. Vienna, Gesellschaft der Musikfreunde.

There was also Salieri, who was only six years Mozart's senior. He had become a part of the musical life of Vienna 15 years before Mozart arrived in the city, and had a perfectly honorable career at court, being in no sense the perpetrator of shameful crimes against Mozart, despite the legend that has persisted ever since he was portrayed as Mozart's murderer in Pushkin's dramatic poem of 1830, on which Rimsky-Korsakov based an opera. Salieri directed concerts in which his own works were performed alongside Mozart's, and he was eager to play a part in the education of Mozart's youngest child, the little orphan Franz Xaver, born four months before his father's death. Salieri acted as the boy's music tutor, and even predicted a brilliant future for him.

During Mozart's ten years in Vienna, two encounters were to prove decisive for him: one was with the music of Bach, the other with Haydn and his works. Both had an enormous impact on him, and it can be said that from then on, in addition to his own father and teacher, Leopold, Mozart regarded Bach and Haydn as two new fathers in his musical life.

In spring 1782 Mozart came across Baron Gottfried van Swieten, to whom he had been introduced some time earlier. A former ambassador and amateur composer, the Baron presided over a circle of high-ranking aristocrats whom he entertained with concerts in his own house or in those of his friends. Van Swieten had a passion for contemporary music (the young Beethoven was to dedicate his first symphony to him) but also for earlier music, and he included works by Handel and Bach and even those of Renaissance composers in his programs. There were regular concerts at his house late on Sunday mornings, which Mozart assiduously attended from April 1782 onward. On April 10 he wrote his father, "I go to the house of Baron van Swieten every Sunday at 12 o'clock and nothing is played there but Handel and Bach. I am making a collection of Bach's fugues, those of Sebastian as well as Emanuel and Friedemann." By April 20 he had already composed a prelude and fugue for piano, in which the fugue is directly influenced by *The Well-Tempered Clavier*.

He sent it to his sister, and was so enthusiastic about the form of the fugue that he stated very clearly to her, "I have purposely written above it 'Andante maestoso,' as it must not be played too fast. For if a fugue is not played slowly, the ear cannot clearly distinguish the theme when it comes in, and consequently the effect is entirely missed." During the next few weeks, he arranged ten fugues by Bach, eight taken from *The Well-Tempered Clavier*, for string quartet, adding a prelude of his own to four of them.

He was keen to make it clear that Constanze shared this new enthusiasm. "My dear Constanze is really the cause of this fugue's coming into the world. Baron van Swieten, to whom I go every Sunday, gave me all the works of Handel and Sebastian Bach to take home with me (after I had played them to him). When Constanze heard the fugues, she absolutely fell in love with them. Now she will listen to nothing but fugues, and particularly (in this kind of composition) the works of Handel and Bach. [...] If Papa has not yet had the works of Eberlin copied I shall be very pleased, for I have gotten hold of them in the meantime and now see (for I could no longer remember them) that they are far too trivial to deserve a place beside Handel and Bach. With due respect for his four-part composition, I may say that his keyboard fugues are just long drawn-out dirges."

Mozart's friendship with van Swieten was to remain firm. When the Baron sought to make Handel's music more widely known through orchestrations adapted to contemporary techniques and tastes, he turned to Mozart for the purpose. This was to be of great assistance to Mozart in the financial and psychological distress of the last years of his life. Mozart had already directed two oratorios by Carl Philipp Emanuel Bach at the Baron's house, and in 1788 he produced a modern orchestration of *Acis and Galatea*, followed by *Messiah* in 1789 and *Alexander's Feast* and the *Ode for St. Cecilia's Day* in 1790.

From his move to Vienna in 1781 until the failure of *Don Giovanni* in the same city in 1788, Mozart's fame grew steadily. Conscious of his own genius and of the unique value of each of his new works, on February 9, 1784, he started a catalogue of his works, which he was to continue until the end of his life.

Leopold, as we have seen, became aware of his son's rise to fame and public recognition when he visited him in Vienna in February 1785. The very evening he arrived, having traveled through a snowstorm, he attended the hugely successful first performance of the Piano Concerto in D minor. He spent the next evening at his son's, where they were joined by two aristocrats. Together the four of them sight-read three quartets that Wolfgang was going to dedicate to his great friend Joseph Haydn, who was also visiting. Leopold later recounted the event, in French: "M. Joseph Haydn and the two Barons Tinti called in, the new quartets were played, but only the three new ones he composed to complement the three we have already got; they may be a little easier, but are remarkably well composed. M. Haydn said to me, 'Before God, and as an honorable man, I tell you that your son is the greatest composer known to me either in person or by name: he has taste and, what is more, the most profound knowledge of composition.'"

Collection from 1773 of twelve themes with variations for pianoforte. Berlin, Archiv für Kunst und Geschichte.

Mozart had first met Haydn, who lived most of the time at the castle of the Esterházy family in Hungary, the previous year in Vienna, during a soirée at the house of the Storace family at which, again, quartets were being played. Haydn was playing first violin and Mozart viola, Dittersdorf second violin and Vanhal cello. It seems likely that the enduring friendship between the two musicians dated from that evening and that experience.

Haydn's admiration for Mozart was unceasing, and he expressed it publicly. Friedrich Rochlitz reported that after a performance of *Don Giovanni* in 1787, a group of fashionable people, including numerous musicians, had gathered to comment on what they had just seen and heard. Everyone expressed their reservations and criticisms, while Haydn, also present, said nothing. When asked for his opinion, he responded, with his customary circumspection, "It is not for me to settle the matter," then adding with animation, "but what I know is that Mozart is the greatest composer that the world knows today!" Those present were silenced.

When, during a visit to London, Haydn heard that Mozart had died, he could not believe it. Having finally accepted the truth, he wrote their mutual friend Michael Puchberg, "I have been beside myself for a long time since hearing of Mozart's death, and cannot believe that Providence has so soon

called to the other world a man who was so irreplaceable." Not long after this he declared to a London publisher, "He was truly a great musician. My friends have often flattered me, saying that I had a certain degree of brilliance, but he was my superior by far."

Mozart drew on Haydn's free spirit and his genuineness, and turned to good account everything he had learned from his genius, as well as from their deep friendship, at the same time gleaning all he could from every new encounter—never forgetting Bach.

In April 1789 he set off for Berlin. He stopped off at Leipzig where, at St. Thomas's Church, he heard a motet by Bach, whose music was still being sung in that period. He climbed up to the organ loft and played for one hour. At his side, the incumbent organist and the cantor Johann Friedrich Doles, who had been a pupil of Bach, pulled the stops for him. We are told that the ageing Doles, spellbound, thought that his old master was once again before his eyes.

Mozart then went on to the Prussian capital, Potsdam, where he received fresh recognition outside Vienna: the King commissioned from him a set of six string quartets. Only three, now known as the "Prussian" Quartets, were actually written. On his return to Vienna, Mozart found he had already gone out of fashion. Rejected by the public, he sank further and further into financial difficulty. Yet his genius was at its height.

All who had seen and heard him as a child prodigy had been astonished by his exceptional, almost incomprehensible gifts. The genius of Mozart the composer is certainly difficult to grasp in all its grandeur, but all those who were close to him were struck by his powers: the facility with which he composed, the urgency, the immediacy of creation that marked his works. It was the unfathomable mystery of absolute genius: witnesses recounted what they observed, remarking that they had no way of explaining it. They pointed out that the works had clearly been maturing in the composer's mind for a long time before he wrote them down in what seemed like the mere copying out of something that was already fully formed. Hence the almost total absence of any crossings-out that so impresses anyone

Two sheets of musical sketches by Mozart. Paris, Bibliothèque Nationale de France, Département de la Musique.

reading his manuscripts. The musician himself was well aware not only of his genius, but of the very distinctive, unusual nature of his creative process, as well as the particular mood he had to be in if he was to be able to work. "And I who must always compose must have a relaxed mind and keep my composure," he wrote his father in 1781, at the very beginning of his independent life in Vienna.

Niemetschek tells us, "Mozart wrote all music with such ease and speed as might at first be taken for carelessness or haste. Neither would he go near a keyboard when he was writing. Once it was conceived, his imagination held the whole piece before him in its full clarity and verve. His thorough grasp of composition enabled him to achieve an overall view of the harmonic structure. It is rare to find improved or erased passages in his scores. But it does not follow that his works were hastily jotted down. The piece was already complete in his mind before he sat at his desk."

All contemporary eyewitness accounts agree with this. The most significant is that of the young Friedrich Rochlitz, a critic, writer, and publisher who was close to Mozart in his final years, and who relayed what the composer had confided to him about the way he worked. "When I am on form, in good shape, as it were, say traveling in a carriage or having a walk after a good meal, or at night if I can't manage to sleep, that's when ideas most readily come to me, in their droves. Where from? How? I have no idea, I can't help it. I keep the ones I like in my head and hum them to myself—that's what I'm told, at any rate. If I stick at it, the way to turn all these pieces into a good dish comes to me gradually, in accordance with the rules of counterpoint, the timbres of the instruments, and so on. My brain is fired up, especially if I am not disturbed. It grows, I elaborate it further, ever more clearly. The work is then complete in my head, or as good as, even if it is a long piece, and I can then embrace it all at a glance, like a painting or a statue. In my mind, I do not hear the work in progress, I hold it there in full, so to speak. And that is such a joy! Invention and elaboration do take place in me, but as if in a wonderful, magnificent dream, and when I get to hearing the mustered whole, that's just the best of all. How come I don't forget it like a dream? That could well be the greatest gift for which I have to thank my Creator."

J. S. Bach: a revelation

Portrait of Johann Sebastian Bach in 1746, by Elias Gottlob Haussmann. Leipzig, Museum für Geschichte der Stadt.

It was to the erudite Baron van Swieten that Mozart owed his discovery of the fugues of Bach. For Mozart, it was a revelation. He immediately applied himself to studying Bach's counterpoint, which instantly fed into and greatly enriched his own musical language. Moreover, Bach's music strengthened Mozart's and gave it a gravitas that he had been striving for but which had not yet fully developed in his work. Nothing would ever be the same again, right up to *The Magic Flute*, which was so deeply influenced by Bach's counterpoint. So when Mozart's journey to Berlin in 1789 took him through Leipzig, he went straight to St. Thomas's Church, where Bach had been employed. Nine years later, the music critic Friedrich Rochlitz gave an account of his visit: "At the instigation of the then cantor of St. Thomas's School, the late Doles, the choir surprised Mozart by performing a motet for double choir, 'Singet dem Herrn ein neues Lied,' by the patriarch of German music, namely Sebastian Bach [...]. The choir had sung no more than a few bars when Mozart gave a start. After a few more bars he exclaimed, 'What is that?' His whole soul seemed to have settled in his ears. When the work was over, he cried out in delight, 'Now here is a piece one can learn from!' He was informed that this school, where Sebastian Bach had once been cantor, possessed a complete collection of his motets, which were preserved as if they were a saint's relics. 'That is right, that is fine,' he exclaimed, 'Let me see them.' There was, however, no full score of the works. He therefore took the separate parts, and then, what a pleasure it was for the quiet observer to see how eagerly Mozart sat down, the parts all around him, held in both hands, on his knees, on the nearest chairs. Forgetting everything else, he did not stand up again until he had looked through all the music of Sebastian Bach. He asked for copies, which he was to treasure, and unless I am much mistaken, no-one who is familiar with Bach's compositions and Mozart's Requiem, especially the great 'Christe eleison' fugue, could fail to notice the extent to which Mozart had studied, appreciated, and fully understood the spirit of the great contrapuntist."

Title page of J. S. Bach's *The Well-Tempered Clavier*, 1722. Berlin, Staatsbibliothek.

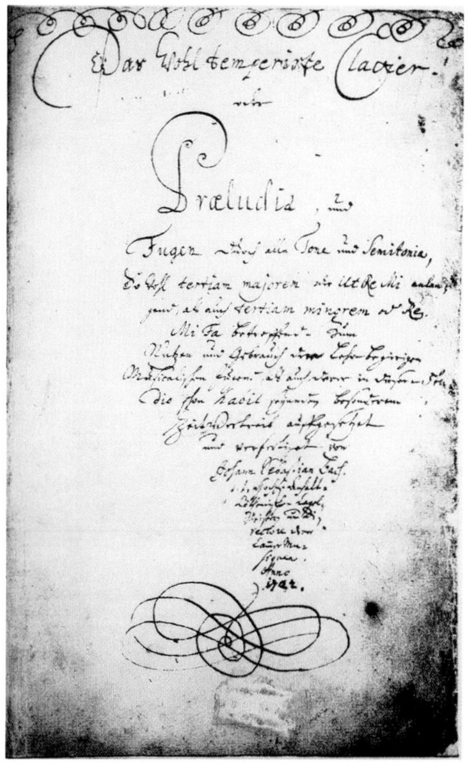

The Gloria from the Mass in C minor (K. 427), last section, Cum Sancto Spiritu, folio 137 verso.
Berlin, Staatsbibliothek, Musikabteilung.

New quartets

Gottfried van Swieten, patron of numerous musicians. Pastel by C. Clavereau. New York, Granger Collection.

As his compositional genius burgeoned, Mozart returned after ten years to the string quartet. Now settled in Vienna, and having immersed himself in the quartets of the celebrated Joseph Haydn, the scores of which he had been able to study, he applied himself once again to this major discipline of musical thought. Reflecting on Haydn's superb models and at the same time on what he had learned from Bach's counterpoint, he sought through this rigorous exercise to reach into the innermost depths of his own personality. His originality exploded in a wonderful group of six quartets, which he produced in just over two years. It is known from the composer's own account that these works cost him more pain and effort than any other. In them, a new Mozart is expressing himself, in the density of the writing, the meticulous attention to their composition. The first quartet came out in December 1782, a second six months later, and then a third; after which, at the end of 1784 and the beginning of 1785, the other three erupted onto the scene. In the meantime, Mozart had met Haydn, and he was to show his gratitude and admiration for him by dedicating the six works to him. The String Quartet in C major is the last in the set, completed on January 14, 1785. Its nickname "Dissonance" derives from the strange chromaticism of its slow introduction. It is probable that Mozart, who had joined the freemasons a month earlier, wanted to depict in it, as Haydn would do in *The Creation*, the primeval chaos that reigned before the divine light burst forth. And here it is a brilliant light of perfect clarity, even if challenged by the incomparable chiaroscuro quality that is one of the essential characteristics of Mozart's genius.

String Quartet in C major (the "Dissonance" Quartet, K. 465), completed on January 14, 1785.
London, British Library.

Return to the piano

Extract from the sheet reproduced on page 159.

Mozart had written no major work for solo piano for six years when the powerfully moving Sonata in C minor appeared. There is no biographical information to shed light on the circumstances of its composition, nor on the composition, eight months later, of the extraordinary Fantasia in C minor, completed on May 20, 1785. There is, however, evidence to suggest that it was a moment of deep crisis in the composer's private life. It was around this time that, for some unknown reason, the Mozarts suddenly left the lodgings they had occupied in the home of the composer's beloved pupil Theresa von Trattner and her husband, an important music publisher. It seems it was a new experience of sorrow and suffering, and Mozart went through a period of deep reflection and searching, which led him to take the step of joining the freemasons. Although composed after the sonata, the fantasia has so many links to it that it seems to be its prelude. Dedicated, like the sonata, to Theresa, it displays a range of emotional moods in sharply contrasting episodes set side by side, indicative of severe inner turmoil. Despairing interjections, explosions of violence, and passages of painful introspection alternate with exquisite moments of tenderness, in an exploration that reaches into the depths of a faltering soul. Mozart seems almost to be improvising here, indulging in the bold gestures that so captivated his audiences. The pathos of the introduction is straightaway indicated by a kind of tonal drifting. The work may well be in the key of C minor, with its three flats in the key signature. But in the sonata's wandering path, the note inflections—sharps, flats, and naturals—are constantly changing. At the beginning of Mozart's autograph score it is just possible to make out that, freeing himself from the straitjacket of tonality, he has scratched out the three flats to leave the stave without a key signature at all, the inflections being inserted note by note—as Schoenberg would later do.

Fantasia in C minor (K. 475), opening.
Salzburg, Mozarteum.

Homage to Haydn

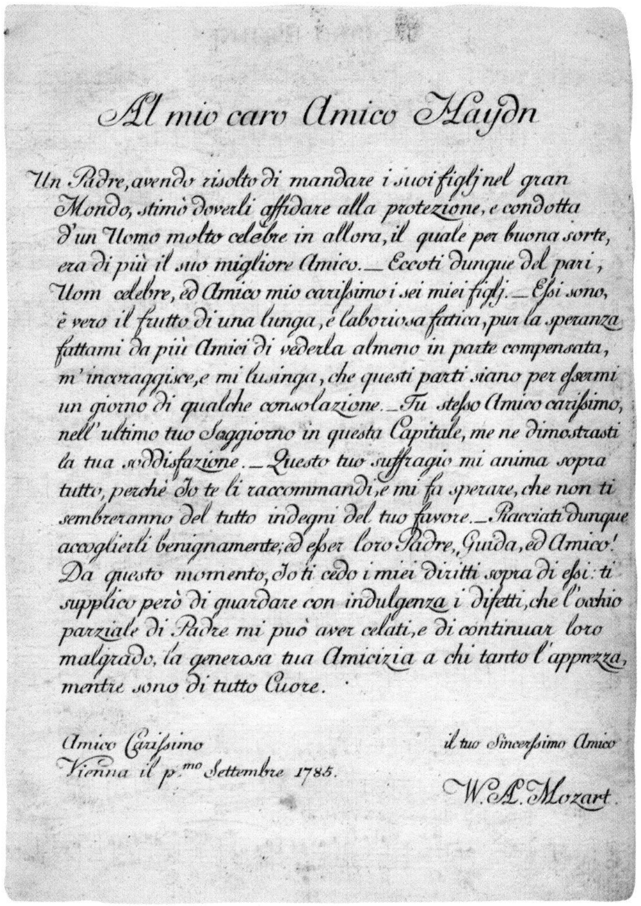

Al mio caro Amico Haydn

Un Padre, avendo risolto di mandare i suoi figlj nel gran Mondo, stimò doverli affidare alla protezione, e condotta d'un Uomo molto celebre in allora, il quale per buona sorte, era di più il suo migliore Amico. _ Eccoti dunque del pari, Uom celebre, ed Amico mio carissimo i sei miei figlj. _ Essi sono, è vero il frutto di una lunga, e laboriosa fatica, pur la speranza fattami da più Amici di vederla almeno in parte compensata, m'incoraggisce, e mi lusinga, che questi parti siano per essermi un giorno di qualche consolazione. _ Tu stesso Amico carissimo, nell'ultimo tuo Soggiorno in questa Capitale, me ne dimostrasti la tua soddisfazione. _ Questo tuo suffragio mi anima sopra tutto, perchè Io te li raccommandi, e mi fa sperare, che non ti sembreranno del tutto indegni del tuo favore. _ Piacciati dunque accoglierli benignamente; ed esser loro Padre, Guida, ed Amico! Da questo momento, Io ti cedo i miei diritti sopra di essi: ti supplico però di guardare con indulgenza i difetti, che l'occhio parziale di Padre mi può aver celati, e di continuar loro malgrado, la generosa tua Amicizia a chi tanto l'apprezza, mentre sono di tutto Cuore.

Amico Carissimo
Vienna il p.mo Settembre 1785.

il tuo Sincerissimo Amico
W. A. Mozart

The dedication to the first edition of the quartets that Mozart dedicated to Joseph Haydn, dated September 1, 1785. Salzburg, Mozarteum.

Portrait of Joseph Haydn in 1783, by Christian Ludwig Seehas. Schwerin, Gemäldegalerie.

The friendship that bound Mozart to Joseph Haydn, who was old enough to be his father, was filial and fraternal at the same time. Founded on mutual trust and admiration, it is one of the most attractive chapters in the whole history of music. Mozart's admiration for his friend is evident in his work: referring to his discovery of Haydn's works, he declared that it was from them that he had learned to write quartets. Under the impact of this discovery, and in homage to the master who was to become his friend, Mozart composed six new string quartets—all of them masterpieces—which he dedicated to Haydn on September 1, 1785.

"To my dear friend Haydn

A father who had decided to send his children into the world at large thought best to entrust them to the protection and guidance of a famous man who fortunately happened to be his best friend as well. Behold here, famous man and best friend, my six children. They are, to be sure, the fruit of long and arduous labor, yet some friends have encouraged me to assume that these children will not go quite unregarded, and this flatters me into believing that they may one day bring me some comfort.

You yourself, dearest friend, showed me your approval of them during our last stay in the capital. Your praise above all sustained me and that is why I recommend them to you, in the hope that they will not seem entirely unworthy of your good will. May it please you therefore to receive them kindly and to be their father, their guide, and their friend. From this moment I surrender to you my rights over them, and accordingly implore you to look with kindness on the faults that an indulgent father's eye might have overlooked, and to uphold, in spite of them, your generous friendship toward him who has such a high opinion of you. For I am with all my heart, dearest friend,

Your most sincere friend,
W. A. Mozart"

Third movement (Andante cantabile) of the String Quartet in G major (K. 387), completed on December 31, 1782, the first of six quartets dedicated to Joseph Haydn. In the margin, a note in Mozart's own hand reads, "written just after dinner."
London, British Library.

Trio in a garden

Music with his family
(Mozart, his father, and his sister),
in 1770.
Augsburg, Mozart-Gedenkstätte.

The apparent and legendary ease with which Mozart composed (in fact, after a long period of maturation in his mind) showed itself once again in the summer of 1786, when, during a game of skittles in the garden of his friends the Jacquins, he wrote down in fair copy a trio for the unusual combination of piano, clarinet, and viola. Once again, the work appeared on the page in a perfect state, with no alterations. It was after the short-lived success of *The Marriage of Figaro* in the spring of that year that Mozart's financial difficulties began. He had confided in fellow members of his masonic lodge, one of whom was the clarinetist Gottfried von Jacquin, asking for their assistance. During this period Mozart was devoting himself to the composition of chamber music, and on a fine and carefree summer's day he wrote this trio, dated August 5, known ever since as the "Skittles" Trio. Everything suggests that it was performed at once with the daughter of the house, Franziska von Jacquin, on piano, her father on clarinet, and Mozart himself on viola. Commentators have pointed to the work's masonic symbols, including the three flats in the key signature, the three movements, and the use of the clarinet, the instrument played in lodge rituals. But the most important thing is the wonderful feeling of friendship and insouciance that pervades the score, its warm and simple tone, with no outward show of bravura. It is a perfect masterpiece of its kind.

Trio for piano, clarinet, and viola (the "Skittles" Trio, K. 498), composed in 1786.
Paris, Bibliothèque Nationale de France, Département de la Musique.

From quartet to quintet

A quartet playing a work by Mozart. Engraving, early 19th century. Prague, villa Bertramka, Mozart Museum.

Extending and broadening the sound world of the string quartet, Mozart began to take a close interest in a much less common form, that of the string quintet, made up of two violins, two violas, and cello. For this he had had a model in Michael Haydn, the younger brother of Joseph and a friend from Salzburg days. Mozart found that, playing first viola, his favorite instrument (together with the piano, of course), he was at the very heart of the polyphony: two violins above him and two other instruments, second viola and cello, below. In this central position, he was immersed deep in the instrumental dialogue. It was from Mozart that the string quintet gained its real credentials (even though it was never to have a large repertory), and he wrote for it some of the finest masterpieces of chamber music ever written. Besides a transcription and one youthful attempt at the genre, he produced four great string quintets, which are among his major compositions. Two things are immediately clear: they came after the quartets dedicated to Haydn, as an extension of their discourse, and were the fruits, deliberately chosen, of Mozart's creative will, not commissioned pieces. The composer dated his String Quintet in G minor May 16, 1787. Returning from his first triumphant stay in Prague to Vienna, where his financial problems were growing, he discovered that his father was gravely ill just as he began work on *Don Giovanni*. The quintet he then wrote was in G minor, the key that expresses tragedy—and here, even deadly anguish. The work is very unusual in its construction, full of lamenting, sighing, and expressions of grief, until it reaches the major-key finale, whose feigned joy is an attempt at exorcizing the sorrow. Twelve days later, Mozart learned that his father had died.

Opening of the String Quintet in G minor (K. 516), completed in 1787.
Cracow, Biblioteka Jagiellonska.

Jokes and games

A key aspect of Mozart's personality that tends to be overlooked is his love of jokes. As a little boy, like all children he loved to play; but throughout his life he retained his cheerful nature, always ready for a good laugh, for practical jokes, lampooning, and clowning, and he loved to enjoy himself at skittles, billiards, and target shooting. He was only ten when, in The Hague, he wrote a *Gallimathias musicum*, a potpourri of popular airs orchestrated in a comical style. Four years later he went back to his *Gallimathias* and turned it into the *Petite Symphonie burlesque*. His correspondence is full of play on words (untranslatable, of course), nonsense words and phrases, *bouts-rimés* (verses written to set rhymes), assonance, jokes of all kinds, disjointed sentences, and a kind of multilingual pidgin—since, in addition to German, his mother tongue, he spoke French, Italian, and English and also knew Latin. His wit sometimes seemed inexhaustible. He loved to write backward, including his own name, which he distorted in various ways, into Trazom, Mozartus, De Mozartini, and so on. All this contrasts oddly with his father's interminable and entirely sensible letters. Both Mozart and his father, however, used to insert words, names, and even entire sentences in code, in order to protect themselves from the censor. Mozart, so profound a thinker, was nevertheless capable of making fun of everything and everyone, including himself. His friend from Salzburg Ignaz Leitgeb, a horn player who had switched to selling cheese, was one of his favorite targets. He frequently referred to him as "that ass Leitgeb." One day he even shut him inside the stove in his room while he worked on a horn concerto for him. In due course he freed him, and wrote the dedication "Wolfgang Amadé Mozart finally took pity on Leitgeb, ass, ox, and fool, in Vienna, May 27, 1783." An indication of the extreme changes of mood of which he was capable is the fact that the first work he wrote after the String Quintet in G minor and his father's death in June 1787 was *Ein musikalischer Spass* (A Musical Joke), for string quartet and two horns; in this rather harsh caricature, he ridicules mediocre composers.

Title page of the first French edition of
Ein musikalischer Spass,
illustrated by Bergeret.
Paris, Bibliothèque Nationale de France,
Département de la Musique.

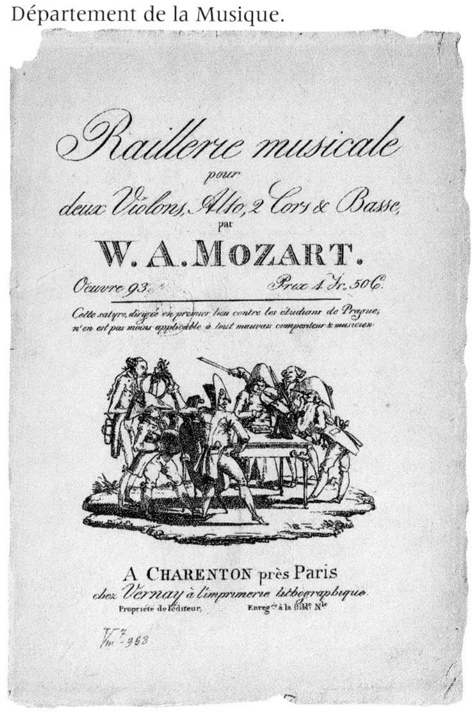

Raillerie musicale
pour
deux Violons, Alto, 2 Cors & Basse,
par
W. A. MOZART.
Oeuvre 93. Prix 4 fr. 50 C.
Cette satyre, dirigée en premier lieu contre les étudians de Prague, n'en est pas moins applicable à tout mauvais compositeur & musicien.

A CHARENTON près Paris
chez Vernay à l'imprimerie lithographique.
Propriété de l'éditeur, Enreg.ᵉ à la Bibl.ᵉ N.ˡᵉ

Ein musikalischer Spass (K. 522), composed in June 1787.
Berlin, Staatsbibliothek, Musikabteilung.

Bach revisited

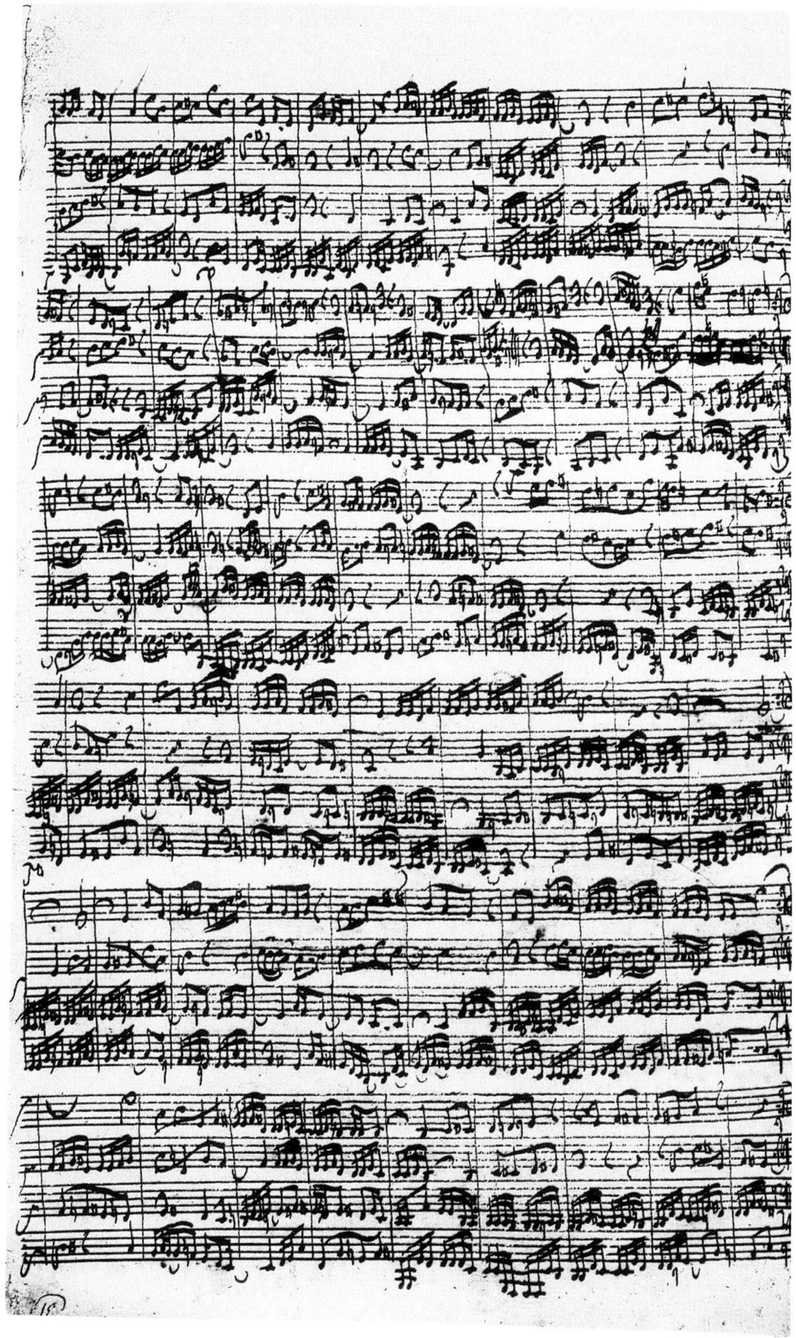

J. S. Bach, *The Art of Fugue*, 1748,
detail of page 31.
Berlin, Staatsbibliothek.

After the failure of the Viennese production of *Don Giovanni* in May 1788, Mozart's financial situation became more and more precarious. He sought commissions and opportunities for potboilers in order to survive. Yet his passion for composing seemed to be keener than ever. The catalogue he kept of his works bears witness to this. A trio for piano and strings was followed by a second, an "easy" sonata for beginners, and then, in the course of the summer, three symphonies, which were to be his last, and the "Puchberg" Divertimento. Among this group of works there was also a very unusual piece, an Adagio and Fugue in C minor for string quartet—effectively, a string orchestra. Mozart went back to a fugue he had written five years earlier for two pianos, transcribed it for strings, and added an introduction, so as to create a prelude and fugue in the manner of Bach. The prelude (the Adagio) is massive, tough, violent, and full of dark, untamed heroism; its modulations and chromaticism create a strange path, sometimes plumbing unfathomable depths. The subject of the fugue is finely chiseled, one of the richest and most beautiful ever written, worthy of the Bach of the *Musical Offering*. The treatment of this motif is incredibly complex: the subject, or theme, is even superimposed on itself in its inverted form. The effect is one of a teeming, evolving world. Beethoven copied out this passage, such was his admiration for it.

Adagio and Fugue in C minor (K. 546),
composed in 1788.
London, British Library.

Fuga
Allegro
Fuga. Allegro.
stacc:
3
144

The *Symphony in G minor*

The Zur Mehlgrube inn, in Vienna, where Mozart gave numerous concerts in 1785. Engraving by Johann Adam Delsenbach after Johann Bernard Fischer von Erlach. Augsburg, Stadtarchiv.

Although he had composed many symphonies while he was still tied down in Salzburg, Mozart had not attempted to win over the Viennese public with new works in this genre. The three written in Vienna were in fact intended for other cities, Mozart having decided to make his mark with two other genres (in which he excelled equally)—opera and the piano concerto. By 1788, however, no-one was commissioning operas from him, and the concertos that had formerly won him great acclaim no longer interested a fickle public. And yet it was in this extraordinary summer of 1788 that he produced these three symphonies, all absolute masterpieces. Nothing is known of the reason for their composition. Was it merely the hope that they might be performed, in Vienna or elsewhere, or had there been a commission, all trace of which has been lost? We have no information at all. There has never been any text, any document to shed light on their genesis. The only thing that is more or less certain is that they were never performed in Mozart's lifetime; he was to die three and a half years later without ever having heard them, and without having had any others to write. Immensely popular today, a century ago the Symphony in G minor was generally regarded as merely a charming work in the *galant* style. It was only with the symphony's rehabilitation by inspired conductors such as Richard Strauss and Bruno Walter that audiences became aware of the brilliant and tragic quality of this score, which had been much admired in the Romantic era. The wild energy of despair that erupts in the music, and the inspired fervor with which Mozart crafted this tempestuous work, still retain their impact of astonishing novelty.

First movement (Molto allegro) of the Symphony no. 40 (K. 550), completed on July 25, 1788.
Vienna, Gesellschaft der Musikfreunde.

"Jupiter," the final symphony

The opening bars of the "Jupiter" Symphony, 1788.

Was it possible for Mozart to plumb the depths of pain even further than he had in the Symphony in G minor? Surely not; but he could go beyond that point, to reclaim light and joy. Less than three weeks after finishing the previous symphony, he completed a new one, which was to be his last. After the G minor, with all its sorrow, came the C major, expressing triumph. The three last symphonies should be heard in succession in order to realize how, after the passages of spirituality and faith that characterize the first, the tumultuous and relentless conflict of the second opens out into, and is resolved in, the third. None of the vital energy has been lost, but now it is channeled into an affirmation of human victory in the struggle between light and darkness. The proud nobility of this symphony earned it the nickname "Jupiter," which may or may not be apt. What matters is to hear in the music the process through which metaphysical joy is recovered, to be proclaimed in the finale, toward which everything converges in a triumphant Alleluia. In this compelling fugal exposition, with its urgent development, Mozart seems to bring together his three "fathers" in music: Leopold, in what he has retained of the *galant* style, here rendered sublimely; Haydn, in the brilliance of the symphonic construction; and Bach, in the vigor of the counterpoint. Perhaps nowhere more than here does Mozart demonstrate the extent to which his three fathers enabled him to achieve the full potential of his genius.

St. Thomas's Church and School, Leipzig. Bach was cantor at St. Thomas's School for over 25 years and Mozart went there on his way to Potsdam in 1789. Copper engraving by Johann Gottfried Kruegner, 1723.

Second movement (Andante cantabile) of the Symphony no. 41 (the "Jupiter" Symphony, K. 551), completed on August 10, 1788.
Berlin, Staatsbibliothek, Musikabteilung.

Mozart c. 1790, by Joseph Grassi. Moscow, Glinka State Central Museum of Musical Culture.

"Most dear friend and brother"

"Most dear, excellent friend!
Most honorable brother
[...]
Ever your most devoted servant,
your true friend and brother."

Mozart, letter to Michael Puchberg,
Vienna, July 12, 1789

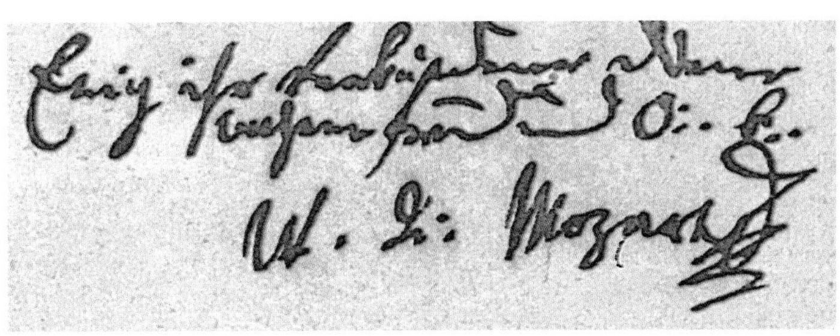

"Ever your grateful servant, true friend and B. O. W. A. Mozart."
Detail of the letter reproduced on page 189.

Like love in its widest sense, friendship played an essential role in Mozart's life. He drew sustenance from friendship not only in sharing moments of boisterous relaxation but also in reflecting on and exchanging views about what was for him of fundamental importance: the study of a particular concept of the world and of man's place in society. Brought up in the Catholic faith, from his earliest years Mozart displayed great religious fervor, at times bordering on mysticism; in Catholicism he found the expression of his ideal of spirituality. This combination of a sense of friendship, philosophical thinking, and spiritual commitment was a fertile mix that made him receptive to the ideas of the masonic movement that was then spreading all over Europe and making itself felt among much of society's intellectual elite.

From an early age Mozart had been in contact with freemasons such as Mesmer in Vienna and Marchand in Mannheim. It was through Mesmer that Baron von Gebler, also a mason, called on the young Mozart to write the interludes and choruses for his "heroic drama" *Thamos, König in Ägypten*, a vindication of the ideals of freemasonry which foreshadowed the philosophical concerns of *The Abduction from the Seraglio* and *The Magic Flute*. Already the composer is using, 18 years ahead of time, certain inflections prefiguring the choruses of *The Magic Flute*.

As a man of the *Aufklärung*, the Germanic Enlightenment, Mozart shared its rationalism, and was enthusiastic about the new ideas regarding society and universal brotherhood. He was a deeply spiritual being, but opposed to all kinds of superstition, and he possessed a lively intellectual curiosity. He believed that everyone could contribute to the progress of humanity, through virtue and through wisdom. And he believed in human dignity. In 1781, at the start of hostilities with his Archbishop and Count Arco, he fulminated, "I have only to listen to my reason and my heart, and therefore have no need of any great lady or person of rank in order to do what is just and good, to do what is neither too much nor too little; it is the heart that makes a man noble, and though I might not be a count, I perhaps have more honor in my body than many counts have." One can almost hear Figaro ranting.

It was not until 1784 that Mozart decided to become a member of the freemasonry movement. At that time he was going through a serious crisis, and everything suggests that it was the prospect of formalizing and fulfilling the ideals that he had always carried inside him that led him to take this decision. It was made all the easier for him because Austrian masonry was not constrained by papal condemnation. Choosing to enter a rationalist lodge did not involve any conflict between his Catholic religion and his philosophical adherence to the ideals of freemasonry.

Initiation Ceremony at the Lodge "Zur neugekrönten Hoffnung" (*New-Crowned Hope*), attributed to Ignaz Unterberger, c. 1784. Mozart appears at the far right of the painting. Vienna, Wienmuseum.

Poster for the first Munich performance of *The Magic Flute* in 1791.
Berlin, Staatsbibliothek, Musikabteilung.

Unfortunately, a large number of letters and autograph manuscripts directly relating to Mozart's masonic activities are now lost, particularly letters to Michael Puchberg, so that we have only partial information about this very important chapter in the Mozartian biography. The same applies to autograph scores: at present, at any rate, we do not have Mozart's autograph manuscripts for the "Puchberg" Divertimento, the Clarinet Concerto, or the cantata *Die Maurerfreude* (The Mason's Joy).

Who was it who, at a particular point in Mozart's life, when he was inwardly ready, persuaded him to join the freemasons? His friend and protector Baron Gottfried van Swieten? Possibly. Or, more likely, another friend, the nobleman Ignaz von Born. Geologist, Egyptologist before the term was coined, and distinguished mineralogist, von Born was also a great humanist. Worshipful Master of the lodge "Zur Wahren Eintracht" (The True Harmony), he had gathered there a brilliant circle, attracting some of the most famous Viennese intellectuals. His essay *On the Mysteries of the Egyptians* was to provide the basis for Schikaneder's libretto for *The Magic Flute*. In honor of this paternal figure, in 1785 Mozart wrote the cantata *Die Maurerfreude*, setting a poem that praises von Born's intellectual virtues: "See how, under the inquiring eye of the researcher, nature reveals her face little by little! How she fills his spirit with great wisdom, and his heart with virtue! There's delight for a mason's eyes, the real, fervent joy of the mason!" Von Born died on July 24, 1791, when Mozart was completing *The Magic Flute*. The figure of the High Priest Sarastro can be seen today as an incarnation of von Born, with whom Mozart is said to have worked on the outline of the opera's libretto.

Ignaz von Born in 1785, detail of a portrait by Johann Baptist Lampi. Von Born was Worshipful Master of the lodge "Zur Wahren Eintracht" (The True Harmony), and was used by Mozart as the model for Sarastro in *The Magic Flute*. Vienna, Mozart Gedenkstätte Figarohaus.

At any rate, in November 1784 Mozart wrote his letter applying to join the lodge called "Zur Wohltätigkeit" (Beneficence), whose mother lodge was "Zur Wahren Eintracht," over which von Born presided. Mozart was initiated on December 14, 1784, and admitted as an Apprentice. This event marked a decisive step in his personal and social life.

On December 24 he paid a visit to the mother lodge and von Born. It is interesting to note that five days later, obviously influenced by his very dear friend Mozart, Joseph Haydn also applied to join the freemasons. He chose the lodge "Zur Wahren Eintracht," and his letter of application seems to echo Mozart himself: "The extremely favorable opinion that I formed long ago with regard to freemasonry has awakened in me the most sincere desire to join the order whose principles are wisdom and love of humanity."

There were only eight masonic lodges in Vienna at the time, several of them established only recently. However, their members included numerous intellectuals, important merchants and businessmen, music publishers, and performers and artists, such as the actor Emanuel Schikaneder, who wrote the libretto of *The Magic Flute* and created the role of Papageno, the tenor Valentin Adamberger, who created, among other roles, that of Belmonte in *The Abduction from the Seraglio*, the virtuoso clarinetist Anton Stadler, and Gottfried von Jacquin. This created an atmosphere effervescing with ideas, a milieu where members exchanged views that were new and knowingly contentious with regard to the established order, the world, and society, therefore representing a potential threat to imperial power. It is thus not surprising that in December 1785

Emperor Joseph II, who relied on the masonic lodges in connection with his efforts to introduce reforms, ordered the merger of the eight Viennese lodges into two, so that they were easier to keep under control. Those frequented by Mozart became a single lodge, "Zur neugekrönten Hoffnung" (New-Crowned Hope).

Following his visit to the lodge "Zur Wahren Eintracht," Mozart was promoted to the rank of Companion on January 7, 1785, and then to that of Master on January 13. A month later, on February 11, it was Haydn's turn to be initiated. He did not appear again at the lodge, but there is every reason to believe that he practiced masonry at Eberau with the Esterházy family, almost all of whom were masons. Being in close contact with masonic circles, he moreover received commissions and invitations from French and English lodges.

Ardent neophyte that he was, Mozart now persuaded his father to join the freemasons as he had Haydn. It happened that Leopold was visiting his son in Vienna, where he was to pass the late winter and early spring. So, during his stay, on April 6, 1785, Leopold was initiated. He was admitted as Apprentice in the lodge "Zur Wohltätigkeit," was promoted to Companion of the lodge "Zur Wahren Eintracht" on April 16, and, since he had to return to Salzburg very shortly, was elevated to the rank of Master on April 22. The lodge "Zur neugekrönten Hoffnung" gave a banquet in his honor.

For Mozart, joining the freemasons had nothing to do with formality; it was a sign of his deep commitment. He took very seriously the meetings to which his lodge invited him, and right to the end he was to display great diligence with regard to the practices and ceremonies, composing and conducting pieces for particular masonic occasions. He was unable to attend the inaugural session of his new lodge, "Zur neugekrönten Hoffnung," on January 14, 1786. He seems to have been sincerely contrite about this and apologized to the presiding Master, Count Wenzel Paar: "Dear brother, I returned home an hour ago, struck down by bad headaches and stomach aches. I was hoping to feel better, but since the contrary is the case, I see that I shall not be in a condition to attend our first formal occasion today. Therefore I pray you, dear brother, to excuse me for this, and to give my apologies to the appropriate person. The loss is all mine; I am ever your sincere brother, Mozart."

The friendships formed within masonic circles, where mutual assistance between brothers was greatly prized, were to prove of great value in the difficult final years of Mozart's life. The entrepreneur Michael Puchberg, unflagging provider of financial support, was to play a decisive role in the composer's material life, Mozart continually appealing to him for help. In the summer of 1789, for example, when Constanze was at death's door and the family's debts were mounting, it was again to Puchberg that Mozart turned: "Here I am, in a situation that I would not wish even on my own worst enemy. And if you, my best friend and brother, if you abandon me, I am lost, alas, and am unable to do anything about it, as are my poor sick wife and my child! [...] Unfortunately, fate is so much against me, although only in Vienna, that I am unable to earn anything, however much I want to; I have been sending round a list for the past fortnight, but the only name on it is that of van Swieten!" And it was Puchberg who paid for the treatment needed by Constanze at Baden where she went to take a cure.

The influence of masonry is plain to see in a number of Mozart's works. There are pages directly linked to masonic practices, there are cantatas and odes, songs for the opening and closure of the lodge's proceedings, but there are also works that develop a system of symbolism, a sensibility, or an ethos connected to masonic ideals: the last two of the string quartets dedicated to Haydn and the Piano Concerto no. 21 in C major, all composed immediately after his initiation, and the "Puchberg" Divertimento are the most famous examples, together with, of course, *The Magic Flute* and the Clarinet Concerto.

Mozart had a particular liking for the clarinet, which for him resonated with tones of warm, brotherly friendship, of trusting partnership, of great tenderness. He had already heard the clarinets of the famous Mannheim court orchestra, and was fascinated by them: "Ah! If only we too had clarinets! You can't believe the wonderful effect produced by a symphony with flutes, oboes, and clarinets!" He was to write his first masterpieces for this instrument.

Associated with the clarinet is the basset-horn, a kind of alto clarinet, whose sound is thinner and at the same time more somber than that of the clarinet. It is the instrument of masonic rituals, and

Designs by Karl Friedrich Schinkel for the Queen of the Night, for the Berlin performance of *The Magic Flute* on January 18, 1816.

Mozart held it in special regard: he was to use it in several works, from the famous, brilliant "Gran partita," of 1781, to his unfinished Requiem. He had started sketching a concerto for basset-horn in 1787, intending it for his lodge brother Anton Stadler, but had set it aside, later making it into his concerto for clarinet, his last concerto, of course dedicated to Stadler.

With regard to *The Magic Flute*, the premiere of which Mozart conducted on September 29, 1791, a few days before completing the Clarinet Concerto and two months before his death, it is well known that the opera is based on a masonic initiation rite, with its philosophy, symbols, and trials. Mozart planned the outline of the opera together with his lodge Master, von Born, and conceived the text together with Schikaneder. In 1815, the architect and painter Karl Friedrich Schinkel showed that he understood the meaning of the opera in the scenery he conceived for the Unter den Linden opera house in Berlin, in which he used appropriate ritual emblems. Goethe, too, had an understanding of masonic ideas, and this enabled him to appreciate and admire *The Magic Flute*, to which he dreamt of writing a sequel.

On November 17, Mozart attended a meeting of his lodge for the last time. Even though he was unwell, he went there to conduct the cantata *Laut verkünde unsre Freude* (Loudly Proclaim Our Joy), which he had composed expressly for the occasion. Two days later, he took to his bed, never to rise from it; meanwhile *The Magic Flute* was proving to be a triumphant success.

"O sacred bond of friendship"

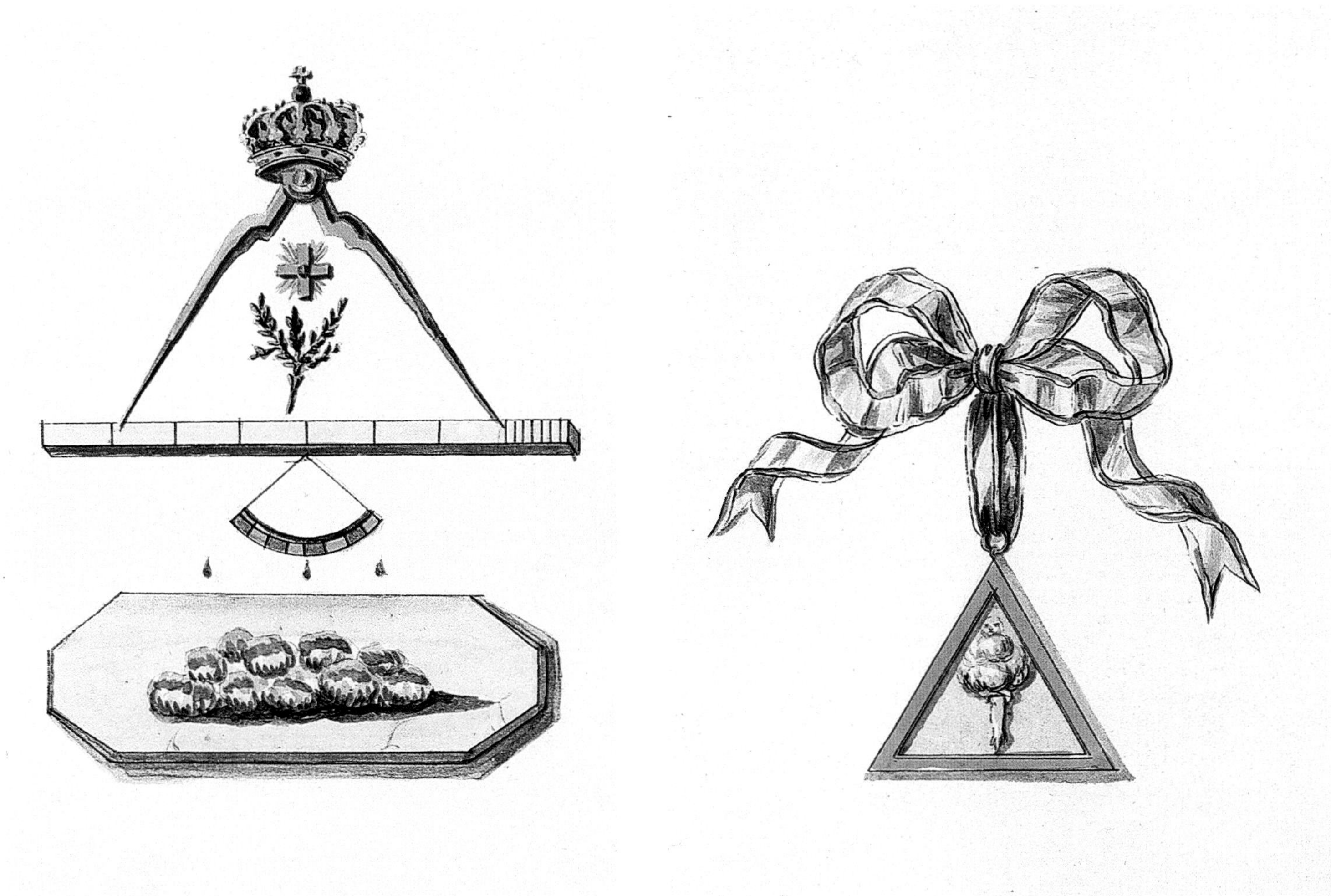

Masonic symbols from the end of the 18th century. Watercolor.
Paris, Musée de la Franc-Maçonnerie.

Long before he ever dreamt of joining the freemasons, Mozart had been in contact with masonic circles, and had written music for them. An example is the incidental music for *Thamos*, which was possibly his first masonic composition. Another is the hymn celebrating the lodge of St. John, a short lied for tenor and piano, setting a poem by a certain Lenz. Long thought to date from 1772, during Mozart's years in Salzburg, it is now believed to have been written at least ten years later. At any rate, the text is very clear in its intent.

> "O sacred bond of friendship between brothers,
> True to the Supreme Good, to the delights of Eden,
> Friend of faith, which it never betrays,
> Known to the world and yet so mysterious!
> So sing, masons! Today let the world know
> That the day to which this song is dedicated
> Is a magnificent day, a great day of honor,
> A solemn celebration of loyalty and unity!"

As was the custom at the time for odes and lieder intended for domestic use and family devotions, the hymn is notated on two staves only, enough for a very simple accompaniment to the vocal line.

The song "O heiliges Band der Freundschaft" (K. 148), 1772.
Salzburg, Mozarteum.

A funeral rite

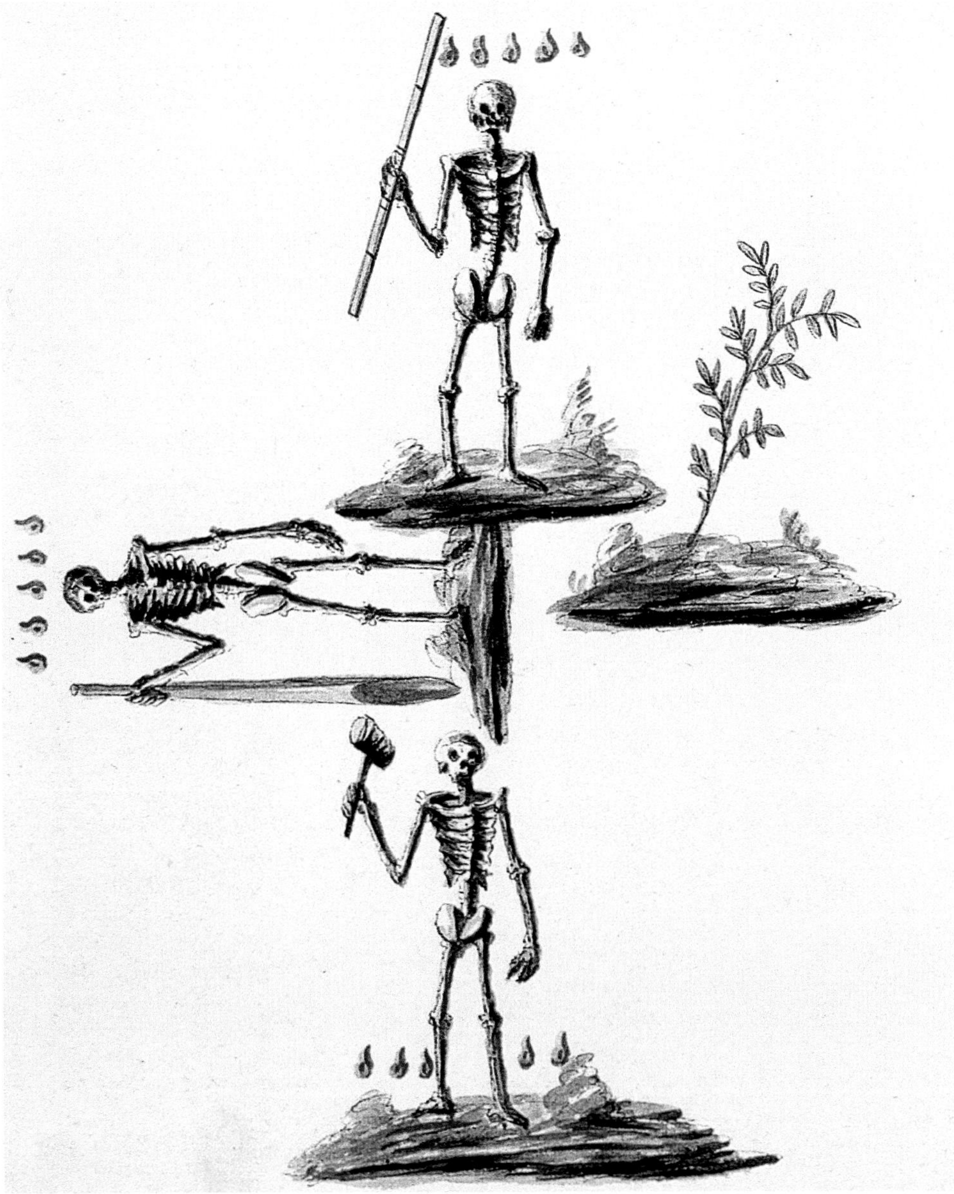

Symbolic representation of Death. Watercolor. Paris, Musée de la Franc-Maçonnerie.

The wonderful orchestral music entitled *Maurerische Trauermusik* (Masonic Funeral Music) was in fact written for a ceremony in which one of Mozart's friends and brother masons was promoted to the rank of Master, in July 1785. The composer conducted the work for a second time in November of the same year, at a funeral ceremony for two aristocrats, and then for a third time three weeks later. It was called "funeral music" not because it had been written for use at funerals, but because it was intended to evoke the idea of death during masonic rituals. It reflects an idea articulated by St. Paul, who declared that when a man casts off his failings and weaknesses, he goes through a symbolic death from which he will return, reborn, with the features of a new man, having overcome his former self. This idea underlies the tone of gravity of this ritual piece, which makes use of liturgical themes, including that of the Requiem Mass. The original orchestration calls for two oboes, one clarinet, two basset-horns, two horns, and a string quartet. The sound quality produced by the group of wind instruments is that of the ensembles used for playing the ritual music of masonic lodges—"columns of harmony."

Maurerische Trauermusik (K. 477), composed in July 1785.
Berlin, Staatsbibliothek, Musikabteilung.

"Cure our distempers ..."

Vienna. View of the Kohlmarkt from the Michaelplatz, 1786. Aquatint.

It was the custom at the time for private households to keep a visitors' book, in which guests could leave their signature together with a maxim or comment. Mozart himself kept one, as did a number of his friends. On March 30, 1787, probably after a soirée at the house of Johann Georg Kronauer, a language professor living in Vienna who taught English and was a member of the same lodge as Mozart, the composer wrote in his host's visitors' book the phrase shown opposite. It is not known whether it reflects a conversation that had just taken place, is a tribute to the teacher, or perhaps a quotation. At any rate, the inscription, in slightly imperfect English, is easy to decipher.

The signature is written in the form of abbreviations and masonic signs, including the rectangle that indicates the lodge. The lodge "Zur neugekrönten Hoffnung" was one of the two that were created on the orders of Emperor Joseph II when the masonic lodges of Vienna, including Mozart's, "Zur Wohltätigkeit," were reorganized. Four weeks later, Mozart wrote in English again, in the visitors' book of Joseph Franz von Jacquin, the brother of his friend and fellow mason Gottfried von Jacquin, "Never forget your sincere and faithful W.A.M."

Patience and tranquillity of mind contribute more to cure our distempers as the whole art of medicine.

Vienna, March 30, 1787

Wolfgang Amadè Mozart
Member of the most honorable lodge
"Zur neugekrönten Hoffnung" in the east
of Vienna

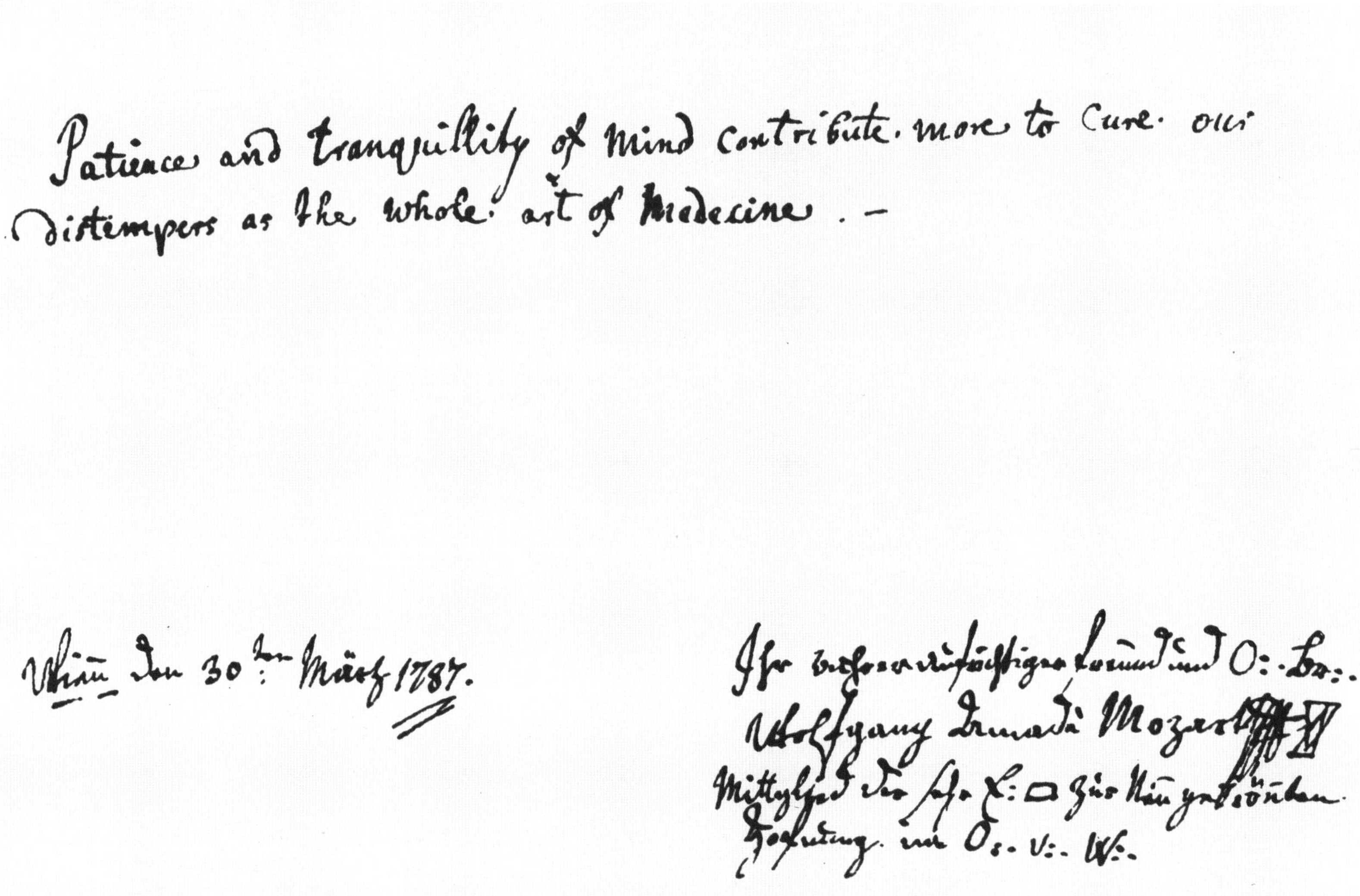

Patience and tranquillity of mind contribute. more to Cure. our
distempers as the whole. art of Medecine. –

Wien den 30:ten März 1787.

Ihr wahrer aufrichtiger Freund und O:. Br:.
Wolfgang Amadè Mozart
Mittglied der sehr Ehrw:. □ zur Neugekrönten
Hofnung im O:. v:. W:.

Inscription by Mozart in a visitors' book, 1787.
Vienna, Österreichische Nationalbibliothek.

His friend Puchberg

Initiation of Masters in a masonic assembly. Colored etching, 18th century. Paris, Musée de la Franc-Maçonnerie.

As Mozart's financial situation worsened, despite the regular salary he received as lodge musician, he increasingly borrowed from his friends and fellow lodge members, obliged to ask for more and more in order to repay earlier debts. His calls for help became increasingly pitiable. For example, in June 1788:
"Esteemed brother, Most dear, excellent friend! I had intended to come into town one of these days so that I could thank you in person for the friendship you have shown me. Now I have not the heart to present myself before you, because I must frankly admit that I am not yet able to repay you the money you have lent me and am forced to beg you to continue waiting! [...] If you could at least do me the favor of getting the money for me by any other means! I will willingly pay the interest, and anyone lending to me has, I feel, sufficient guarantees regarding my character and my earnings. I truly regret being in this situation, and it is precisely for this reason that I should like to obtain a rather larger sum for a slightly longer period, so that I can ensure that this does not happen again. If you, most dear brother, do not help me in this situation, I will lose my honor and my credit, which are the only two things I am anxious to preserve; but I count totally on your friendship and your brotherly love."

Five years younger than Mozart, Michael Puchberg, head of a textile firm, had met the musician the year before, at the lodge to which they both belonged. On numerous occasions he acceded to his friend's insistent requests, and never made any claims after the composer's death. Moreover, he continued to lend money to Constanze, who paid him back. He himself died in poverty ... but he certainly deserved to be the dedicatee of the famous divertimento that today bears his name.

[...] I must frankly admit that I am not yet able to repay you the money you have lent me and am forced to beg you to continue waiting! That circumstances are so, and you cannot support me as I would wish, concerns me deeply! My situation is such that I need to raise money immediately. But dear God, whom can I confide in? No-one but you, my dear friend! [If you could at least do me the favor of getting the money for me ... but I count totally on your true friendship and your brotherly love] and confidently expect you to come to my assistance in word and deed. If my wish is fulfilled, I shall be able to breathe once more, for then I shall be able to put my affairs in order and keep them there. Come and see me, then, visit me; I am always at home; for the ten days I have been here I have worked more than in two months in other lodgings, and if such black thoughts did not come to me so often (and I literally have to force them from my mind), things would be even better, for my lodgings are pleasant, comfortable—and *cheap*! I shan't detain you any longer with this drivel, just *keep quiet* and *hope*.

Ever your grateful servant
true friend and B.O. [Brother of the Order]
W. A. Mozart

June 27, 1788

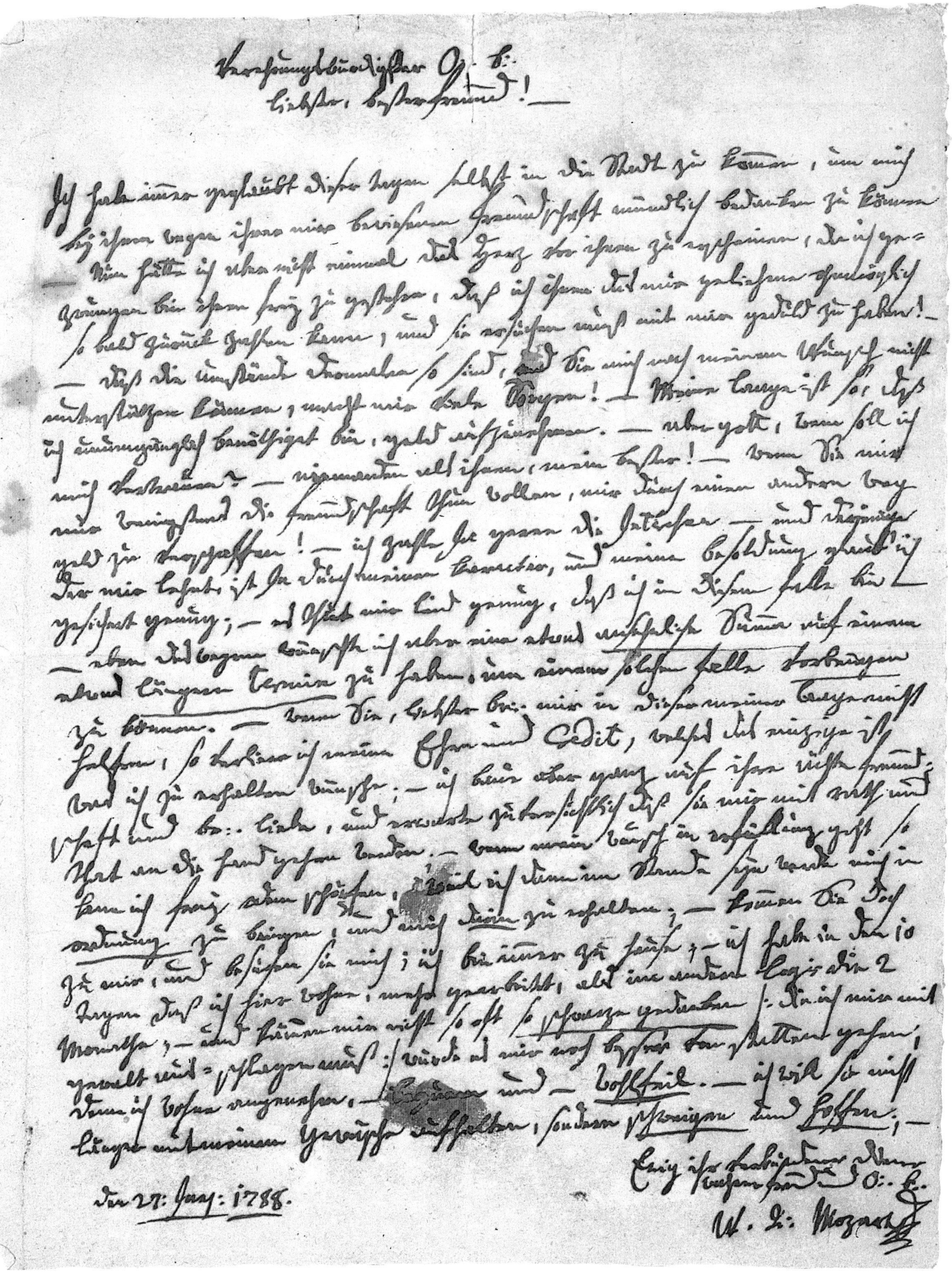

Letter from Mozart to Michael Puchberg, June 27, 1788. Salzburg, Mozarteum.

Nature and culture

Papageno's costume for the Berlin performance of *The Magic Flute* on January 18, 1816. Aquatint by Karl Friedrich Thiele.

"Hier, meine Schönen, übergeb'ich meine Vögel." *The Magic Flute*, Act 1, Scene 3. Tamino, the Three Ladies, Papageno and the serpent cut into pieces. Etching by Peter Schaffer for a performance at the Freyhaustheater, Vienna, on September 30, 1791.
Salzburg, Mozarteum.

At the center of the network of symbolism in *The Magic Flute* is the dual personage represented by Tamino and Papageno, the young prince and the bird-catcher, respectively embodying the worlds of culture and nature. Just as Don Giovanni and Leporello might be seen as two complementary faces of the same being, so Tamino and Papageno appear as two faces of a single character that is perhaps Mozart himself—and perhaps the audience's natural sympathies are rather for the decent, jovial Papageno. Both will go through dangers and deadly ordeals, both will be subjected to an initiation ritual to test their individual levels of fortitude. Right from their respective first arias, the psychological characterization of the two men is very clear-cut. They are a bit like Phoebus and Pan—Tamino sensitive and elegant, an idealistic poet, whose polished aria sets him in contrast with the somewhat rough and ready good humor of the bird-catcher and his popular song.

Yes, I'm the bird-catcher,
Always happy, hopsasa!
I'm known as the bird-catcher
By young and old throughout the land.
I know how to lure
And how to play my pipe.
I can always be gay and merry
For all the birds are mine.

The introduction to Papageno's song "Der Vogelfänger bin ich ja" from Act 1 of *The Magic Flute* (K. 620). Berlin, Staatsbibliothek, Musikabteilung.

Ordeals overcome

Design by Giuseppe Quaglio for the Temple in *The Magic Flute* (detail), for a performance in Munich in July 1793. Watercolor. Munich, Deutsches Theatermuseum.

Sarastro's costume for the Berlin performance of *The Magic Flute* on January 18, 1816. Aquatint by Karl Friedrich Thiele.

Everyone can attain wisdom, we are told by the masonic opera *The Magic Flute*, and the circumstances of our life can at any moment put us to the test through what turns out to be an initiation ritual. Tamino will have to renounce his received ideas, prosaic trivialities, and the ease of his everyday life, discard the person he was in order to reach the inner Man. The whole of the action in this fable without tragedy brings to life for the audience the difficult inner journey that is necessary in order to gain entry, by stages, into the heart of the temple of Wisdom, where the venerable High Priest Sarastro reigns. Tamino cannot be united with Pamina, whose image has guided him toward the temple of the person he believes has abducted her, until he has triumphed over the trials that have been set for him. In this process of overcoming the ordeals one by one, it is Woman, Pamina herself, contrary to what one might have imagined, who is to lead Tamino through those ordeals and who will help him reach the highest level of his humanity. The ageing Goethe, who had dreamt of writing a sequel to *The Magic Flute*, was to state precisely the same thing in the final line of Part Two of *Faust*: "It is the eternally feminine principle that guides us toward the heights."

The priests' chorus "O Isis und Osiris!" from Act 2 of *The Magic Flute*.
Berlin, Staatsbibliothek, Musikabteilung.

The golden chain of brotherhood

Manuscript and printed scores for a masonic cantata and a piano concerto, 1790.
Vienna, Gesellschaft der Musikfreunde.

The last work completed by Mozart is a short masonic cantata for male soloists, male choir, and orchestra, *Laut verkünde unsre Freude*, dated November 15, 1791. Written for the inauguration of a new temple for his lodge, "Zur neugekrönten Hoffnung," its text is by a brother of the lodge, none other than Emanuel Schikaneder, the librettist of *The Magic Flute*; not surprisingly, the cantata contains echoes of Sarastro and the male choruses of the opera.

> "Let the instruments' joyous notes loudly proclaim our joy,
> Let every brother's heart feel the echo of these walls.
> For through the golden chain of brotherhood and the sincere union of hearts,
> We consecrate today this place, this temple.
> For the first time, noble brothers, this new seat of wisdom and virtue receives us.
> [...]
> Let harmony firmly tie the precious bond woven out of brotherly love.
> [...]
> In this place our hearts and words have become entirely accustomed to virtue.
> Longing, o joy! is now satisfied, and the vow fulfilled, crowning our hope."

Two days later, Mozart himself conducted the cantata at his lodge.

The figure in this scene, painted on a shooting target, is that of the freemason Emanuel Schikaneder, who wrote the libretto for *The Magic Flute*.
Salzburg, Mozarteum.

Laut verkünde unsre Freude (K. 623), masonic cantata, composed on November 15, 1791. Mozart was to die on December 5.
Vienna, Gesellschaft der Musikfreunde.

Mozart at the Piano, unfinished portrait by Mozart's brother-in-law Joseph Lange, 1789. Salzburg, Mozarteum.

“This best friend of man”

“As death is the last stage of our life, for several years I have been familiarizing myself with this true best friend of man, so that not only does its image no longer hold any terrors for me, but rather it is something reassuring and consolatory.”

Mozart, letter to his father, Vienna, April 4, 1787

The first sheet of the score of the Requiem (K. 626), composed in 1791.
Vienna, Österreichische Nationalbibliothek.

These words, so moving in their tranquil serenity, appear in the very last letter that Mozart addressed to his father—the very last known letter, at any rate. This air of detachment with regard to death was much more common at that time than it is today: the combination of factors such as the high rate of infant mortality, low life-expectancy in general, being resigned to inevitable pain and having the fortitude to bear it, meant that suffering, illness, and death were often regarded with relative indifference.

In Mozart's case, moreover, there was the dual spiritual teaching he received from his Catholic faith and his masonic involvement. Long before he joined the freemasons, he had displayed not only this serenity but also a calm familiarity with regard to death. The understanding and direction that the masons gave him was coupled with that of the Christians. For a mason, the death of self enables the new man to be born, triumphing over what was the ordinary man. This is the message of *The Magic Flute*. And it is by experiencing the death of the earthly body that man can rise again in his new glorious body for eternal and supernatural life. This is what is expressed in the Requiem. Thus death is not a frightening prospect, but is indeed "the best friend of man," providing consolation for the vicissitudes of life.

While masonic teaching did not actually instill this attitude in Mozart's mind, it helped to reinforce it by giving it greater formality. Certainly it is the attitude that emerges from this letter, whose text leaves no room for doubt on the subject. The barely concealed allusions scattered through the letter include, "You understand me," placed within parentheses, the reference to those "keys" to happiness which he had had the fortune to learn, and the phrase "I beg of you—by all that is sacred to us." Mozart is all the better placed to express himself in this way as it was he who had arranged for his father to be initiated into freemasonry, reversing the roles and becoming the spiritual father, in masonry, of his own father; just as he had recently done in respect of the man who was his "older brother and father" in musical matters, Joseph Haydn. In this final letter, Mozart speaks to his father not only as an adult, but as a father.

Mozart's liveliness of spirit brought an additional element to this apparent detachment in the face of death, even when it was the death of those dearest to him. He was not a man to be depressed for long about anything—not because of indifference, but rather because he was driven by a vital energy that was quite out of the ordinary. He had an inimitable manner of speaking about the most serious matters and then abruptly changing the subject completely. The most striking example of this is the letter he wrote from Paris to his father and sister in Salzburg, telling them of the death of his mother and describing her last moments. Written in a very lofty tone, his account comes at the start of a long letter: "In these sad circumstances, three things brought me consolation: my total and trusting submission to the will of God, and the observation that her death, so beautiful and so simple, allowed me to imagine how happy she would be in the next instant—how she is now happier than us—so that at that moment I could have wished to depart with her; this wish and this desire gave rise finally to my third consolation, knowing that we have not lost her forever, that we will see her again, that we will one day be reunited, more joyful and happier than in this world. It is only that we don't know when that moment will be. But that does not worry me: when God wishes it, I too shall wish it." These thoughts take up about one-fifth of the letter. After which there is no further mention of the deceased mother, not even of her funeral, and the composer turns abruptly to speak of all kinds of things, mainly bits of gossip from the musical world.

The same applies to his attitude toward his children. In nine and a half years of married life, the Mozarts had six children, only two of whom survived, just as Wolfgang himself was one of two surviving children of the seven that Leopold and Anna Maria had had. The Mozarts' first child, Raimund Leopold, died when he was in the care of his nurse at the age of two months, when his parents were in Salzburg. They did not hear the news until their return, three months later. A few days afterward, Mozart confided to his father in the course of a letter, "We are both very sad about the poor chubby little fellow." Of the death at an early age of the three other children, there is no trace of a mention, at least in the correspondence that has come down to us.

As for the death of his own father, had Mozart prepared himself inwardly? Had relations between them become so inharmonious that his father's death would no longer break his heart? As always, the

Franz Xaver and Karl Thomas Mozart, two of the sons of Wolfgang and Constanze, painted by Hans Hansen in 1798.
Salzburg, Mozarteum.

correspondence on this subject is particularly laconic. First of all, in a letter to his friend Jacquin, Mozart refers to it only in a postscript: "I must tell you that today, on returning home, I received the sad news of the death of my excellent father. You can imagine the state I am in!" And a few days later, to his sister Nannerl: "You can well imagine my sorrow on learning the sad news of the sudden death of our beloved father, since the loss is the same for both of us." That's all. Is this serenity? Or indifference? Perhaps just, "That's life, after all."

Nevertheless, four or five days after learning of his father's death, Mozart experienced the sadness of seeing his pet starling die. He buried it in his garden and composed a little poem in its memory. Perhaps this was a way of giving vent to what he had been unable to write about his father.

A little fool lies here
Whom I held dear,
A starling in the prime
Of his brief time,
Whose doom it was to drain
Death's bitter pain.
Thinking of this, my heart
Is riven apart.
O reader! Shed a tear,
You also, here.
He was not naughty, quite,
But gay and bright,
And under all his brag
A foolish wag.
This no-one can gainsay
And I will lay
That he is now on high,
And from the sky
Praises me without pay
In his friendly way.
Yet unaware that death
Has choked his breath,
And thoughtless of the one
Whose rhyme is thus well done.

The last pages, written between July and November 1791, of the thematic catalogue that Mozart made of his own works. At the top of the right-hand page, part of the score of *La clemenza di Tito* may be seen between two phrases from *The Magic Flute*. The page ends with a movement from the masonic cantata (K. 623).
London, British Library.

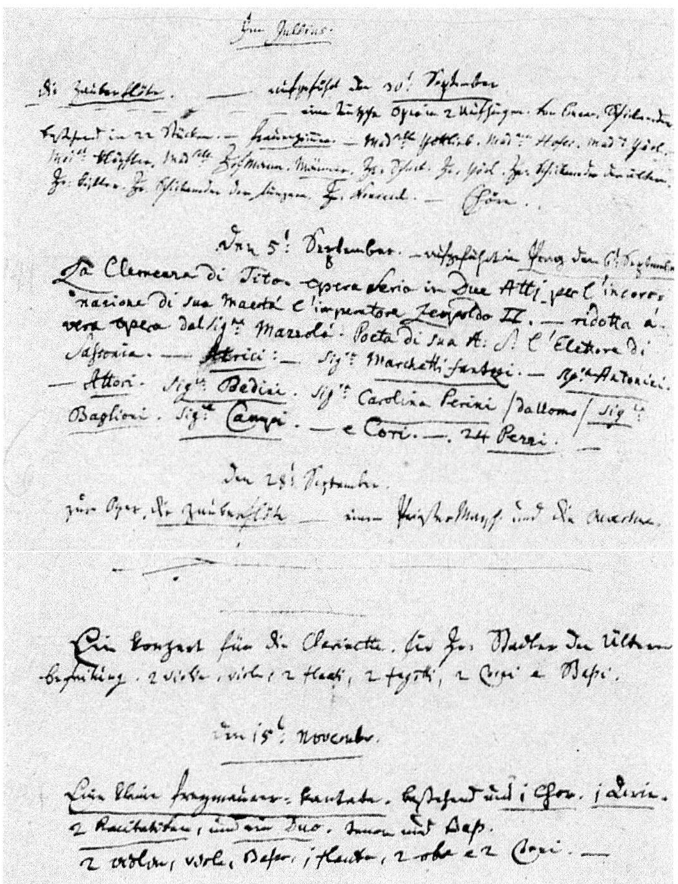

Mozart's last hours, as depicted by Henry Nelson O'Neill, 1849. Leeds, City Art Gallery.

Sometimes, however, a corner of the veil is lifted. In July 1789, for example, the pregnant Constanze fell seriously ill. She was suffering a great deal and the worst was expected. Writing his friend Puchberg, Mozart confided in him that "she accepts her fate in an astonishing manner, and awaits recovery or death with truly philosophical resignation. I am writing this to you with my eyes full of tears."

The final months of this dazzling life arrived. Between late August and early September 1791, Mozart was in Prague to stage *La clemenza di Tito* for the Emperor's coronation. His friend Niemetschek, who met him regularly there, recounted that "already in Prague Mozart was not feeling well and had to keep consulting the doctors; his complexion was pale and he looked sad, even though when he was in the company of friends, his cheerful disposition often broke through in merry joking."

On his return to Vienna, no-one guessed he was ill. He engaged in intense activity, devoting himself totally to the rehearsals and first performances of *The Magic Flute*, after which he wrote his Clarinet Concerto. The success of *The Magic Flute* brought him some tempting offers from abroad. Full of happiness at the success of his opera, he wrote Constanze, who was in Baden again for a cure, describing in detail the pranks he had been up to and the good meals he had been enjoying. Despite his fatigue and his money worries, he was still in a very good mood. He was obliged to return, albeit half-heartedly, to composing the Requiem, because this was a commission that would bring him some money, and time was pressing. Yet he never experienced in this period, as legend would have it, the somber presentiment of approaching death, even less so the urgent need to complete the Requiem that was to be his own. Good fortune even seemed to be smiling on him again, when, during the second half of October, he fell seriously ill. On November 20 he took to his bed, exhausted, never to rise from it.

Constanze's younger sister Sophie Haibel visited her frequently during this period, as Constanze was recovering from the birth of her latest child. These were intense and painful times, as Sophie later recounted. On December 4, she wrote, she arrived at the house on Rauhensteingasse. "Oh! My God, how alarmed I was when my sister, panic-stricken but at the same time trying to keep calm, came to meet me and said, 'God be praised, Sophie, that you have come. Last night he was so ill that I thought he would not survive until morning. Stay with me today, because if that starts again, he will die tonight. Go and see him, see how he is.' I tried to pull myself together and I approached his bedside. He said to me straight away, 'Oh! Dear Sophie, thank goodness you are here; stay here tonight, to see me die.' I tried to give myself strength and to prevent him from talking like this, but he had a reply for everything. 'I already have the taste of death on my tongue; and who will console my dear Constanze if you do not stay here?'" A few hours later, Mozart died, on December 5, at one o'clock in the morning.

What did Mozart die of? Certainly not from poison given to him by Salieri, as is often claimed, even if the suffering of his final weeks did make him imagine that he might have been poisoned. In the light of historical evidence, it is now thought that he had probably succumbed to the terminal phase of rheumatic fever, a debilitating illness that began to affect him as early as 1784.

The Poor Man's Funeral Procession. Colored engraving, French, c. 1800. This image remained so symbolic of Mozart's pitiful funeral that Beethoven kept a copy of it at his house. Vienna, Austrian Archives.

On the morning of that December 5, Baron van Swieten went to the Mozarts' house to pay his last respects to the dead composer. The next day, a modest service took place at St. Stephen's Cathedral, followed by burial in a common grave in the cemetery of St. Marx, a fairly standard practice at that time. (At the end of the 20th century, the composer's coffin was identified and his remains exhumed.) The weather was mild that day, without the least sign of the snowstorm invented by legend. Constanze, exhausted, was looked after by friends. A few close acquaintances followed the funeral procession: van Swieten, Süssmayr, a handful of musicians, three women—their identity is unknown, but they must have been women whom Mozart had loved (and were there any women whom Mozart did not love?)—and ... Salieri.

In her husband's visitors' book, Constanze later wrote down a little poem in free verse by way of an epitaph, on the same page where Mozart himself had written a poem in memory of his doctor and friend who had just died:

> "What you wrote long ago, in honor of your friend,
> I repeat here for you, weighed down as I am by grief.
> Beloved husband! Mozart, immortal for me and for the whole of Europe,
> You too, you are at rest now—forever!!
> At one hour after midnight, during the night of December 4 to 5 of this year,
> He departed, in his 36th year—too soon, oh! how much too soon—
> This world, which is good, it is true, but ungrateful! Oh, God!
> Eight years bound us together with an affectionate, indelible bond!
> Oh! that I may soon be united with you forever.
> your wife, distraught with grief
> Vienna, December 5, 1791
>
> Constanze Mozart, née Weber"

Just before the finale of *The Magic Flute*, at the moment when Tamino and Pamina are going through the ordeals by fire and water, they sing, together with the two men in armor: "Through the power of music, we walk joyously through the dark night of death." It says all there is to say.

Tamino and Pamina, watercolors by Josef Hoffmann for the 1866 production at the Vienna Hofoper. Vienna, Österreichische National-bibliothek.

“The saddest day of my life”

When his mother had just died before his eyes, Mozart wrote his father and sister, telling them that she was very ill, and also a friend in Salzburg, telling him that she had died; he would convey the bad news to his father and sister only a few days later, once they had been prepared for it by the Abbé Bullinger.

“My very dear friend!

For you alone.

Weep with me, my friend! This day was the saddest in my life. I am writing this at two o'clock in the morning. But I still have to tell you: my dear mama is no more! God has called her to Him. He wanted to have her, I could see that clearly, and therefore I gave myself up to the will of God. He gave her to me, He could also take her from me. Imagine the anxiety, distress, and worries that I have endured during this past fortnight. She died without realizing it, she was simply extinguished, like a lamp. She had made her confession three days earlier, taken Communion, and received the last rites. These past three days, she was constantly delirious, and today, at twenty-one minutes past five, her death agony began, she immediately lost all her senses and consciousness. I squeezed her hand, talked to her, she could no longer see me, no longer hear me, and felt nothing. She stayed like that for five hours up to the moment when she died, at twenty-one minutes past ten. There was no-one there but myself, one of our good friends (whom my father knows), M. Haina, and the nurse. I am unable to tell you about her illness today. I am of the opinion that her death was inevitable, God wanted it like that. All I ask of you now is that you do me the kindness of preparing my father very gently for receiving this sad news. I have written him by the same post, but saying only that she is gravely ill. I am just waiting for your reply before I tell him the truth. May God give him strength and courage! My friend! I am comforted, and not only now, but have been for a long time! By God's special grace, I have been able bear everything steadfastly and calmly. When her condition worsened, I asked God to grant me two things—a blessed death for my mother, and strength and courage for me—and God, in His goodness, answered me and granted me these two favors in the highest degree.

I beg you, my very dear friend, look after my father for me, give him courage so that he does not take the grievous news with too much distress or sorrow when he learns of it. Likewise I entrust my sister to you with all my heart. Go immediately to see them, I beg you, don't tell them yet that she is dead, but prepare them for the news. Do whatever you want, use any means, so long as I can feel reassured and do not have to face yet another misfortune. Look after my dear father and my dear sister for me. Give me your reply straight away, I beg you. Adieu, I am your most obedient and most grateful servant

Wolfgang Amadè Mozart”

Nannerl, Wolfgang, and Leopold Mozart by Johann Nepomuk della Croce, c. 1780–81 (detail). The deceased Anna Maria is represented by her portrait. Salzburg, Mozarteum.

Paris, July 9, 1778

Monsieur, mon trés cher Pére!

I hope that you will now be strong enough for me to tell you the saddest, most painful news—my letter of July 3 will have prepared you for the worst. On the same day, the 3rd, my mother fell blessedly asleep in the Lord, at twenty-one minutes after ten in the evening. When I wrote you, she was already tasting the joys of Heaven—everything was already over. I wrote you the same night. I hope you and my sister will forgive me this slight piece of deception, but I thought it most necessary: understanding from my own pain and sadness what yours would be, I could not find it within me to announce such dreadful news to you brutally. I hope you are now prepared to hear the worst and, after you have allowed your pain and tears to take their natural, understandable course freely, to surrender yourselves finally to the will of God and worship His ineffable, unfathomable, and all-wise Providence.

Letter from Mozart to his father, Paris, July 9, 1778 (folio 1). Salzburg, Mozarteum.

From carnival to poetry

Carnival and masked ball at the end of the 18th century. Copper engraving from Augsburg. Munich, Münchner Stadtmuseum.

Known as the "Gran partita" (it is not known who gave it that name), the Serenade in B flat major is written for an ensemble of 12 wind instruments—two oboes, two clarinets, two basset-horns (the first time they appear in a piece by Mozart), four natural horns, and two bassoons—supported by a double bass. It occupies a very special place in Mozart's career as a composer: first sketched in Munich for carnival in 1781, it was completed in Vienna some years later, when the hostility between the composer and the Prince-Archbishop of Salzburg, who was still his employer, was coming to a head. In this serenade the composer asserted his independence and his pride as a human being, faced with an employer who was as narrow-minded as he was demanding. The work represents a turning point; one hears in it echoes of the *galant* style of his Salzburg days, but also an affirmation of the free-spirited genius, the shadow of intense seriousness, dazzling jubilation, and, as always, moments of infinite tenderness and ineffable poetry. One has only to listen to the clarinet's dreamy phrase unfolding in the first Adagio to experience the serene and contemplative quality of Mozart at his greatest.

The "Gran partita" (K. 361), composed in 1784.
Library of Congress, Music Division, Collection Gertrude Clarke Whittall.

The dying Leopold

Portrait of Leopold Mozart by an unknown artist. Vienna, Gesellschaft der Musikfreunde.

Vienna, end of May 1787

Dearest friend!
Please tell Herr Exner to come at nine o'clock tomorrow morning to bleed my wife.
I enclose your Amynt and the canticle. Please be so good as to give the sonata to your sister, with my compliments; and tell her she should set to work on it at once as it is rather difficult. Adieu.

Your true friend,
Mozart.

I must tell you that today, on returning home, I received the sad news of the death of my excellent father. You can imagine the state I am in!

Learning that his father was seriously ill, in April 1787, Wolfgang wrote him a grave, reflective letter, in which he expressed his feelings about death, but in which he also included, in veiled terms, numerous allusions to freemasonry. This was to be the last letter that Mozart wrote his father, who died suddenly on May 28 of that year.

"As death is the last stage of our life, for several years I have been familiarizing myself with this true best friend of man, so that not only does its image no longer hold any terrors for me, but rather it is something reassuring and consolatory. And I thank my God for having granted me the fortune to be able to seize the chance (you understand me) to learn how to understand death as the key to our true bliss. I never go to bed at night without reflecting that the next day perhaps (young though I am) I might not be here any more, and yet nobody among all those who know me could say that I am despondent or sad when I am in their company. Every day I thank my Creator for this bliss and I wish it cordially for every one of my fellow humans [...]. I hope and wish for your recovery as I write these lines; if, despite all expectations, you are not getting better, I beg of you ... not to hide it from me but to tell me, or to get someone else to tell me, the absolute truth, so that I can come and nestle in your arms, as quickly as humanly possible; I beg of you—by all that is sacred to us."

liebster freund! — ich bitte sie dem Hr: Exner zu sagen er möchte morgen um 9 uhr kommen, um meiner frau Aderzulassen. — hier schicke ihnen ihren Amynt und das kirchen lied — die Sonate haben sie die güte ihrer frl: Schwester nebst meiner Empfehlung zu geben; — sie möchte sich aber gleich darüber machen, denn sie seye etwas schwer. — adieu. —

ihr wahrer freund
Mozart

Ich benachrichtige sie dass ich heute als ich nach Hause kam die traurige Nachricht von dem tode meines besten Vaters bekamm. — Sie können sich meine lage vorstellen! —

geb. 27. Jäner 1756, + 5 Dez. 1792

29 mai 1787
O. Jahn I. 714
II. 12

Mechanical music

The catafalque of Emperor Joseph II on February 20, 1790. Engraving, late 18th century. Vienna, Wienmuseum.

Around 1790 a Viennese aristocrat, Count Deym, alias Müller, acquired a gallery where he put on show a life-size waxwork image of the famous Marshal Laudon, who had died in June of that year. An artificially lit glass structure served as a mausoleum. Shortly afterward, he added a memorial to Emperor Joseph II, who had just died. The Count wanted funeral music to be heard in this place. He therefore commissioned from Mozart three pieces to be performed by a small mechanical organ. The most deservedly famous of these three pieces is a Fantasia in F minor, which has a tragic, grandiose feel to it despite the modest nature of the instrument, and which today is played in a transcription for full-size organ. The instrument's mechanism allowed Mozart to ignore the constraints imposed by playing with the fingers and to give his imagination free rein. The challenge posed resulted in a wonderful contrapuntal piece, extremely complex and intensely expressive in style. The autograph copy of the music is lost, as is the copy that Beethoven made of it in a great surge of admiration for the work. But four early copies survive, proof of Mozart's fame and of the enthusiasm aroused by this extraordinary funeral piece.

Fantasia for mechanical organ in F minor (K. 608), dated March 3, 1791.
Cracow, Biblioteka Jagiellonska.

"My beloved, my only one"

Portrait of Constanze Mozart in 1802, by Hans Hansen. Puchberg continued to lend Constanze money after Wolfgang's death. Salzburg, Mozarteum.

During the summer and autumn of 1791 Constanze Mozart was in poor health and went to Baden to take a cure before and after the birth of her last child, Franz Xaver, in Vienna, on July 26. Mozart wrote her often, up to October 14. His tone is always impetuous, and always overflowing with tenderness and affection for his wife, whom he addresses with the familiar nickname that he gave her, Stanzi-Marini. On June 6, he sent her a long letter, the first part of which was entirely written in French, which, it seems, Constanze knew perfectly. When writing in French he addressed her with "vous" rather than the informal "du" that he used when writing her in German.

"My dearest wife! I write this letter in the little garden room at Leutgeb's, where I have spent an excellent night—and I hope that my dear wife has passed this last night as well as I have. I will stay here tonight too, because I have dismissed Leonore [the maid], and should be all alone in the house, which would not be very nice. I wait very impatiently for a letter telling me what your day was like yesterday; I tremble when I think of the St. Anton baths, for I am always afraid of the risk of your falling on the steps when coming out of them, and I find myself between hope and fear—a very disagreeable state! If you were not pregnant I would worry about it less—but let's leave this sad thought! Heaven will certainly take care of my dear Stanzi-Marini."

And further on, in German but with the odd word in French: "Adieu—my beloved, my only one!—catch in the air—2,999 and one kisses from me—as they fly toward you, waiting to be caught. Now, I'll whisper something in your ear — — —, and you in mine — — —. Now, we open and close our mouths—more and more—and more—at last we say: it's because of Plumpi-Stumpi—you can interpret that how you like. In fact, it's the *commodité*. Adieu—1,000 tender kisses, forever your Mozart."

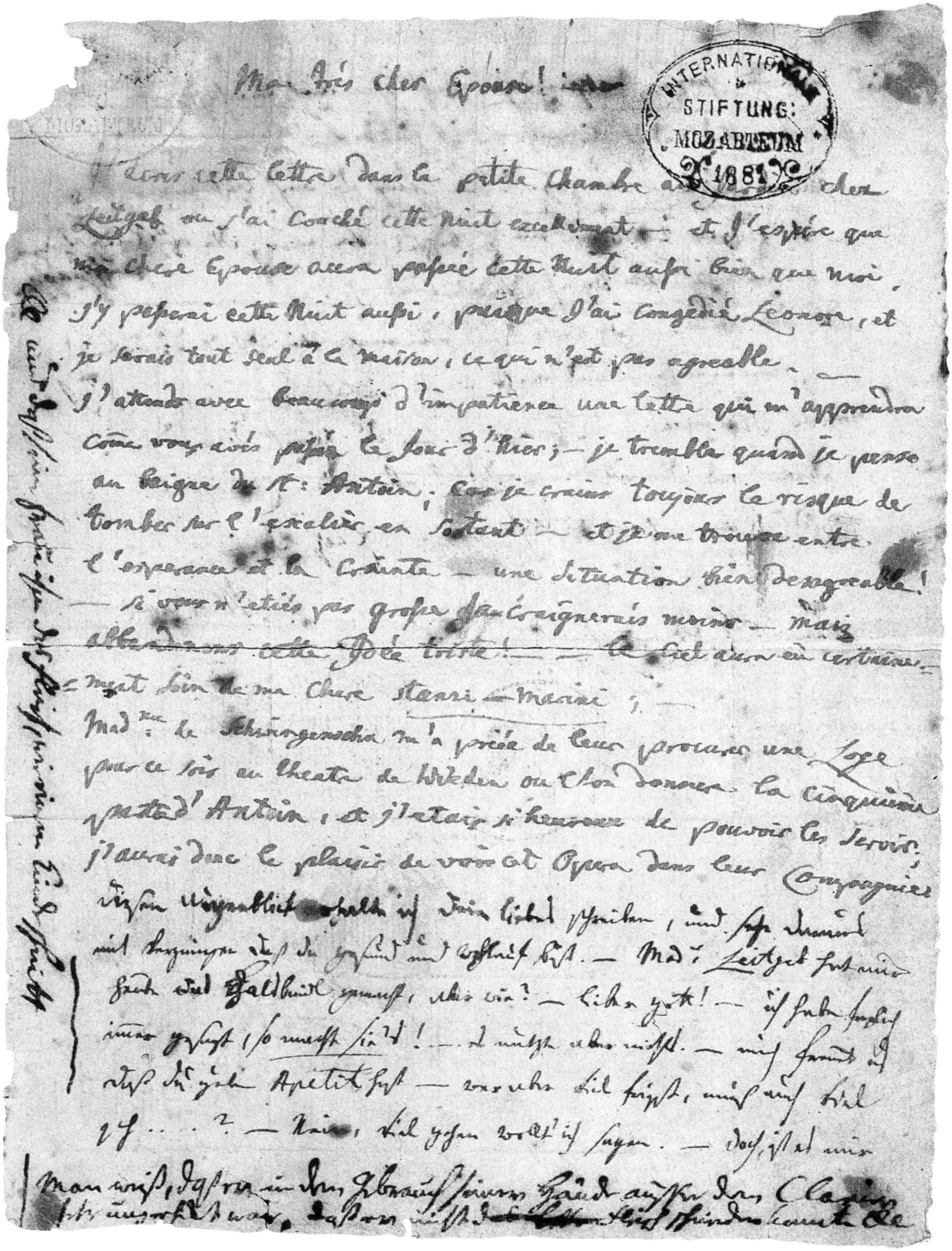

Letter from Mozart to his wife, partly written in French. Salzburg, Mozarteum.

A mysterious messenger ...

The word "requiem" sounds from the very first bars of the Kyrie.

The first two pages of the Kyrie from the Requiem (K. 626), composed in 1791. Vienna, Österreichische Nationalbibliothek.

A dense fabric of fanciful stories has for two centuries surrounded the commissioning and the gestation of the Requiem that Mozart left unfinished. But musicologists have disentangled the historical reality from the romantic imagery. Toward the end of July 1791, a mysterious messenger called on Mozart with a commission for a Requiem for someone whose identity would not be revealed to him. He must compose it without delay, and he would be well paid for the work. As he had just finished *The Magic Flute*, Mozart got down to work and composed the Introit and the Kyrie. Then the commission for *La clemenza di Tito* arrived, and the Requiem was put aside. After *La clemenza*, *The Magic Flute* was being performed. So it was not until October that Mozart was able to resume work on the Requiem. He was never to finish it, and would never learn who had commissioned it, nor for what purpose. We know today that the mysterious messenger had been sent by Count von Walsegg zu Stuppach. The latter had lost his wife at the beginning of the year and wanted to have performed in his private chapel, during a service in her memory, a Requiem that he would conduct himself and pass off as his own composition. It seems that this did indeed take place—and the intention was clearly that the real composer should never hear of it.

allo
Kyrie
Christe ele

Christe ele
Kyrie

Ultima verba

Mozart Composing His Requiem, by William James Grant, 1854. Salzburg, Museum Carolino Augusteum.

It was when he was again working on the Requiem, toward the end of October, that Mozart, suffering from extreme fatigue, began to feel the effects of the illness that was to kill him. Struck by a sense of foreboding, and soon sure that he was nearing the end of his life, he worked on the Requiem until he finally had no more strength left. His sister-in-law Sophie recounted that "the last thing he did was to make with his mouth the sound of the kettle drums in his Requiem, I can still hear it." Left unfinished, Mozart's work was completed by his pupil Süssmayr, who had been close to him in his last weeks, and we now know precisely what his additions and revisions consisted of. Did Süssmayr possess some of Mozart's sketches? Had Mozart given him some instructions? Opinions vary and the evidence is unreliable. The fact remains that the composer's pupil, who had no great talent himself, did not feel he could put his own signature to his master's work; he contented himself with making use of some earlier scraps of music by Mozart, together with those parts of the score that he had managed to finish, in order to arrive at a work that was performable. Van Swieten had the Requiem performed in Vienna in 1792, and then Count Walsegg in 1793, under his own name ... It seems that it was at the first verse of the "Lacrimosa" that Mozart, overcome by the effects of his fatal illness and extreme weakness, finally put down his pen.

"Lacrimosa dies illa,	(That day shall be one of weeping,
Qua resurget ex favilla	When shall rise up from the ashes
Judicandus homo reus.	The guilty man, to be judged.
Huic ergo parce, Deus.	Therefore pardon this one, O God.
Pie Jesu Domine,	Merciful Lord Jesus,
Dona eis requiem!"	Grant them rest!)

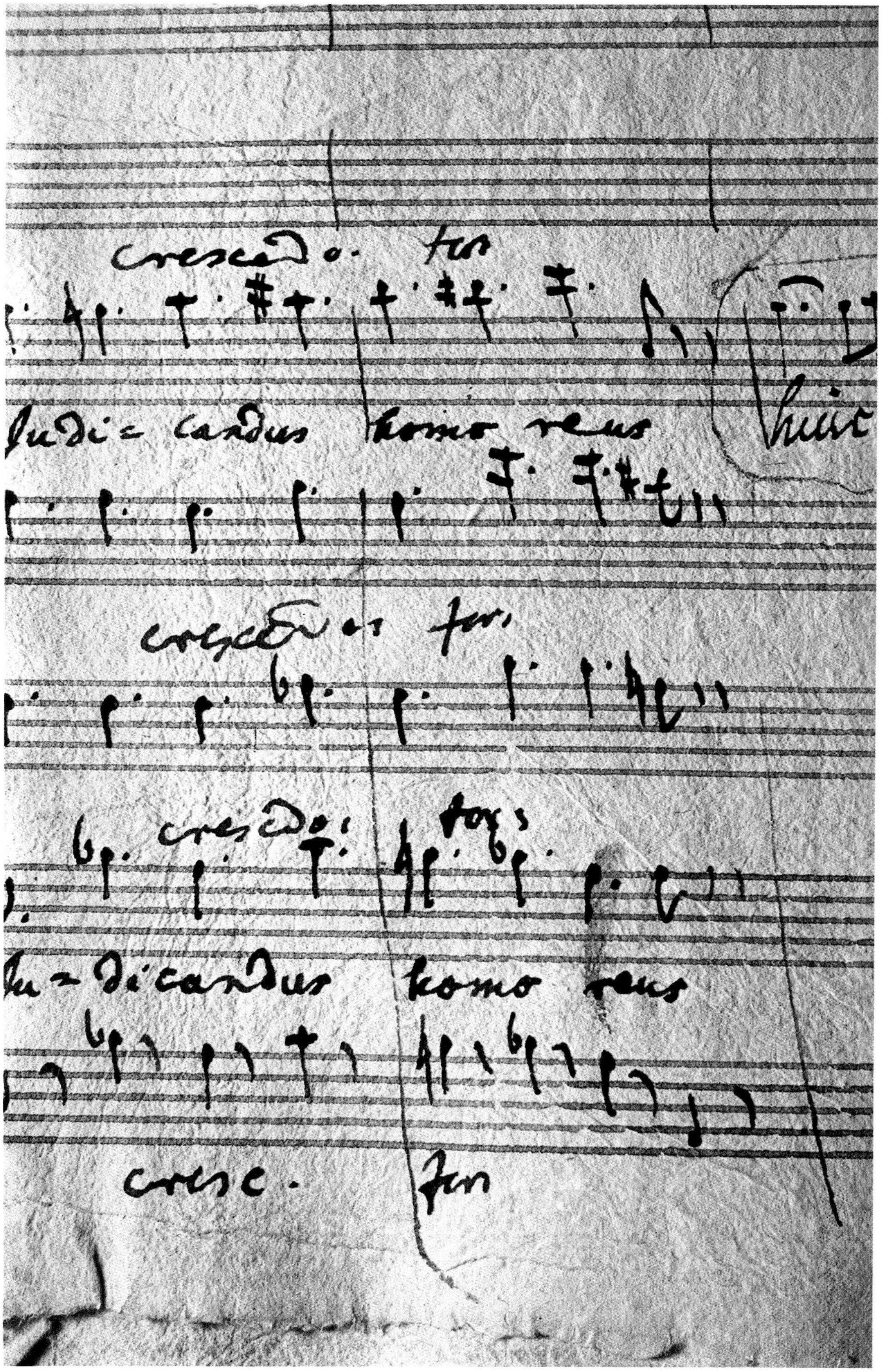

The last words and last musical phrases to come from Mozart's hand: the final page of the "Lacrimosa" from the Requiem. Vienna, Österreichische Nationalbibliothek.

Chronology

1756

January 27, Joannes Chrysostomus Wolfgangus Theophilus Mozart born in Salzburg, the seventh and last child of Leopold Mozart, composer, violinist, theorist, and teacher, and Maria Anna Pertl, though only the second to survive. His elder sister, Maria Anna Walburga Ignatia, nicknamed Nannerl (1751–1829), was to become a pianist.

1759

Wolfgang displays an astonishing talent for music.

1760

First harpsichord lessons with his father.

1762

January, first composition by Wolfgang, a Minuet for harpsichord in F major, notated by his father. Mozart is barely six. First pieces for the keyboard. First of many trips around Europe, during which Leopold puts his children on show. Spring in Munich. September–December in Vienna. Mozart plays before Empress Maria Theresa.

1763

In June, the Mozarts set out on a European tour which will last three and a half years. Passing through Munich, Augsburg, Schwetzingen, Frankfurt, and Brussels, they reach Paris in November, where they remain for five months, to considerable acclaim. The object of great interest, taken up by Baron Friedrich Melchior von Grimm, Wolfgang is feted and received in the best salons. He is welcomed by Mme de Pompadour and the Prince de Conti, and invited to perform at Versailles. He meets various composers, including Schobert. During his stay, he composes two pairs of sonatas for keyboard and violin, the first of which is dedicated to Mme Victoire de France, daughter of Louis XV.

1764

The Mozarts remain in Paris until April 10, when they set off for London. On their arrival, they are invited to St. James's Palace by the King and Queen. They remain in London for 16 months, until July 1765. The eight-year-old Wolfgang forms friendships with Johann Christian Bach, the youngest son of Johann Sebastian, 21 years Mozart's senior, and with Karl Friedrich Abel, the son of a friend of J. S. Bach and a leading figure in the musical life of London. Mozart's six keyboard and violin sonatas are dedicated to Queen Charlotte.

1765

On August 1, the Mozarts leave London for The Hague, traveling via Lille, Ghent, and Rotterdam. Nannerl falls ill, and then young Wolfgang, who is overworked, succumbs to a severe case of typhoid fever. He takes several months to recover.

1766

From The Hague they return to Paris, arriving in May to a rapturous welcome. Two months later, in July, they leave for Salzburg, which they had left three years earlier, arriving at the end of November. First vocal works, first attempts at concertos.

1767

After nine months in Salzburg, the family sets off for Vienna, intending to perform for the wedding celebrations of Maria Theresa's daughter, Archduchess Maria Josepha, and the King of Naples. But this was not to be: a smallpox epidemic kills the bride and disfigures her sister. Leopold and his family flee before the scourge, only to fall prey to it in Olmütz. After their recovery, they return to Vienna via Brünn.

1768

The Mozarts arrive in Vienna in January. Wolfgang receives a commission for his first *opera buffa*, *La finta semplice* (The False Simpleton), and his first *Singspiel* (a comic opera with spoken dialogue in German), *Bastien und Bastienne*. The whole year is spent in Vienna.

1769

January 5, the Mozarts arrive back in Salzburg. Now aged 13, Wolfgang begins to compose more prolifically. First religious and orchestral pieces (Mass in C, *Te Deum*, cassations, serenades). At the end of the year (December 11), Leopold and Wolfgang set out on yet another long trip, to Italy, in order to improve Wolfgang's compositional skills and musical culture.

1770

The Mozarts visit Milan, Bologna, Florence, Rome, and Naples, returning via Rome—where they are received by the Pope—Bologna, and Milan. Their "grand tour" brings Wolfgang into contact with many of the best musicians, most notably the famous Padre Martini, an eminent theorist, in Bologna. Mozart is commissioned to write an *opera seria*, *Mitridate, re di Ponto* (Mithridates, King of Pontus), which is first performed in Milan, to great acclaim, at the end of the year (December 26).

1771

From Milan, the Mozarts travel to Padua, where Wolfgang receives a commission for an oratorio, *La Betulia liberata* (Bethulia Liberated). They return home via Vicenza and Verona, reaching Salzburg on March 28, after a 15-month tour, only to set off again very soon, for a four-month trip to Milan, where Mozart's *festa teatrale Ascanio in Alba* is performed. They return to Salzburg at the end of the year (December 16).

1772

Salzburg appoints a new Prince-Archbishop, Hieronymus Colloredo, who, unlike his predecessor, has little time for the Mozarts. On August 15, Wolfgang is formally appointed *Konzertmeister* of the Salzburg court. Spending the best part of the year in his native city, he composes, among other things, seven symphonies. In October, he sets off for a third and last trip to Italy. First performance in Milan of the *opera seria Lucio Silla*.

1773

In March, Mozart is back in Salzburg, where he will remain for the next five years, barely traveling at all. From July to September, during a visit to Vienna, he composes the Serenade in D major K. 185 and the six string quartets known as the Viennese quartets. In December, in Salzburg, his first great symphony, no. 25, in G minor.

1774

A year spent in Salzburg. Mozart is by now composing a great deal: the symphonies nos. 28–30, the Serenade in D major K. 203, the Bassoon Concerto, and the *opera buffa La finta giardiniera* (The False Gardener).

In December, he is on the road again with his father, spending three months in Munich.

1775

In January, first performance of *La finta giardiniera*, in Munich. Composition, at Colloredo's request, of the opera *Il re pastore* (The Shepherd King), together with four concertos for violin and orchestra and the "Durnitz" Sonata for piano.

1776

Wolfgang spends the whole year in Salzburg. Now 20, he devotes himself tirelessly to composition: several serenades, among which the "Serenata notturna" and the "Haffner" Serenade, the piano concertos nos. 6–8, and several Masses.

1777

In January, Mozart completes one of his important early masterpieces, the Piano Concerto no. 9 in E flat major, known as the "Jeunehomme." Conflict with Archbishop Colloredo, who rejects a request by the Mozarts for leave. Leopold yields but Wolfgang resigns his position. Aged 21, he decides to leave Salzburg, taking his mother with him. They journey to Munich and then to Augsburg, before spending four months in Mannheim.

1778

At the beginning of the year, Wolfgang makes the acquaintance of the young and talented soprano Aloysia Weber, and falls very much in love with her. Having been unable to secure any sort of position, he sets off to try his luck in Paris, arriving on March 25. Here he manages to obtain several commissions: the Symphony no. 31 (the "Paris") and the *Sinfonia concertante* for wind for the Concerts Spirituels, the ballet *Les Petits Riens* for the Paris Opera, the Concerto for flute and harp, and the Piano Sonata in A minor, with its "alla turca" finale. But the musician is no longer the little prodigy he once was, and the visit is a bitter disappointment, echoes of which may be heard in the tragic Piano Sonata in A minor. On July 3, Mozart's mother dies. Disheartened, Wolfgang returns to Salzburg via Nancy and Strasbourg, where he stays for a month with the composer Franz Xaver Richter.

1779

January 17, Wolfgang is appointed court organist in Salzburg. He composes a number of important sacred works.

1780

At the end of the summer, the Elector of Bavaria commissions an *opera seria* from Mozart for the Munich carnival. This was to be *Idomeneo, re di Creta* (Idomeneus, King of Crete), now regarded as the first of Mozart's "great" operas. In November, Mozart leaves Salzburg for Munich, to oversee rehearsals for his opera.

1781

January 29, first performance of *Idomeneo*. Mozart stays in Munich until March, when he is summoned to Vienna by Colloredo. This does not prevent him from composing five violin sonatas and a Rondo in C major for violin and orchestra. But the tensions between the musician and his employer reach breaking point and Mozart leaves Salzburg for good to settle in Vienna. Now 25, he takes lodgings with the widowed Frau Weber, the mother of Aloysia, who is now married to the actor and painter Joseph Lange. Having lost Aloysia, Mozart turns his attentions to her younger sister Constanze. In Vienna, Mozart meets with instant success. Emperor Joseph II commissions from him the *Singspiel The Abduction from the Seraglio*, whose heroine is called Constanze.

1782

In Vienna, Mozart attends the salon of Baron Gottfried Van Swieten, a diplomat, man of letters, and music lover, who is passionate about the works of Bach and Handel. He introduces Mozart to *Das wohltemperierte Klavier* (The Well-Tempered Clavier), which will be influential for Mozart's musical thinking. On July 16, *The Abduction from the Seraglio* is staged at the Burgtheater in Vienna, and on August 4, Wolfgang marries Constanze Weber. Mozart's style reaches new heights, as seen in the Symphony no. 35 (the "Haffner"), the Serenade for wind in C minor, and the piano concertos nos. 11–13. This period probably sees the beginning of the friendship between Mozart and Joseph Haydn, a friendship that is based on profound mutual admiration and that will prove both unclouded and unchanging. At the end of the year, Mozart completes the String Quartet in G major K. 387, the first of a set of six dedicated to his eminent friend that will be completed only two years later.

1783

Mozart gives piano lessons, and organizes concerts (or "academies") in which to introduce new works, conducting the other players from the piano. The first academy takes place on March 23. Mostly dedicated to social activities, the year yields little in the way of new works.

1784

On February 9, Mozart begins a catalogue of his works, which he will maintain until his death, with the Piano Concerto no. 14 in E flat major. Five more piano concertos will follow that same year, written for public concerts. A new string quartet also appears.

1785

The set of six string quartets dedicated to Haydn is completed. In February, Leopold visits his son in Vienna and hears three of these quartets performed, with Mozart on the viola. This year also sees the composition of the piano concertos nos. 20–22. Mozart becomes a freemason, and writes the first of his works intended to accompany the rituals of his lodge. After many months in search of a good libretto he begins work on a new opera, *The Marriage of Figaro*, to a text by Lorenzo Da Ponte.

1786

At the beginning of the year, the Emperor commissions a *Singspiel* from Mozart, *Der Schauspieldirektor* (The Impresario), which is performed at Schönbrunn on February 7. On May 1, the first performance of *The Marriage of Figaro* at the Burgtheater in Vienna is well received. The year also brings new concertos, chamber music (including the "Skittles" Trio), and, for his beloved Nancy Storace, the concert aria "Ch'io mi scordi di te." Mozart is invited to Prague, the capital of Bohemia, and in December composes the Symphony no. 38 for his many friends in that country.

1787

Mozart arrives in Prague on January 11. From January 17, *The Marriage of Figaro* is performed there to great acclaim. Mozart returns to Vienna in February and starts work on *Don Giovanni*. On May 28, his father dies after a short illness, aged 68. Mozart concentrates on vocal music (lieder, concert arias) and chamber music, with the string quintets in C major and G minor, the Piano Sonata for four hands in C major, the Sonata for piano and violin in A major, and "Eine kleine Nachtmusik," which is completed in August. Throughout the summer, however, he is hard at work on *Don Giovanni*. On October 29, *Don Giovanni* is premiered in Prague, conducted by the composer, who had completed the overture only two nights before. It is an unqualified success. He returns to Vienna in November, and on December 7 is appointed Musician of the Royal Imperial Chamber, with a salary.

1788

Mozart spends the year in Vienna. Unable to manage his financial affairs, he has to agree to various potboilers in order to meet his family's needs (including a new orchestration for Handel's *Messiah*). The Austrian capital has lost interest in him, and rejects a style of music it finds too complex and bereft of charm. Over the summer, Mozart composes his three last symphonies, nos. 39–41, three masterpieces he will never hear performed. He suffers from low morale and experiences great financial hardship.

1789

In the spring (April–June) Mozart tours Bohemia, Saxony, and Prussia. In Leipzig, he plays the organ in St. Thomas's Church and examines Bach's scores with great enthusiasm. In Potsdam, he is given a very positive reception by the King of Prussia, Frederick William II, who, as an accomplished cellist, commissions music from the composer. The first "Prussian" Quartet is written in June, but work on it is interrupted by a commission from the Emperor for a divertissement for the following carnival. This will be *Così fan tutte* (All Women Behave Thus), the third of Mozart's operas to a libretto by Da Ponte. With his friend the clarinetist Anton Stadler in mind, he composes the Quintet for clarinet and strings.

1790

January 26, first performance, in Vienna, of *Così fan tutte*. Again Mozart has to accept a number of potboilers. Composition of the second and third "Prussian" Quartets and of the String Quintet in D major, in addition to an array of rondos, minuets, and contredanses.

1791

The last year in the musician's life, and that of his final masterpieces: the Piano Concerto no. 27 in B flat major, the String Quintet in E flat major, the "Ave verum," and the Clarinet Concerto. Early in the spring, at the request of a fellow freemason, the actor-manager Emanuel Schikaneder, Mozart begins work on a "fairy-tale opera," *The Magic Flute*. He receives a commission from the Prague National Theater for a work to celebrate the coronation of Emperor Leopold II as King of Bohemia, and composes, in great haste, the *opera seria La clemenza di Tito* (The Clemency of Titus), his pupil Franz Xaver Süssmayr helping with the recitatives. On July 26, a son, Franz Xaver, is born, his sixth child, the second to survive. *La clemenza di Tito* is premiered on September 6, and *The Magic Flute* on September 30, in Vienna, to great acclaim. Two months later, on December 5, Mozart dies, leaving unfinished a Requiem commissioned by Count von Walsegg zu Stuppach. This too will be completed by Süssmayr.

Bibliography

Correspondence

E. ANDERSON, ed. *The Letters of Mozart and His Family*. London 1938. Revised by S. Sadie and S. Smart, 1985.

Life and works

E. J. DENT. *Mozart's Operas: A Critical Study*. London 1913. 2nd edn. 1947.

A. EINSTEIN. *Mozart: His Character, His Work*. New York 1945. 3rd edn. 1968.

C. M. GIRDLESTONE. *Mozart et ses concertos pour pianos*. Paris 1939. Eng. trans. 1948; 3rd edn. 1978.

R. HALLIWELL. *The Mozart Family: Four Lives in a Social Context*. Oxford 1998.

D. HEARTZ and T. BAUMAN. *Mozart's Operas*. Berkeley 1990.

W. HILDESHEIMER. *Mozart*. Frankfurt 1977. Eng. trans. 1982.

J. IRVING. *Mozart: The "Haydn" Quartets*. Cambridge 1998.

A. H. KING. *Mozart Chamber Music*. London 1968.

H. C. ROBBINS LANDON. *Mozart and the Masons*. London 1982. 2nd edn. 1991.

H. C. ROBBINS LANDON. *Mozart: The Golden Years, 1781–1791*. London 1989.

J. ROSSELLI. *The Life of Mozart*. Cambridge 1998.

N. ZASLAW. *Mozart's Symphonies: Context, Performance Practice, Reception*. Oxford 1989.

Index

Entries cover principal cities, compositions, people, and topics. Page numbers in italics indicate illustrations. "WAM" stands for "Wolfgang Amadeus Mozart."

Photographic credits

Agence photographique des musées nationaux/photo Gérard Blot pp. 31, 47.
Agence photographique des musées nationaux/photo Bulloz p. 34 b.
AKG (Archiv für Kunst und Geschichte), Berlin pp. 7 8, 10, 16 l, 16 r, 22, 24, 26 (t and b), 28, 30, 34, 36 b, 40, 42 b, 44, 48–49, 50, 52, 56 b, 58, 60, 64 t, 66, 74, 78 l and r, 82 t, 84, 89, 90, 92, 94 b, 96, 100, 106–107, 110, 116 t, 118, 122, 125, 126–127, 132, 136 b, 138 b, 140 l, 142, 146, 150, 151, 154 b, 157, 160 r, 162, 168, 172 t and b, 174, 179, 181, 186, 187, 190 l and r, 192 t and b, 194 b, 196, 199, 203, 204, 206, 212, 216.
AKG, Berlin/Elie Bernager pp. 182 l and r, 184, 188.
AKG, Berlin/Erich Lessing pp. 12 (detail of page 13), 13, 14, 15 (detail of page 14), 20, 73, 98, 154 t, 177–178, 194 t, 217.
AKG, Berlin/Jérôme da Cunha pp. 54 b, 105,
AKG, Berlin/Nimatallah pp. 18, 38, 112,
AKG, Berlin/Rabatti-Domingie p. 136 t
Augsbourg, Stadtarchiv, p. 17.
Bayerisches Nationalmuseum, Munich p. 56 t.
Biblioteka Jagiellonska, Cracow pp. 43, 61, 62 b, 77, 81, 83, 94 b, 95, 97, 115, 119, 131, 135, 165, 211.
Bibliothèque Nationale de France, Département des Estampes p. 42 t.
Bibliothèque Nationale de France, Département de la Musique pp. 34 l, 35, 45, 55, 69, 71, 103, 111, 116 b, 141, 143, 152, 153, 163, 166.
Bridgeman Art Library cover plate and pp. 36 t, 68, 80 t and b, 120, 130, 134, 138 t, 140 r, 178, 201.
British Library, London pp. 37, 75, 161, 169, 200.
Deutsche Mozart-Gesellschaft e. V., Augsburg p. 19.
D. R. pp. 11, 29, 46, 47, 51, 54 t, 62 t, 70, 76, 86, 87, 91, 114, 117, 123.
G. Dagli Orti, Paris pp. 82 b, 94 t, 108, 144, 148, 164, 170, 208, 210.
Gesellschaft der Musikfreunde, Vienna pp. 102, 113, 171, 195.
IMAGNO/Austrian Archives/Scala, Vienna p. 202.
Internationale Stiftung Mozarteum (ISM), Salzburg pp. 21, 23, 25, 27, 53, 67, 79, 121, 133, 158, 159, 160 l, 183, 205, 213.
Library of Congress, Washington p. 207.
Musée des Autographes et Manuscrits, Paris, Suzanne Nagy pp. 137 b, 209.
Musée Bargoin, Clermont-Ferrand, p. 129.
Museo San Martino, Naples p. 82
Oesterreichische Nationalbibliothek, Vienna pp. 101, 197, 214, 215.
Pierpont Morgan Library, New York pp. 59, 65, 139, 149.
RMN/Bulloz p. 64 b.
Rue des Archives, Paris p. 109.
Rue des Archives/The Granger Collection, New York p. 156.
Sotheby's/AKG, Berlin p. 33.
Staatsbibliothek, Musikabteilung, Berlin. © BPK/Dist. RMN, pp. 9, 39, 41, 57, 63, 85, 93, 99, 137 t, 145, 147, 155, 167, 173, 175, 183, 189, 191, 193.

Contents